Green Banking and Green Central Banking

Institute for Law and Finance Series

Edited by
Theodor Baums
Andreas Cahn

Volume 24

Green Banking and Green Central Banking

Edited by
Andreas Dombret
Patrick S. Kenadjian

DE GRUYTER

ISBN 978-3-11-075287-8
e-ISBN (PDF) 978-3-11-075289-2
e-ISBN (EPUB) 978-3-11-075292-2

Library of Congress Control Number: 2021941760

Bibliographic information published by the Deutsche Nationalbibliothek
The Deutsche Nationalbibliothek lists this publication in the Deutsche Nationalbibliografie; detailed bibliographic data are available on the Internet at: http://dnb.dnb.de.

Typesetting: jürgen ullrich typosatz, Nördlingen
Printing und binding: CPI books GmbH, Leck
Cover image: Medioimages/Photodisc

www.degruyter.com

MIX
Papier aus verantwortungsvollen Quellen
FSC www.fsc.org
FSC® C083411

Foreword

ILF Conference "Green Banking and Green Central Banking: What are the right concepts?"

By Christian Edelmann, Managing Partner Europe, Oliver Wyman

Climate change is a challenge for everybody – individuals, institutions, and society more broadly. To reach net-zero carbon emissions by 2050, the world needs to halve its emissions in the next decade. Many businesses have already committed to this – both in their own footprint and through influencing and enabling their customers and suppliers.

But there's much more work to be done. It is time to reimagine the world we operate in today.

The costs of transitioning to a net-zero carbon economy are immense. Investments are needed to make it a reality. Financing can be both a barrier and an enabler for climate transition. The financial sector will have to play a central role in allocating resources towards a sustainable and green economy. This also means engaging with carbon-intensive activities, not necessarily avoiding them.

Capital markets play a pivotal role in financing lower-carbon solutions and resilient infrastructure and are in a unique position to help accelerate the transition. Allocating money where it is most effective can help mobilize and drive change in industries that need the large-scale financing required to reach net-zero.

Policy makers have recognized the urgency and have started to explore their roles in tackling the challenges arising from climate change. Central banks in particular play an important role, directly through monetary policy, but also indirectly through the incentives they set as part of their micro- and macroprudential policies.

Individuals across the financial sector have a role to play and the journey to net-zero starts with a strong vision and strategy. But collective effort is needed to make change happen and the time to act is now.

The contributions in this book reflect the current thinking of central bankers, regulators, supervisors, public officials, and leaders of the financial services industry, who have come together to drive greater understanding of the contributions everyone can make towards responding to climate change.

We thank the authors for sharing their perspectives and expertise, as well as the Institute of Law and Finance for their work in advancing this important conversation. We would also like to express our thanks to Andreas Dombret and Patrick Kenadjian for their partnership and their dedication to make this conference happen.

https://doi.org/10.1515/9783110752892-202

We hope these insights will be an impetus to stimulate further discussion and research in all these areas.

Preface

The Future of the Financial Sector Series

This book is the ninth in the series on the future of the financial sector sponsored by the Institute for Law and Finance (ILF) at Johann Wolfgang Goethe University in Frankfurt and published by De Gruyter, Berlin. Each book corresponds to a day long conference held by the ILF at which leading representatives from the public sector, industry and academia met to examine key issues of the day concerning the future of the financial sector. Together they trace the arc of our concerns for the sector following the Great Financial Crisis.

The first three volumes, as well as the seventh, concern themselves with the resolution of financial institutions, as well as other potential solutions to the "too big to fail" dilemma in the wake of the crisis, and show the remarkable progress we have made in Germany and in Europe on that topic. The first volume was based on a conference held in November 2010, a point at which the term bank resolution was so unfamiliar in Germany that we felt it best to call the conference "Brauchen wir ein Sonderinsolvenzrecht für Banken?", do we need a special insolvency law for banks. For the book, which appeared in 2012, we stuck in Too Big to Fail in the title. Contributors included Andreas Dombret, John Douglas, former General Counsel of the Federal Deposit Insurance Corporation, Thomas Huertas, member of the Executive Committee at the UK Financial Services Authority and Alternate Chair of the European Banking Authority (EBA), Martin Hellwig, Director at the Max Planck Institute for Research on Collective Goods and Charles Randell, who was soon to become external member of the UK Prudential Regulation Committee and later Chair of the UK Financial Conduct Authority.

By May 2012 we were already able to discuss what was then being called the EU Crisis Management Directive, although the actual text itself had been delayed and was only published after the conference. By the time the book appeared in 2013 we were able to call it by its definitive name, the Bank Recovery and Resolution Directive, and actually deal with the text itself. It was clear that by then resolution had been adopted by the EU as its preferred solution to too big to fail, although its complexities were still being sorted through, especially the topic of "living wills" and the then very controversial "bail-in tool". Contributors included Eva Hüpkes, advisor to the Financial Stability Board, Thomas Huertas, Charles Randell and Paul Tucker, Deputy Governor of the Bank of England.

By January 2014 we were considering more radical proposals, as the recommendations of the Liikanen Commission joined the Volcker Rule and the conclusions of the Vickers Commission in the United Kingdom in pointing towards a variety of so-called structural reforms, separating various kinds of banking ser-

https://doi.org/10.1515/9783110752892-203

vices. So we asked “Should We Break Up the Banks?” Contributors included Paul Achleitner, Chairman of the Supervisory Board of Deutsche Bank, Jan Krahnen, member of the High level Expert Group on Structural Reforms of the EU Banking Sector and Adam Posen, President of the Peterson Institute for International Economics. At the end of the day, most contributors ended up advocating or conceding that, without a credible bank resolution system, structural proposals to break up the banks would not suffice to solve too big to fail.

We returned to the question of resolution in the spring of 2018 with our program entitled “Resolution in Europe: The Unresolved Questions”, the fourth in our series on too big to fail, in which we narrowed our focus to Europe but broadened our scope to include insurance and central counterparties (CCPs). The book was published in 2019 with contributions by José Manuel Campa, the future Chair of the EBA, Benoît Cœuré, member of the Executive Board of the European Central Bank (ECB), Adam Farkas, Executive Director of the EBA, Levin Holle, Director General, Financial Markets Policy Department, German Federal Ministry of Finance, Felix Hufeld, President of the German Federal Financial Supervisory Authority, Elke König, Chair of the Single Resolution Board, Steven Maijoor, Chair of the European Securities and Markets Authority, Fausto Parente, Executive Director of the European Insurance and Occupational Pensions Authority and Sir Paul Tucker. The contributors concluded that significant progress had been made on bank resolution, although significant open issues remained, especially with respect to cross-border cases, but that less progress had been made on insurance and that CCP resolution required significant additional attention.

In March 2015 we turned our attention from the past to the future to consider the European Capital Markets Union in response to the European Commission’s Green Paper in a session where we questioned whether it was a viable concept and a real goal. The book appeared, in the same year, with contributions from Benoît Cœuré, Sir Jon Cunliffe, Deputy Governor for Financial Stability of the Bank of England, Philipp Hildebrand, Vice Chairman of BlackRock, Anshu Jain, Co-chief Executive Officer of Deutsche Bank and Wim Mijs, Chief Executive Officer of the European Banking Federation. There was a broad consensus on the desirability of the project, but considerable reservations on the tactics being pursued to accomplish it.

In November 2015–2015 was a busy year for us – we turned our attention back to one of the nagging questions left over from the Great Financial Crisis: to what extent was the crisis due to culture and could we hope to restore public confidence in financial institutions without tackling the issue of ethics. “Getting the Culture and the Ethics Right, Towards a New Age of Responsibility in Banking” appeared in 2016, with contributions from Lorenzo Bini Smaghi, Chairman of Société Générale, John Cryan, Chief Executive Officer of Deutsche Bank, Georg Fahrenschon, President of the German Savings Banks Association, Douglas Flint,

Group Chairman of HSBC Holdings, John Griffith-Jones, Chairman of the UK Financial Conduct Authority, Danièle Nouy, Chair of the Supervisory Board of the ECB Single Supervisory Mechanism, Jean-Claude Trichet, Chairman of the Group of Thirty, Sir Paul Tucker and Axel Weber, Chairman of the Board of UBS Group. There was unamimity among the contributors as to the importance of culture and ethics, but less clarity on whether the goals could best be reached through external pressure from regulation and supervision or bankers' codes, or internally through boards of directors and structural changes.

We had intended to hold a conference in 2016 on the final Basel III accord, scheduled for finalization by year end. When the negotiations collapsed we pushed our session back to December 2017 and the book, "Basel III: Are We Done Now?" appeared in 2019 with contributions from Claudio Borio, Head of the Monetary and Economics Department, Bank for International Settlements, William Coen, Secretary General of the Basel Committee on Banking Supervision, Andrea Enria, Chairperson of the EBA, Charles Goodhart, Emeritus Professor at the London School of Economics, Levin Holle, Stefan Ingves, Governor of the Swedish Riksbank and Chairman of the Basel Committee for Banking Supervision, Sabine Lautenschläger, Member of the Executive Board of the ECB, Christian Ossig, Chief Executive of the Association of German Banks, Isabel Schnabel, Member of the German Council of Economic Experts and Shunsuke Shirakawa, Vice Commissioner for International Affairs, Financial Services Agency of Japan, The contributors emphasized both the magnitude of the accomplishment Basel III represented and the issues which still remained to be resolved in the implementation of the accord as well as those items about which no agreement had been reached.

Finally, in 2019 we tackled the questions standing in the way of completing the European Banking Union. The book, entitled "EDIS, NPLs, Sovereign Debt and Safe Assets", appeared in 2020 with contributions by Andrea Enria, Chair of the Supervisory Board of the ECB, Edouard Fernandez-Bollo, Secretary General, French Prudential Supervision and Resolution Authority, Martin Helling, Levin Holle, Dominique Laboureix, Director of Resolution Planning at the Single Resolution Board, Christian Ossig, Fabio Panetta, Senior Deputy Governor of the Bank of Italy, Isabel Schnael, Joachim Wuermeling, member of the Executive Board of the Deutsche Bundesbank and Jeromin Zettelmeyer, Deputy Director in the Strategy and Policy Review Department at the International Monetary Fund.

The full list of the titles and contributors is set forth below. We are very grateful for all of them for the efforts they put into these volumes, which we hope have contributed to advancing thinking in Europe on the various topics we covered.

Andreas Dombret
Patrick Kenadjian — Frankfurt am Main, April 2021

Institute for Law and Finance Series; Titles on the Future of the Financial Sector

Vol. 9: *Too Big To Fail – Brauchen wir ein Sonderinsolvenzrecht für Banken? Ed. Patrick S. Kenadjian (2012)*

Authors: Dirk H. Bliesener, Andreas Dombret, John L. Douglas, Martin Hellwig, Thomas F. Huertas, Patrick S. Kenadjian, Wolfgang M. Nardi, Klaus Pannen, Carl Pickerill, Leo Plank, Matthias Raphael Prause, Wolfgang M. Nardi, Charles Randell, Christoph Thole.

Vol. 13: *The Bank Recovery and Resolution Directive: Europe's Solution for "Too Big to Fail?", Ed. Andreas Dombret and Patrick S. Kenadjian, De Gruyter Recht Berlin (2013)*
Authors: Andreas Cahn, Dirk H. Bliesener, Andreas Dombret, Randall D. Guynn, Thomas F. Huertas, Eva Hüpkes, Patrick S. Kenadjian, Simon Gleeson, Mathias Otto, Charles Randell, Paul Tucker.

Vol. 16: *Too Big to Fail III: Structural Reform Proposals Should We Break Up the Banks? Ed. Andreas Dombret and Patrick S. Kenadjian, De Gruyter Recht Berlin (2015)*
Authors: Paul Achleitner, Andreas Dombret, Douglas J. Elliott, Simon Gleeson, Randall D. Guynn, Patrick S. Kenadjian, Jan P. Krahnen, Adam S. Posen, Miguel de la Mano, Debra Stone.

Vol. 17: *The European Capital Markets Union A viable concept and a real goal? Ed. Andreas Dombret and Patrick S. Kenadjian, De Gruyter Recht Berlin (2015)*
Authors: Cyrus Ardalan, Andrew Bosomworth, Benoît Cœuré, Sir Jon Cunliffe, Andreas Dombret, Alexandra Hachmeister, Philipp Hildebrand, Anshu Jain, Patrick S. Kenadjian, Wim Mijs, Christian Ossig, Dirk Schoenmaker.

Vol. 20: *Getting the Culture and the Ethics Right Towards a New Age of Responsibility in Banking and Finance, Ed. Patrick S. Kenadjian and Andreas Dombret, De Gruyter Recht, Berlin (2016)*
Authors: Lorenzo Bini Smaghi, John Cryan, Andreas Dombret, Georg Fahrenschon, Leonhard H. Fischer, Douglas Flint, Simon Gleeson, John Griffith-Jones, Klaus J. Hopt, Patrick S. Kenadjian, Jan P. Krahnen, Sylvie Matherat, Wim Mijs, Alberto G. Musalem, Danièle Nouy, Dominik Treeck, Jean-Claude Trichet, Sir Paul Tucker, Axel A. Weber.

Vol. 21: *Basel III: Are We Done Now? Ed. Andreas Dombret and Patrick S. Kenadjian, De Gruyter Recht Berlin (2019)*
Authors: Claudio Borio, William Coen, Andreas Dombret, Douglas J. Elliott, Andrea Enria, Michael S. Gibson, C.A.E. Goodhart, Stuart Graham, Paul Hilbers, Levin Holle, Stefan Ingves, Patrick S. Kenadjian, Sabine Lautenschläger, Laurie Mayers, Martin Merlin, Sandie O'Connor, Christian Ossig, Shunsuke Shirakawa, Isabel Schnabel.

Vol. 22: *Resolution in Europe: The Unresolved Questions, Ed. Andreas Dombret and Patrick S. Kenadjian, De Gruyter Recht Berlin (2019)*
Authors: José Manuel Campa, Benoît Cœuré, Andreas Dombret, Wilson Ervin, Joachim Faber, Adam Farkas, Helmut Gründl, Levin Holle, Thomas F. Huertas, Felix Hufeld, Patrick S. Kenadjian, Elke König, Daniel Maguire, Steven Maijoor, Fausto Parente, Giulio Terzariol, Sir Paul Tucker, Mark E. Van Der Weide, James von Moltke.

Vol. 23: *EDIS, NPLs, Sovereign Debt and Safe Assets, Ed. Andreas Dombret and Patrick S. Kenadjian, De Gruyter Recht Berlin (2020)*
Authors: Klaus Adam, Roland Boekhout, Thiess Büttner, Rebecca Christie, Andreas Dombret, Colin Ellis, Andrea Enria, Edouard Fernandez-Bollo, Martin Hellwig, Joachim Hennrichs, Georg Huber, Thomas F. Huertas, Patrick S. Kenadjian, Nikki Kersten, Slawek Kozdras, Jan P. Krahnen, Dominique Laboureix, Álvaro Leandro, Nicoletta Mascher, Sylvie Matherat, Wim Mijs, Arthur J. Murton, Charles Nysten, Christian Ossig, Fabio Panetta, Jörg Rocholl, Karl-Peter Schackmann-Fallis, Isabel Schnabel, Anita van den Ende, Nicolas Véron, Klaus Wiedner, Joachim Wuermeling, Jeromin Zettelmeyer.

Contents

I. The Role of the Financial Sector

II. The Chance for Europe

Introduction

"Green Banking and Green Central Banking: what are the right concepts?" was the eighth conference we have co-chaired and the ninth in the series on the future of the financial sector sponsored by the Institute for Law and Finance ("ILF") at Goethe University in Frankfurt. We began planning it in January 2020, aiming for a June 2020 event. Then COVID-19 intervened, bringing with it postponement, then format changes from full presence, to hybrid to fully virtual event, the format in which we were finally able to hold it, thanks to the steadfastness and flexibility of the ILF, the support of our Knowledge Partner for the conference, Oliver Wyman and the commitment of our speakers and moderators, on January 25, 2021. Over 1,000 people from all over the world signed up for the program, by far the largest audience we have ever addressed.

Our goal was to go beyond repeating the commonplaces often heard at climate related conferences to drill down to identify the right concepts by asking the tough questions of financial institutions, government officials and central bankers. Where will the money to finance the transition to a low carbon environment come from, how far do the banks' balance sheets stretch and where will the rest of the money come from? How much can we rely on the capital markets, especially in the European Union, to get money to the parts of the economy which really need it, without greenwashing? How do governments organize not just a transition, but a just transition to a low carbon environment? Is it time to revisit received ideas about the proper role for central banks? And while the conference's title asked "what are the right concepts" our goal was to move the discussion beyond concepts to deliver concrete proposals to guide us forward.

The morning sessions were devoted to the private sector. The first panel, made up entirely of European and African bank CEOs, discussed how financial institutions are using their own resources to contribute to financing the transition to a lower carbon environment out of their own balance sheets and through the services they provide to industry, especially to those sectors in transition, including how well equipped they are for the task, the size of the financing needs to be met, the challenges of financing at scale sometimes risky investments in untried technologies, how to manage and price risk properly and what support they need from the public sector to fulfil their role.

In the second panel we broadened the focus to move beyond financial institutions' balance sheets to examine how financial institutions can marshal funds from outside investors, especially through the capital markets. Capital markets have long been an Achilles heel of the European Union and, while we are now on to what we might call Capital Markets Union 2.0, not as much progress has been made in this area since the first conference on the topic which we co-chaired some

https://doi.org/10.1515/9783110752892-205

six year ago in 2015 at the ILF. But the European Union's fragmented and objectively too small capital markets are not the only obstacles to mobilizing savings and capital. These range from the confusing multitude of competing standards being developed in the market for green products – bringing with them the ever present fear of greenwashing – to the lack of appropriate products to attract investors and help corporates make the needed investments in their transitions to a less carbon intensive world.

The afternoon was devoted to the role of the public sector in providing both funds and the structure and infrastructure within which private sector funds can be meaningfully mobilized and put to best use. The third panel thus discussed the role of government authorities as providers of funds, infrastructure and rules and, most importantly as architects of not just a transition to a lower carbon economy, but as the guarantors of a just transition in the global context of the need for national governments to revise and increase the Paris Agreement goals in the run up to COP26 in Glasgow in November.

The fourth panel centered on the role of central banks, regulators and supervisors of the financial sector and dealt with the key question of the proper role for central banks in the context of climate change. The discussion of the role for central banks was introduced by two exceptional speeches. The first was the stirring keynote address by Christine Lagarde, President of the European Central Bank, who used the fable of belling the cat to ask if not us and if not now, who and when. The second were the remarks of Jens Weidmann, President of the Deutsche Bundesbank, who methodically set forth the issues raised by extending central bank mandates too far and proposed a thoughtful potential alternative at the European Union level.

Andreas Dombret
Patrick Kenadjian

Frankfurt am Main, April 2021

The Authors

John Berrigan

John Berrigan is the Director General in DG FISMA (Directorate-General for Financial Stability, Financial Services and Capital Markets Union) of the European Commission. DG FISMA is responsible for EU-level policy making and legislative initiatives with respect to the financial sector, including Banking Union, Capital Markets Union, sustainable finance, digital finance, anti-money laundering and sanctions. In this context, John represents the European Commission on the Economic and Financial Committee and the Financial Services Committee, which report to EU Finance Ministers. He also represents the Commission on the Financial Stability Board, which reports to G20 Finance Ministers. He attends the European Systemic Risk Board and is a permanent observer on the Single Resolution Board.

John has been a Commission official since the mid-1980s and has spent most of that time working on financial-sector issues – first in DG ECFIN (where he contributed to macro-financial analysis in general and more specifically to financial-sector aspects of the assistance programmes for Member States) and now in DG FISMA. He worked on preparations for the introduction of the euro in 1999 and was secretary of the so-called Giovannini Group, which produced reports, inter alia, on issues related to euro-denominated debt issues and post-trading in EU securities markets in the early 2000s. In the mid-1990s, he worked for several years with the International Monetary Fund. John has a Master's degree in economics from University College Dublin.

Jean Boivin

Jean Boivin, PhD, Managing Director, is the Head of the BlackRock Investment Institute (BII). The institute leverages BlackRock's expertise and produces proprietary research to provide insights on the global economy, markets, geopolitics and long-term asset allocation – all to help clients and portfolio managers navigate financial markets. Dr. Boivin oversees all of BII's activities and is responsible for ensuring that BII integrates research insights on portfolio construction, economics and markets with the long-term, whole-portfolio perspective that BlackRock's clients need today. Dr. Boivin, who is a member of BlackRock's EMEA Executive Committee, also is BII's Global Head of Research. He is responsible for economic and markets research, and for developing the core principles and intellectual property that underpin BlackRock's approach to portfolio design, such as capital market assumptions and optimization tools.

Prior to joining BlackRock in 2014, Dr. Boivin served as Deputy Governor of the Bank of Canada and Associate Deputy Finance Minister, serving as Canada's representative at the G7, G20 and Financial Stability Board. Dr. Boivin has also

https://doi.org/10.1515/9783110752892-206

taught at Columbia Business School and HEC Montreal, and has written widely on macroeconomics, monetary policy and finance. Dr. Boivin earned a B.Sc. degree in economics from the Universite de Montreal in 1995, an MA in economics from Princeton University in 1997 and a PhD in economics from Princeton University in 2000.

Günther Bräunig

Dr. Günther Bräunig, born in 1955, has been CEO of KfW since January 2018. Bräunig studied law and was awarded a German doctorate in law. He began his professional career in 1984 at Commerzbank in the Investment Banking Division. Bräunig then worked for Airbus as Sales Finance Director in Toulouse and Washington, D.C. In 1989, he joined KfW as Head of its International Capital Markets Division. Subsequently, Bräunig held various senior positions in the departments of Credit and Management Affairs. In 1996, he was promoted to Senior Vice President in charge of the Secretariat of Management Affairs. Four years later, in 2000, he was appointed Executive Vice President, and in 2006, Member of the Executive Board of KfW. In September 2017 Bräunig was named Deputy CEO of KfW. During the financial rescue of IKB AG by KfW in 2007/2008, Bräunig served as CEO of IKB AG.

Bräunig is also Chair of the Supervisory Board of Deutsche Pfandbriefbank AG and member of the Supervisory Boards of Deutsche Post AG and Deutsche Telekom AG. He is married and has two adult children.

José Manuel Campa

Chairperson of the European Banking Authority.

After studying law and economics at the University of Oviedo and earning his PhD in economics from Harvard University, Mr. Campa taught finance at New York University and the IESE Business School and consulted for a number of international organisations including the World Bank, the IMF, the Bank for International Settlements and the European Commission.

He then served as the 10th Secretary of State for Economy of the Spanish government and was most recently Director of Regulatory affairs of the Santander Bank.

Andreas Dombret

Dr Andreas Dombret was born in the USA to German parents. He studied business management at the Westfälische Wilhelms University in Münster and was awarded his PhD by the Friedrich-Alexander University in Erlangen-Nuremberg.

From 1987 to 1991, he worked at Deutsche Bank's Head Office in Frankfurt, from 1992 to 2002 at JP Morgan in Frankfurt and London, from 2002 to 2005 as the Co-Head of Rothschild Germany located in Frankfurt and London, before serving

Bank of America as Vice Chairman for Europe and Head for Germany, Austria and Switzerland between 2005 and 2009. From May 2010 to May 2018, he has been a member of the Executive Board of the Deutsche Bundesbank with responsibility for Financial Stability, Statistics, Markets, Banking and Financial Supervision, Economic Education, Risk Controlling and the Bundesbank's Representative Offices abroad. He was also responsible for the IMF (Deputy of the Bundesbank), Financial Stability Commission (Member), Supervisory Board of the SSM (Member), Basel Committee on Banking Supervision (BCBS) (Member) and has been a member of the Board of Directors at the Bank for International Settlements (BIS), Basel, until the end of 2018. Since 2009, Andreas holds a professorship at the European Business School in Wiesbaden and teaches, as Adjunct Senior Fellow, at Columbia University in New York since May 2018.

Wiebe Draijer

Chairman of the Managing Board, Rabobank

Wiebe Draijer took over as Chairman of the Rabobank Managing Board on 1 October 2014. He studied mechanical engineering in Delft and in 1992 received an MBA from the Insead Business School. From 1990 to 2003, he was employed as a consultant at the McKinsey consultancy firm. In 2004, he was appointed the company's managing partner for The Netherlands and in 2006 for the Benelux countries. As from 1 September 2012, he was appointed president of the Social and Economic Council of The Netherlands.

Wiebe Draijer is also Member of the Board of the Dutch Banking Association (NVB), Member of the Executive Committee of the World Business Council for Sustainable Development (WBCSD), Member of the Board of the Dutch Council for Cooperatives (NCR), Member of the Supervisory Board of Staatsbosbeheer (State Forest), Chairman of the Supervisory Board of the Dutch Cancer Society and Member of the Dutch Cybersecurity Council (CSR).

Christian Edelmann

Christian Edelmann is Managing Partner Europe at Oliver Wyman. He is based in London. Prior to his current role he was Co-Head EMEA Financial Services and Global Head of Wealth & Asset Management. He previously led the firm's business in the Asia-Pacific region.

Christian holds a Master's degree in Law and a Master's degree in Business and Economics from the University of Basel and he holds the designations of Chartered Financial Analyst (CFA) and of Financial Risk Manager (FRM). Christian has advised major financial institutions in North America, Europe, Asia, and the Middle East. He loves how working in diverse environments helps him develop unique relationships and deliver strategic change for our clients.

Ed Fishwick

Ed Fishwick, Managing Director and Global Co-Head of Risk & Quantitative Analysis at BlackRock. In addition he is a member of the European Executive and Global Operating Committees of the firm, and is a member of the Board of BlackRock Group Ltd. Mr. Fishwick has worked in quantitative finance for over 30 years in London, New York and Boston. Previously he was Head of Risk Management and Investment Process Research at AXA Investment Managers, and Director of Research at Quantec. Mr. Fishwick is a member of the Editorial Board of the Journal of Asset Management, and is the Chairman of the London Quant Group.

Sylvie Goulard

Second Deputy Governor of the Banque de France

Sylvie Goulard was appointed second deputy governor of the Banque de France on 17 January 2018. Her portfolio includes international issues, research, public financial education and climate related financial stability issues. She served as Minister of the Armed Forces (May-June 2017) in the first government of President Macron. She carried out most of her career in European institutions. From 2009, she was Member of European Parliament. As a member of the Alliance of Liberals and Democrats for Europe (ALDE) group, she sat on the Parliamentary Committee on Economic and Monetary Affairs (ECON) where she served as coordinator/spokesperson for the ALDE group. She was rapporteur or co-rapporteur for various legislative texts, in particular on the governance of the euro, the banking union and the role of the EU in global finance. From 2010 to 2017, she chaired the European Parliament Intergroup against Extreme Poverty. Between 2001 and 2004 she was political adviser to the President of the European Commission, Romano Prodi.

Born in 1964, Sylvie Goulard holds a law degree from the University of Aix-en-Provence (1984). She then graduated from the Institut d'études politiques in Paris (1986) and the Ecole nationale d'administration (1989). Upon leaving the ENA, she worked at the Ministry of Foreign Affairs on legal and European affairs. Sylvie Goulard is the author of several books on Europe.

Philipp Hildebrand

Philipp Hildebrand, Vice Chairman of BlackRock, is a member of the firm's Global Executive Committee. He also oversees the BlackRock Investment Institute (BII) and BlackRock Sustainable Investing (BSI). Mr. Hildebrand joined BlackRock in 2012. Prior to that, he served as Chairman of the Governing Board of the Swiss National Bank (SNB). In that capacity, he was also a Director of the Bank for International Settlements (BIS), the Swiss Governor of the International Monetary Fund (IMF) and a member of the Financial Stability Board (FSB), of which the Leaders of the G20 appointed him Vice Chairman in 2011. He was also Chairman of the Administrative Committee of the Board of Directors of the BIS, and part of the Steering Committee and the Plenary of the Financial Stability Board (FSB). Previously, Mr. Hildebrand was Chief Investment Officer of a Swiss private bank and a partner at Moore Capital Management in London.

Mr. Hildebrand is a Trustee of the British Museum, a member of the Group of Thirty and an Honorary Fellow of Lincoln College, Oxford. He sits on the International Advisory Board of Oxford University's Blavatnik School of Government and the International Leadership Council for Europe for the University of Toronto. He is a Chevalier de L'Ordre National du Mérite (France). Mr. Hildebrand earned a BA from the University of Toronto, an MA from the Graduate Institute of International Studies in Geneva, and a DPhil from the University of Oxford.

Werner Hoyer

Werner Hoyer has a PhD (economics) from Cologne University where he also started his career in various positions. Dr Hoyer served for 24 years as a Member of the German Bundestag. During this period, he held the position of Minister of State at the Foreign Office on two separate occasions. In addition, he held several other positions, including that of Whip and FDP Security Policy Spokesman, Deputy Chairman of the German-American Parliamentary Friendship Group, FDP Secretary General and President of the European Liberal Democratic Reform Party (ELDR). Upon appointment by the EU Member States, Dr Hoyer commenced his first term as EIB President in January 2012. His mandate was renewed for a second term commencing on 01 January 2018.

Otmar Issing

Prof. Dr. Dr. mult. h.c. Otmar Issing, born in 1936, held chairs of economics at the University Erlangen-Nuremberg and Wuerzburg. He was a member of the Council of Economic Experts (1988–1990). From 1990 to 1998 he was a member of the Board of the Deutsche Bundesbank with a seat at the Central Bank Council. From 1998 to 2006 he was a founding member of the Executive Board of the European Central Bank, responsible for the Directorates General Economics and Research. He has Honorary Doctorates from the Universities Bayreuth, Frankfurt and Konstanz and received many awards. He was Head of the Advisory Group on the New Financial Order appointed by Chancellor Merkel (2008–2010) and member of the High Level Group of the European Commission chaired by J.De Larosiere (2008–2009). In 2017 he was appointed member of the G20 Eminent Persons Group on Global Financial Governance.

He is President of the Center for Financial Studies and Chairman Kuratorium House of Finance, Goethe University Frankfurt. He is Honorary Professor of the

Universities Frankfurt and Wuerzburg, and was (inter alia) International Advisor to Goldman Sachs (2006–2018). He has published numerous articles in academic journals and is the author of two textbooks. Die Einführung in die Geldtheorie (Introduction to Monetary Theory) 15th edition 2011 (also translated into Chinese and Bulgarian). His Book "Der Euro", 2008 has been translated into English and Chinese.

Patrick Kenadjian

Patrick is currently an Adjunct Professor at the Goethe University in Frankfurt am Main, Germany, where he teaches courses on the financial crisis and financial reform and mergers and acquisitions at the Institute for Law and Finance. Since 2012, Patrick has co-chaired a series of conferences at the University on financial reform, including the need for and design of resolution regimes for banks, insurance companies and CCPs and other potential solutions for "too big to fail", the proposed European Capital Market Union, the importance of culture and ethics in financial institutions, the final agreement on Basel III and collective action clauses in sovereign debt issues. Since 2015 he has served on the Advisory Council to the Salzburg Global Forum on Finance in a Changing World where he served as Program Director in 2013 and 2014.

Patrick is also Senior Counsel at Davis Polk & Wardwell London LLP. He was a partner of the firm from 1984 to 2010, during which time he opened the firm's Tokyo and Frankfurt offices in 1987 and 1991, respectively and spent over 25 years in its European and Asian offices. He speaks French, German and Italian.

Matthias Kopp

Matthias Kopp is Director Sustainable Finance at WWF Germany and a leading member of the WWF Finance Practice worldwide. Previously with PwC Management Consulting Services, he has been responsible for several projects and publications on carbon accounting, decarbonisation strategies, climate strategy reporting, etc. He co-initiated the German Finance Sector Climate Commitment 2020, represents WWF at the UN Net Zero Asset Owners Alliance, and serves on the advisory boards to the German Government on Sustainable Finance, the Climate Champions Germany (Klimaschutz-Unternehmen e.V.) and Hannover Stock Exchange (Global Challenges Index), among others.

Christine Lagarde

President of the European Central Bank since November 1st, 2019

Born in Paris in 1956, Christine Lagarde completed high school in Le Havre and attended Holton Arms School in Bethesda (Md, USA). She then graduated from law school at University Paris X, and obtained a Master's degree from the Political

Science Institute in Aix-en-Provence. After being admitted as a lawyer to the Paris Bar, Christine Lagarde joined the international law firm Baker & McKenzie as an associate, specialising in labour, anti-trust, and mergers and acquisitions. A member of the Executive Committee of the Firm in 1995, Christine Lagarde became the Chairman of the Global Executive Committee of Baker & McKenzie in 1999.

Christine Lagarde joined the French government in June 2005 as Minister for Trade. After a brief stint as Minister for Agriculture and Fisheries, in June 2007 she became the first woman to hold the post of Finance and Economy Minister of a G7 country. From July to December 2008 she also chaired the ECOFIN Council, which brings together Economics and Finance Ministers of the European Union. As a member of the G20, Christine Lagarde was involved in the Group's management of the financial crisis, helping to foster international policies related to financial supervision and regulation and to strengthen global economic governance. As Chair of the G20 when France took over its presidency for the year 2011, she launched a wide-ranging work agenda on the reform of the international monetary system.

In July 2011 Christine Lagarde was elected the 11th Managing Director of the International Monetary Fund (IMF), and the first woman to hold that position. In February 2016 she was selected to serve a second five-year term. She resigned from the IMF on 12 September 2019 following her nomination as the first woman to be appointed President of the European Central Bank. In 2020 Christine Lagarde was ranked the second most influential woman in the world by Forbes magazine. She has often been named by Time magazine as one of the 100 most influential people in the world. Christine Lagarde was named Officier in the Légion d'honneur in April 2012.

Dr. Valentin von Massow

Dr. Valentin von Massow, an Agricultural Economist by training, is Chairman of the Board of Trustees of WWF Germany and Vice President of the Board of WWF International. He spent close to 20 years with The Boston Consulting Group based in Germany, UK and India, covering a wide range of consulting assignments and internal leadership positions. Since leaving BCG in 2005, he has been serving as an Independent Director on a number of plc, private company, start-up and NGO Boards in the environmental services and renewable energy sectors.

Wim Mijs

Chief Executive Officer, European Banking Federation

Wim Mijs (b. 1964) was appointed Chief Executive Officer of the European Banking Federation in 2014. Between 2007 and 2014 Wim served as CEO of the Dutch banking association NVB. During this tenure he transformed the NVB into a modern industry association, positioning it as the key representative of the banking sector in the wake of the financial crisis. Wim studied law at the University of Leiden in the Netherlands, specialising in European and International law. After his studies he worked at the International Court of Arbitration at the Peace Palace in The Hague. In 1993he joined ABN AMRO in Amsterdam before moving to Brussels to head up the bank's EU liaison office. Wim moved back to The Hague in 2002 where he became the Head of Government Affairs for ABN AMRO. Wim is a member of the Advisory Board of the BBVA Center for Financial Education and Capability, the Industry Chair of the European Parliamentary Financial Services Forum and member of the Advisory board of Leiden Law School. Between 2011 and 2018, Wim held various institutional roles within the international and European financial/banking community: chairman of the International Banking Federation; chairman of the Executive Committee of the EBF; and chairman of the Board of Euribor, now known as the European Money Market Institute.

Daniel Mminele
Daniel served as Group CEO at Absa Group from 15 January 2020 to April 2021 when he resigned from this role.

Prior to joining Absa, he was a Deputy Governor of the South African Reserve Bank since July 2009 where he served two terms. His responsibilities included Financial Markets, International Economic Relations and Policy as well as the Human and Operations Cluster. He was a member of the Governors' Executive Committee, the Monetary Policy Committee, Financial Stability Committee, Risk Management Committee and the Prudential Committee. He was the Chairperson of the Reserves Management Committee as well as the Chair of the Board of the Corporation of Public Deposits. He served as the G20 Central Bank deputy for South Africa as well as the Chairman for the IMFC Deputies.

His experience before the SARB included credit-risk analysis, corporate banking, and project and structured finance at private banking institutions in Germany, The United Kingdom (UK) and South Africa.

Ted Moynihan
Ted Moynihan is Managing Partner and Global Head of Industries at Oliver Wyman. He has led Oliver Wyman's Financial Services practice globally since 2016 and previously served as the Global Head of the Corporate & Institutional Banking Practice. Ted personally has concentrated on banking strategy, operating structure, financial management and operations. He advises several industry bodies, policy makers and regulatory bodies assisting in the development of strong policy and regulatory rule-making. Ted specialised in control engineering and mathe-

matics for a number of years before joining Oliver Wyman. He is a graduate of University College, Dublin, and holds a degree in Engineering from Cambridge University.

Simona Paravani-Mellinghoff

Simona Paravani-Mellinghoff, Managing Director, is the Global CIO of Solutions, MASS at BlackRock. The Multi-Asset Strategies & Solutions (MASS) team is the investment group at the heart of BlackRock's portfolio construction, asset allocation, and active management ecosystem. MASS draws on the full toolkit of BlackRock's index, factor, and alpha-seeking investment capabilities to deliver precise investment outcomes and cutting-edge alpha insights. MASS constructs active asset allocation strategies and whole portfolio solutions across a wide spectrum of commingled funds, separate accounts, model portfolios, and outsourcing solutions in the wealth and institutional channels. Prior to joining Blackrock in 2015, Ms Paravani-Mellinghoff spent ten years at HSBC where she held a number of senior positions in Hong Kong, London and New York including Global Investment Strategist and CIO in the asset management division. During her tenure at HSBC, Ms Paravani-Mellinghoff was responsible for a range of investment solutions covering both institutional and retail clients including being the lead PM on the World Selection global range. Prior to HSBC, she was the quantitative strategist at Julius Baer Asset Management in Zurich. She started her career in 1998 as a quantitative analyst at Orbis in London.

Ms Paravani-Mellinghoff was named for two consecutive years in 2009 and 2010 as a rising star of finance under 40 by Financial News, a sister company of the Wall Street Journal. She is Industrial Professor at the Institute of Finance and Technology at UCL where she teaches Financial Analytics and Machine Learning. She earned both a BA and MA in Economics from Cambridge University. Ms Paravani-Mellinghoff is a published author and sits on the board of financial education charity MyBnk.

Sirpa Pietikäinen

Sirpa Pietikäinen is a member of the European People's Party (EPP) in the European Parliament. She is a former Minister of the Environment in Finland (1991–1995), and a Member of the parliament from 1983 to 2003 and Member of the European Parliament since 2008. At the European Parliament, Ms Pietikäinen is a member of the Economic and Monetary Affairs Committee and Women's Right and Gender Equality Committee, and a substitute member of the Environment, Public Health and Food Safety Committee. Within her work, she seeks to combine her two specialities, that of environment and economics. Ms Pietikäinen is a strong advocate of a transition to a circular economy and sustainable finance, and served as the lead negotiator on behalf of European Parliament and the EPP group on the first Sustainable Finances legislative initiatives, Disclosure and Taxonomy Regulations as well as on the Parliament's Own Initiative Report on Sustainable Finance.

A graduate from the Helsinki School of Economics, Ms. Pietikäinen holds a MSc in Business, and teaches university courses on negotiations theory and practices. She is active in several organisations, her positions of trust including Chairmanship of the Globe EU.

Christian Sewing

Chief Executive Officer, Deutsche Bank

Christian Sewing has been a member of the Management Board since January 1, 2015 and Chief Executive Officer since April 2018. He joined Deutsche Bank in 1989. From January until June 2015, he was responsible on the Management Board for Legal, Incident Management Group and Group Audit, and assumed responsibility for Deutsche Bank's Private & Commercial Bank (including Postbank) between July 2015 and April 2018. He was Head of Group Audit from June 2013 to December 2014, prior to which he held a number of management positions in Risk. From 2012 to 2013, he was Deputy Chief Risk Officer. From 2010 to 2012, he served as the Bank's Chief Credit Officer. He has worked in Frankfurt, London, Singapore, Tokyo and Toronto.

Luiz Awazu Pereira da Silva

Deputy General Manager, BIS

Luiz Awazu Pereira da Silva became Deputy General Manager on 1 October 2015. Before joining the BIS, Mr Pereira da Silva, a Brazilian national, had been Deputy Governor of the Central Bank of Brazil since 2010. Prior to that, he worked in various positions for the World Bank in Washington DC, Tokyo and southern Africa. He also served as Chief Economist for the Brazilian Ministry of Budget and Planning, and as Brazil's Deputy Finance Minister in charge of international affairs.

Jessica Tan

Jessica Tan, Managing Director, is Global Head of Corporate Strategy at BlackRock. She is responsible for developing and implementing strategic priorities and cross-functional initiatives, centered around achieving long-term, sustainable growth. Previously, Ms. Tan served as Chief of Staff to the CEO from 2017 to mid-2019. In this capacity, she was responsible for oversight of the Executive Office of the Chairman and Chief Executive Officer and for leading the firm's Global Strategic Partner Program. From 2010 to 2016, Ms. Tan was a member of BlackRock's Financial Markets Advisory Group, which provides a wide range of advisory, valuation and innovative solutions for its clients, including banks, insurance companies and official institutions. From 2014 to 2016, she was the team's Global COO.

Prior to joining BlackRock, Ms. Tan was a Vice President in the equity sales & trading division of Merrill Lynch, where she covered clients trading international equity portfolios. Prior to that, she was a member of the transition management group, where she was responsible for assisting clients with project management, risk management and execution strategies related to the implementation of asset allocation changes. Prior to that, Ms. Tan was an analyst at Deutsche Bank. Ms. Tan earned an MBA from Harvard Business School and graduated magna cum laude and Phi Beta Kappa with a B.S. in economics from Duke University.

Guenther Thallinger

Member of the Board of Management of Allianz SE

Guenther Thallinger joined Allianz Group in May 2009. He has been a member of the Board of Management of Allianz SE since 2017, responsible for Investment Management and the Center of Competence Life & Health. In 2018 he additionally assumed responsibility for steering ESG topics within Allianz. He is the chairman of the United Nations-convened Net-Zero Asset Owner Alliance (AOA). Until his appointment to the Board of Management, Guenther Thallinger acted as CEO, and before that as CFO, of Allianz Investment Management SE and was Chairman of the Allianz Investment Management Board. Before joining Allianz, he was principal at McKinsey&Company.

Born in Austria, Guenther Thallinger graduated with a BSc from the Technical University Graz and a MSc from the Technical University Vienna in technical mathematics. He holds a PhD in applied mathematics from the Technical University Vienna.

Bouke de Vries

Bouke de Vries is Advisor to the Board on Public Affairs and works at the Sustainability Department of Rabobank. Currently he also chairs the Sustainable Finance Working Group of the European Association of Cooperative Banks in Brussels. From 2009- 2013 Bouke headed the financial sector research team of the Economic Research Department of Rabobank. From 2001 he worked there as an economist and has published several research reports on the cooperative banking sector, the Basel capital standards and the European Banking Union. Prior to joining Rabobank, he worked for three years for the Dutch Association of Insurers. Bouke earned a degree in Economics, specialising in International Economic Relations, from the University of Amsterdam.

Dr. Jens Weidmann

President, Deutsche Bundesbank, Frankfurt am Main

Dr Jens Weidmann (b. 1968) has been President of the Deutsche Bundesbank since May 2011. He is a member of the Governing Council of the European Central Bank (ECB), represents Germany in the International Monetary Fund (IMF) and other international bodies, and has been Chairman of the Board of Directors of the Bank for International Settlements (BIS) since November 2015.

After studying economics in Bonn and Aix-en-Provence, Jens Weidmann obtained his doctorate at the University of Bonn. From 1997 to 1999, he worked at the IMF in Washington before becoming Secretary General of the German Council of Economic Experts. In 2003, he joined the Bundesbank as head of the Monetary Policy and Analysis Division. Dr Weidmann headed the Economic and Fiscal Policy Department at the Federal Chancellery from 2006 to 2011, also serving as the Federal Chancellor's sherpa for the world economic summits of the G8 and G20 countries.

I. The Role of the Financial Sector

Günther Bräunig

The Role of public Financing in Reaching Climate Neutrality

1. Climate Neutrality requires substantial Investments

The path to climate neutrality in 2050 implies that all parts of the economy involving greenhouse gas emissions need to find ways to decarbonize, mainly through increased energy and resource efficiency and the integration of renewable energy sources. This represents a transformation of large parts of the economy, challenging many established business models and production processes. Like other economic, social or ecological challenges, climate change requires new solutions. Innovative technologies will play a key role in making the transformation process a success for society, economy and for our planet. In several areas, new technologies based on green electricity or green hydrogen have started to appear on the market or promise to be available in the near future. Nevertheless, ongoing R&D will be crucial – and the path towards climate neutrality still depends on substantial investments in the next years. Following a study commissioned by the Federation of German Industries (BDI), the level of extra investment to reduce greenhouse gas emissions in Germany by 95 % compared to 1990, amounts to EUR 2.3 trillion by 2050. – And requirements for reaching climate neutrality by 2045 may even be considerably higher.

As these investments heavily rely on access to financial resources, the existing partnership of the financial sector and the real economy has to be refreshed in light of the new challenge. There is little doubt on the general direction we are heading to, as a growing number of countries are committed to becoming climate neutral. Recent pledges from the U.S. and China confirm the common view that markets for green products and technologies will grow, making carbon neutral technologies not only a solution to meet our climate goals, but also an important driver of future economic growth.

Still, a lack of short-term profitability of climate investments, substantial uncertainty about the exact timing and application of specific technologies as well as political frameworks confine investment activities and pose a threat to the transformation. Investors need planning security. It is thus essential to offer a reliable long-term perspective that sharpens the view on the associated risks and benefits, also in financial markets.

https://doi.org/10.1515/9783110752892-001

2. The Role of the Financial Sector

Risk transformation is an important contribution of financial intermediation. The ability to channel high-risk capital to investors willing to engage with new technologies puts financial institutions in the center of any system of innovation. Optimal risk management, however, can only be achieved if all relevant consequences are adequately measured and reflected in the markets, which is currently not the case with respect to climate risks. So how to achieve a better reflection of the economic costs of climate change in financial markets?

Carbon pricing is an important ingredient generally suited to become the key instrument to internalize the damages from climate change. If, however, the CO2 price is too low, as currently the case, the price signal will not provide incentives at the efficient level. A second important ingredient are improvements in measuring individual exposure to climate related risks. The EU taxonomy for sustainable activities represents another milestone on the path to achieve carbon neutrality, offering a classification system to list environmentally sustainable economic activities. Translating this complex and comprehensive framework into business processes and practical implementation is an important next step.

Public financing can make important contributions in this context. There is evidence that market shaping through direct public financing can even be more important than market fixing through other regulatory measures. There are various potential channels of public financing. First, the provision of public funds can immediately help innovative technologies to reach market maturity. Second, public financing can increase the attractiveness for private investors more generally, attracting private capital and increasing bankability of sustainable technologies. Third, public banks can help to establish markets for publicly traded green financial products, like green bonds. Finally, public banks can serve as a role model for the financial sector with respect to the way sustainability and associated risks are reflected in bank steering and disclosure processes.

The different channels will be explored in more depth in the following sections, using concrete examples from Germany to illustrate the potential contributions of public financing, looking both at successful programs from the past as well as promising approaches for the future.

3. Capital Funds supporting green Innovations

Given the technological risks and the need for innovative solutions, the transformation towards climate neutrality requires venture capital to meet investment needs at an early stage. Different to other transformations, the path to climate neutrality is not induced by technological progress, but rather depends on it. Reaching the optimal climate path derived from scientific evidence and corresponding scenario analyses, requires targeted innovation at a given time. As indicated, current market conditions are not likely to stimulate innovation fast enough.

This gives room for capital funds to be directed into high risk investments, typically addressed by private venture capital (VC). While not being a traditional area for public banks, it might become a growing field of action in this context – at least, this is what is currently happening in Germany. At the end of the year 2020, the German Parliament approved a EUR 10 billion future fund to promote venture capital financing in Germany. KfW and its VC subsidiary KfW Capital, established in 2018, will play a central role in the implementation of these funds. There is an increasing number of start-ups focusing on climate-friendly technology development, and we see more of both traditional and impact funds capitalizing on these climate tech investment opportunities. The availability of venture capital is among the key success factors when it comes to new technologies and business models developed by start-ups. Therefore, KfW Capital focusses on the equity finance sector. The objective is to improve access to capital for young technology-oriented growth companies.

KfW Capital aims to sustainably improve the supply of venture and growth capital to innovative technology companies in Germany. An increasing number of these companies have the potential to shape the transformation towards climate neutrality. Moreover, KfW Capital has integrated sustainability criteria in the investment process and has teamed up with international experts to shape the VC and start-up ecosystem by offering a specific ESG framework for start-ups and VCs. This will help VC funds and start-ups to focus on relevant sustainability topics at a very early stage of their growth path to operate sustainably and successfully. In the next ten years, KfW Capital will invest around EUR 2 billion into German and European venture capital funds to improve access to capital for innovative startups and growth companies through enhanced VC funding.

There is also an international dimension to this instrument, in the context of development finance. Recently, KfW has started to structure a green investment fund with a special focus on Africa where development banks take a first loss and one of the world's largest asset managers is sourcing private capital for the second loss. Such forward-thinking approaches not only allow to redirect capital towards sustainable investments but also ensure that developing countries are included in the transformation process, improving their chances to take advantage of future green markets.

4. Public Financing triggers private Money

For established firms and companies, debt financing is the most important financial source in Germany. Promotional loans may therefore be the "classic" way to apply public funds to incentivize economic activities. There is already a successful history of promotional loans in the context of the German energy transition. These are applied to promote climate-neutral technologies and business models that have already reached market maturity and require suitable financing for further market penetration.

For more than 15 years, KfW has been promoting energy efficiency in German buildings. KfW's programs for energy-efficient construction and refurbishment, conducted on behalf of the Federal Ministry of Economics and Energy, enable the long-term financing of investments in the modernization and construction of energy-efficient residential, commercial and municipal buildings at low interest rates. These energy efficiency programs have triggered substantial investments mobilizing private capital for energy efficiency. Over the last 15 years, KfW has issued about EUR 180 billion in loans or grants to builders and renovators, triggering investments totaling EUR 480 billion. The leverage effect even goes beyond the projects directly financed by KfW.

Market shaping even goes beyond the immediate stimulation of private capital. The programs require energy consulting as a prerequisite to receive funding, and helped to establish this service as a new job profile, shaping today's market for energy efficiency services. Also, the clear definition of "Efficiency Houses" and the visibility of the corresponding label helped to spread the idea of energy efficient buildings, establishing new standards in the market. A viable indicator is the fact that we observe new buildings compliant with the Efficiency House standard, even without KfW loans. The impacts of KfW's energy efficiency programs have been validated by independent research institutes, showing that energy-efficiency measures supported by KfW's programs are helping to reduce yearly emissions of carbon equivalents by about 12 million tons. Moreover, the investments secured about 6 million jobs per year in the building industry and regional trades, mainly in SME.

KfW also helped to ramp up the market for offshore wind in Germany. In order to speed up the expansion of offshore wind energy in Germany, KfW supported the financing of offshore projects in Germany on behalf of the Federal Government. At the time, the risks of wind power projects were hard to evaluate, and commercial banks were reluctant to provide financing. KfW's programs benefited from a 95 % state guarantee. KfW joined bank consortia with commercial banks and lent money under conditions same as those of the other consortium partners. The program turned out to be a great success. KfW's commitments of EUR 1.8 billion triggered investments totaling EUR 9 billion. The resulting wind power projects today generate green electricity for 2.3 million households, with a turnover of EUR 9 billion and offering 24,500 jobs. Moreover, subsequent to the program, Germany could switch to competitive auctions. In the last offshore wind auctions, capacity was won by investors who offered to build parks without subsidies, showing how public programs could help to form the market.

5. Green Bonds as an important Instrument for mobilizing Capital

Given the enormous need for capital, it has become apparent that global bond markets must be involved to a greater extent in the financing of the transition towards a sustainable economy and society. In explicitly articulating the use of bond proceeds, green bonds have raised awareness of climate and environmental issues among a broad range of capital market participants. Public entities have been a driver for the development of the green bond market from the outset. From the first "Climate Awareness Bonds" issued by the European Investment Bank in 2007 until today, the green bond market has grown dynamically. Creating a new sense of responsibility, green bonds have also put focus on other sustainability dimensions, serving as a blueprint for social and sustainability bonds as well as sustainability-linked bonds.

In order to promote capital markets-based financing of environmental and climate protection and linking its experience in green finance and its standing in international capital markets, KfW decided to comprehensively support the development of the green bond market. Entering the market as a green bond issuer in 2014, and as a dedicated green bond investor one year later, KfW has been among the most active participants in the market segment. As a leading borrower of green bonds, KfW has issued more than EUR 32.5 billion so far in various currencies. On the investment side, KfW has been building a green bond portfolio since 2015. The initial target volume of the portfolio of EUR 2 billion was reached in February 2021. Going forward, KfW will continue investing in green bonds and will maintain the portfolio volume at a level of EUR 2–2.5 billion.

KfW promotes market harmonization through acting as a vocal advocate of the market in various international initiatives. KfW has been especially engaged in the Green Bond Principles, being a member of the Executive Committee since 2015, and has, most recently, been part of the EU TEG working on the proposals for EU Taxonomy and EU Green Bond Standard.

6. Reflecting Climate Change Mitigation in Bank Steering and Disclosure

Finally, public entities can also be role models with respect to supporting the transformation towards climate neutrality through sustainable bank steering mechanisms and disclosure processes that adequately reflect and quantify climate related risks, enabling financial intermediaries to direct capital towards the most efficient sustainable investment projects.

As Germany's promotional bank, KfW is a frontrunner in terms of sustainability. Just recently, KfW's Board of Supervisory Directors approved a new Sustainable Finance Concept that positions KfW as a transformative promotional bank. To meet the challenges, it is necessary to focus even more on the impact of our financing activities – equally in ecological, economic and social terms. Mapping all new commitments to the sustainable development goals (SDG) is a first step to reach more transparency in this respect. There is a rising interest in these kinds of instruments, which are increasingly based on highly automated data analyses within banking systems.

The SDG mapping allows for further extensions in the future, including the development of more granular SDG-oriented physical impact indicators and their integration in management reporting systems – to pave the way for future impact-based steering mechanisms. Furthermore, KfW's Sustainable Finance Concept comprises sectoral guidelines to ensure that new commitments are aligned with the Paris Agreement. This approach focuses on high-emission sectors such as energy, housing and mobility. It defines clear requirements in terms of climate friendliness of the financed technologies and will increase this level of ambition over time to support the transformation process in the real economy. In this regard, and considering its mandate as a "transformative promotional bank", KfW will go beyond reducing its own footprint from financing and bank operations and further strengthen ESG risk management more generally. There is a clear goal to identify ESG risks as early as possible to protect the asset position and, apart from that, to anticipate future requirements from banking supervision. Of course, ESG risks do not represent a fundamentally new risk category, but given increased importance, they have to be evaluated even more systematically. In this context, public entities can support the goal of making climate risks transparent to stakeholders, e. g. by supporting the Task Force on Climate-related Financial Disclosures (TCFD). In 2020, KfW reported for the first time on the key climate risks for its business, following the recommendations of the Task Force.

7. Conclusion

Transforming the economy towards climate neutrality is among the biggest challenges of our time. We know that this transformation will require substantial investments, but at the same time, we have good reasons to believe that the general conditions for reaching our climate goals are favorable – which turns the current situation into an opportunity we should take.

There is a growing number of countries committed to becoming climate neutral, with recent pledges from the U.S. and China, sending clear signals towards growing markets for green products and technologies. Moreover, given the technological progress, there is little doubt that the path towards climate neutrality is technologically feasible. Finally, there is a lot of capital available in Europe, also thanks to the EU Green Deal, to support the transformation towards climate neutrality – and tailwind from the action plan on financing sustainable growth and the development of a renewed sustainable finance strategy, providing important impulses for a consistent framework.

The financial sector can and must fulfil an important role in directing financial flows towards promising sustainable activities. As market-based incentives are still limited, public financing activities can provide the needed stimuli to corroborate this path, attracting private money, increasing bankability of green projects and stepping forward to shape the market.

In the end, joint efforts of private and public financial intermediaries can make the transformation towards global climate neutrality also an economic success story: Being the world's second largest exporter of climate friendly goods, only surpassed by China, Europe is also in a very good position to benefit from future markets for green products and services. If we strengthen cooperation at the European level, taking advantage of synergies through joint markets and coordinated infrastructure, sustainability requirements can become the basis for future welfare.

Andreas Dombret

The Financial Services Sector needs to be an important Driver for the Corporate Decarbonization Trajectory in Europe

The 2015 Paris agreement to limit global warming to well below 2 °C, preferably 1.5 °C, represents a landmark in the fight against climate change. Fortunately, we are witnessing considerable progress in reducing carbon emissions by many of Europe's largest corporates.

But this progress is uneven, pointing to wide skews in progress to date, as well as differences in business models: Positive developments can be seen in the latest climate change data from European companies disclosing to CDP, a not-for-profit charity that runs the global disclosure system for investors, companies, cities, states and regions to manage their environmental impacts. Last year, the top quarter of corporates in terms of decarbonization reported emission reductions of more than 15 % in absolute terms as well as more than 20 % in emission intensity levels (emissions per unit of revenue). However, there are large differences between companies in the same sector as well as between sectors. Across almost all sub-sectors of the traditionally carbon intensive industries of materials, energy and transport, the CO2 intensity levels of the bottom 25 % of companies are more than double those of the top 25 %. For sub-sectors such as steel, electric utilities and transport services, the levels are more than four times as much.

More importantly however, even if European corporates were to achieve their stated ambitions this would result in an economy on a trajectory towards a global heating of 2.7 °C, well above the Paris target and falling short of the European Union's policy ambition.

The Financial System as an Accelerator

Many financial institutions have the ambition to be Paris-aligned. This means they need the emissions of the companies they lend or invest in to cut emissions at a rate commensurate with the Paris goals. This has the potential to be a major force in accelerating company commitments to reduce emissions.

Banks representing 95 % of all lending to European corporates share this ambition. This contrasts with just 8 % of European corporates having set targets in line with a well-below 2 °C rise, creating a gap of more than €4 trillion between

https://doi.org/10.1515/9783110752892-002

the lending that banks plan to align with Paris and the current available demand for such financing.

This gap has the potential to galvanize industry to greater action, as the financial system acts to start to close this gap. Primarily, this presents an opportunity for the corporate sector.

Change in Motion for Corporates

As financial institutions seek to meet their green targets they ate likely to drive down the price of capital for those companies making progress in reducing emissions. Corporations able to fulfil the growing customer demand for sustainable products – or to pioneer new, green technologies – will enjoy lower funding costs and valuation premia.

The digital revolution over the past 10 years has shown that in major periods of transformation new companies often are the winners, while established players may struggle to move fast enough. Large, diversified companies must attempt to "thread the needle" – maintaining their legacy businesses at a level that can generate the cash needed to support investment in the businesses of the future. This can present a difficult balance to strike and a hard message to sell to investors. As investors increasingly place a premium on companies with a clear and compelling green-growth story, some corporates will seek to tap into this source of finance by carving out those businesses that fit the bill.

In the automotive sector, for example, there exists a vast difference in the valuation multiple applied to the electric car businesses embedded within incumbent auto manufacturers and that is applied to electric specialists. This premium reflects a belief not just in the green credentials of pure electric players but also in their ability to innovate and move with speed towards a model for the future. The different treatment by investors is already causing some automakers to react. Some are separating out specialized activities, such as units developing new powertrains or autonomous vehicles, into separate entities that can attract higher valuations. Incumbent companies will find it challenging to prove the value of their diversified business models and corporate structures. Can they pivot their investment budgets and create the conditions to incubate innovative technologies? Can they then drive these to scale? Can they use their power and influence to create mission-based ecosystems that assemble a diverse group of players to solve complex problems? Those market participants that present convincing answers to these questions and set out a clear path forward are likely to attract strong appetite amongst investors. With these answers they may face increasing questions over both their transition paths and their wider business models.

The Importance of Scope 3 Emissions

How should corporations prepare themselves for financial institutions' and investors' growing focus on transition plans? There is an emerging consensus on the components of a good plan and growing numbers of companies are putting these elements in place. Disclosure, however, remains limited in some important areas, and quality is somewhat mixed. Investors and financiers want and need to see plans that are ambitious, grounded in specific targets and action, and supported by strong governance. They see opportunity as well as risk and are increasingly rewarding those companies that are best prepared to accelerate their decarbonization trajectory. The most ambitious corporate leaders are realizing that, in order to benefit from the new focus in the financial world, they need to rethink the very structures within their industries and of their companies.

All being said, the majority of existing plans fall short of Paris. One of the contributors to this situation can be found in the challenging area of the so-called Scope 3 emissions.

Scope 1 emissions (direct emissions, largely from fossil fuel combustion) and Scope 2 (indirect emissions from the generation of purchased electricity, steam, heating and cooling consumed) are relatively straightforward to identify and to measure. However, for many companies the key drivers of emissions are indirect, and emissions are either embedded in the global value chain through which they source components and products, or they are caused by use of the products they sell. These are the called Scope 3 emissions which account for 80 % of total carbon emissions associated with the activities of the European corporate sector. A recent study confirmed that supply chain emissions are on average over 11 times a company's direct emissions.

A major issue for corporates is the assessment of its Scope 3 emissions, being far more difficult to trace than Scope 1 and Scope 2 emissions. Currently, as a consequence, less than 35 % of companies in high-impact sectors are disclosing meaningful information on Scope 3 emissions. Addressing this requires new forms of collaboration, working across boundaries; to most ambitious market participants are already actively pushing for change in this respect.

Today, Scope 3 disclosure is most consistent in some of the lesser important sectors such as business travel but lacking in many others. For instance, only 5 % of real estate companies disclose emissions relating to the use of the sold products. In fact, less than 35 % of companies in high-impact sectors disclose information for the most important category of their Scope 3 emissions. This shows how challenging it can be to represent Scope 3 emissions accurately, as methodologies can be complex and the data is hard to come by.

The disclosure and interpretation of Scope 3 emissions is an important area requiring further work due of its significance in creating more accurate and higher-quality temperature ratings for companies. Financial institutions cannot properly assess temperature, and reduce ratings, without more high-quality Scope 3 data from companies. Therefore, this lack of corporate Scope 3 data represents a major barrier for banks, asset managers and asset owners to set their own ambitious targets.

Since one company's Scope 3 emission is another's Scope 1 or 2 emission companies will have to collaborate to monitor, and thereby reduce, these emissions. Nowhere is the need to collaborate clearer than in the energy sector. Estimates of Oliver Wyman and others suggest that reductions in emissions relating to energy and fuel will account for more than 50 % of the total reductions needed over the next 10 years.

Banks may need to rotate 20–30 % of their Portfolios

Financial institutions, for their part, will have the opportunity to intermediate between motivated investors and sustainable businesses.

For many financial institutions in Europe climate change has moved from a fringe topic to a board level priority. There have been significant investments to build new capabilities, and a number of statements have been made in the last 12–18 months. Yet the work required to fully embed this ambition within the plumbing of the financial system is only just beginning.

The baseline requirement for all financial institutions is to ensure that financial risks and opportunities presented by climate change are reflected adequately in their decision making. It is now wide accepted that these risks are material and need to be understood as part of a financial institution's core fiduciary responsibility to manage risk and return. Yet implementing it is not at all straightforward.

Most analytical frameworks and decision tools traditionally used by financial institutions to assess and price risk are calibrated based on backward-looking data sets. Assessing climate risk requires a forward-looking approach based on scenario analysis. This means systematically thinking through how a wide range of potential scenarios – from changes in the physical environment to new policies or technologies that hasten the transition to a low- carbon economy – could affect the different types of companies in the lending or investment portfolio. To provide the necessary information, companies report a wide range of risk types. While most financial institutions are now assessing climate risk and opportunity on some level, few are doing this comprehensively across the portfolio.

Regulatory pressure is helping to accelerate progress. The Bank of England has set the bar high for UK-based banks and insurers, pushing them to include a climate scenario analysis as part of their biennial stress test. The European Central Bank has indicated that it will be pushing in a similar direction, requiring banks to not just disclose climate data but also extensively to quantify those risks and embed them into their risk management frameworks.

Shifting the Lending Portfolio

Banks' portfolio temperature ratings are higher than the pathway of the European economy as a whole, indicating that their loan distributions are skewed towards companies that are less advanced in their transitions. Addressing this overshoot is challenging. Banks do not wish to walk away from relationships that may have stood for many years or abandon communities that have been built around heavy, extractive industries. Equally, it would be counterproductive if capital were driven away from pollutive companies which are seeking to invest in technologies and processes to reduce their emissions. As such, the most crucial strategy for a financial institution is to engage with its existing customers and encourage them to develop credible transition plans. This requires strong engagement to drive meaningful action.

However, there are various portfolio strategies open to banks that want to align with Paris. For example, a bank could systematically "drop the worst and pick the best" clients in terms of climate within each sector. Another approach could be to strategically target high-emitting and low returning clients to which the bank has a high exposure, so the bank would maximize progress towards its climate goals while minimizing the adverse business impact. Even so, the shifts required to meet financial institutions' Paris ambitions could be significant. In a scenario which implies a modest acceleration vis-à-vis today's decarbonization trajectory a hypothetical bank would need to re-align 20 to 30 % of their portfolios and clients, to be on track with their commitments for Paris alignment.

Financial institutions have an important role to play in engaging with companies, to encourage and incentivize them to develop credible transition plans and deliver against these. Yet there is a risk that without a step change in progress, probably triggered by a major policy change such as a carbon tax or a tech breakthrough, the corporate sector will not reduce emissions as fast as the Paris agreement requires. In such a scenario only those banks and asset managers willing to proactively align their portfolios will be able to meet their Paris goals.

At least 65 % of European companies need to be Paris-aligned.

There is notable progress in the decarbonization of Europe. Many companies are setting ambitious targets, and the financial sector is gearing up to direct capital more meaningfully in favour of companies taking action to mitigate climate risks and support the transition. Yet there are also important warnings. Despite the increasing corporate ambitions for a transition to low-carbon industry, the pace needs to step up significantly. As mentioned before, assuming European companies achieve their current targets the European corporate sector is in line with a 2.7 °C world by 2100. That falls short of the collective 1.5 °C target and short of the minimum required for Paris alignment.

Therefore, Europe is at a critical inflexion point. This decade will be critical for companies to develop more robust transition plans. They will need to work in collaboration with governments and financiers to shape these plans – and deliver on them. In order to have a good chance of meeting the Paris goal our economy needs to shed 50 % of emissions over the next decade. This means that at least 65 % of companies need to be fully Paris-aligned by then, with many going beyond that ambition level. The financial system can help accelerate the path to Paris by mobilizing capital towards those companies likely to prosper in the transition, but action is needed now.

A supportive policy environment will be key. Governments across the region have an important role to play. Country-level differences in current temperature levels in the European corporate sector, ranging from 2.3 °C to 3.0 °C, point to the different challenges across governments and to the potential of sharing best practices across the region.

As the world steps up to fight climate change, Europe's corporates can and will need to play a leading role. Realizing this potential requires not only ambition but also action – action that is most impactful when taken in collaboration. Corporates, financial institutions and governments all need to build on the momentum that is presently developing and hold each other accountable to deliver.

This contribution is based on 'Running Hot' published by CDP and Oliver Wyman in March 2021. The author thanks both CDP and Oliver Wyman for their cooperation.

Wiebe Draijer and Bouke de Vries

Greening the Economy: The Role of Banks in the Climate Transition and Challenges

Preface

The world is facing major challenges in the areas of climate change, biodiversity loss, and threats to ecosystems. At the same time, more mouths need to be fed. How can we reduce the ecological footprint of economic activities? To do this, we need to reduce emissions, move to more sustainable production methods, make choices about what we consume, and adjust the way in which our food is produced. Banks play an important role in this as financiers of economic sectors and with their knowledge and networks in the economy. This article discusses that role and the opportunities and challenges that go with it.

Section 1 describes the role of banks in the climate transition with examples from several sectors, including the relationship between the food transition and the climate transition. Section 2 discusses the challenges of how to attribute emissions to assets on bank balance sheets, and of assessing climate-related risks and opportunities for companies and sectors, in order to create a picture of the possible impact on bank balance sheets in the future. Section 3 discusses how businesses and consumers can be incentivized to take the next step in the climate transition. Section 4 examines the role of regulation and government policies, from the perspective of how these can help banks to finance transitions, followed by conclusions.

1. The Role of Banks in the Climate Transition

In order to achieve the Paris Climate Agreement target of limiting global warming to well below 2 degrees, preferably 1.5 degrees, we need to significantly reduce greenhouse gas (GHG) emissions. In the Netherlands and Europe, this equates to more than halving greenhouse gas emissions by 2030 compared to 1990 and moving to a net carbon-neutral economy by 2050. Although the use of energy from fossil sources is still a reality and a necessity today, it is essential that we decrease the dependence of the economy on fossil fuels in the coming years. This requires an energy transition. Signatories to the Paris Agreement have drawn up National Determined Contribution plans (NDCs) which set out those emission reduction goals for different sectors of the economy, along with initial ideas on how to

https://doi.org/10.1515/9783110752892-003

achieve them. This is an important achievement, but there is still more to be done: taken together, the current NDCs are still insufficient to meet the goals of the Paris Agreement to get on a net carbon-neutral path (NDC Synthesis Report, Emission Gap report 2020).

The climate transition requires enormous efforts from everyone, including banks. Banks are already greening their own business operations,[1] but their greatest potential contribution lies in the financing they provide their clients and in the intermediation and transformation function of banks in the economy. It is through banks that savings, investments and money from the capital markets find their way to projects and companies and to private investments in infrastructure, for example. An increasing proportion of this will have to be (re) structured to support activities that accelerate the climate transition. Banks can stimulate and facilitate their customers in this through financial solutions and providing access to economic knowledge and the banks' networks.

Business clients taking steps towards sustainability make both a positive contribution to society and limit the risks to which they (and their financiers) are exposed. Risks of tightening environmental laws and policies, and other transition risks such as changing consumer preferences, or the possibility that competitors become more successful in reducing emissions and developing new technologies. Banks and clients therefore have a shared interest in becoming more sustainable, properly assessing the climate-related risks and, where possible, limiting these risks. More about this in section 2.

The Food Transition

A transition which partly overlaps with the climate transition is the food transition. This is about guaranteeing food security in combination with a lower ecological footprint of food. A lot of emissions can be avoided by reducing food waste. Think of measures throughout the supply chain, from production, transport, storage, up to consumption. Banks stimulate the food transition with smart financial incentives and by including sustainability criteria in their terms and conditions for products and services. In addition, banks connect parties in the chain with each other and share knowledge in a number of concrete projects – where there is a logical role for the lender.

1 Banks are becoming increasingly transparent about their own carbon footprint and set annual targets to reduce it. Many banks also offset emissions from their own operations.

What are some concrete Examples of how Banks stimulate the Transitions?[2]

The Dutch real estate market:

- In the Dutch Climate Commitment the financial sector has agreed to commit to making the built environment more sustainable, including the private housing stock (Dutch Banking Association, 2019). For example, at Rabobank we aim for an average energy label B in the residential real estate portfolio by 2024 and label A (almost energy neutral) by 2030. Currently, the average energy label is C. To stimulate this transition, we offer our clients advice and financial incentives to make sustainable investments in their homes, plus a free scan of their home's energy efficiency by a specialized party. Our green mortgages now also carry lower interest rates than our regular mortgages, and we have established a *GroenDepot* (green depot), so that households can borrow for energy efficiency measures such as installing a heat pump or solar panels. The number of clients asking for these solutions is increasing all the time. Yet we still have a long way to go, especially for properties that still have a very low energy performance, such as homes built in the 1930s. Dutch banks will continue to contribute to these developments with financing solutions. These banks, including Rabobank, have also committed to being transparent about the financed emissions of their portfolio through recognized reporting standards, such as the Platform for Carbon Accounting Financials (PCAF)[3].
- The Dutch banking sector's Sustainable Housing Sector Collective offers mortgage advisers a 'Sustainable Housing Adviser' training course to better promote the importance of making people's homes sustainable.

The Dutch Food and Agriculture sector:

- As part of the Dutch Climate Agreement, the agriculture and horticulture sectors have committed to an emission reduction of 6 megatons between 1990 and 2030. Banks, and Rabobank in particular as we finance almost 85 % of primary producers in the sector, support business clients in realizing this ambition and offer various types of sustainable loans. We are also partnering in projects that invest in new agricultural practices to increase emission reductions. These include the development of new barn systems, the production of

---

2 Examples are selected from Rabobank's Climate Report (2020). More examples of other banks can be found in a Dutch Banking Association report (2020) about the Financial Sector Climate Commitment.

3 The PCAF standard provides definitions per asset category for calculating the financed emissions.

renewable energy and feed optimization, including the utilization of waste flows. The Dutch dairy and horticulture sectors are illustrative of what can be achieved. In the dairy sector average emissions per kg of milk are currently 1.14 kg of CO2 – half of the global average of 2.5 kg of CO2. Additional steps are being taken to further reduce this. The horticulture sector in the Netherlands is now 80 % self-sufficient in renewable energy.

- Emissions in Dutch horticulture have decreased by 16 % compared to 1990. This comes mainly from a stronger focus on modernizing (low energy) greenhouses, the transition to geothermal heating and from strengthening entrepreneurship. Most geothermal heating projects in agriculture in the Netherlands are financed by Rabobank, with our exposure topping more than EUR 200 million.
- Initiatives such as the Biodiversity Monitor[4], the *Open Soil Index*[5] and the *Food Waste Challenges*[6] should lead to detailed insight into the performance of entrepreneurs and a revenue model for fewer emissions and a more sustainable agricultural food chain.
- An assessment is currently being made of what will be needed in the coming years for the sustainability transition of food and agriculture sectors in the Netherlands. For a full implementation of the Dutch Climate Agreement and an integrated solution for the nitrogen and water problems the sector is facing, it is crucial that sufficient financing is available. Rabobank has proposed to set up an investment fund of EUR 1 billion to support the transitions. The aim of that fund is to help achieve the Dutch climate, water and nitrogen targets for the countryside, with a specific focus on land around Natura 2000 protected area sites[7] and on stimulating regenerative agriculture. This would provide a new perspective. We are currently investigating the feasibility of this with the Ministry of Agriculture and a large group of stakeholders.

---

4 The Biodiversity Monitor has been set up by Dutch Provincial authorities, the Sustainable Dairy Chain, Friesland Campina and Cono, Aware, banks, insurer ASR, water company Vitens, the representative organisation for Arable Farming, WWF, to encourage farmers to pay more attention to biodiversity and give them a financial benefit for it. They are also committed to ensuring that the customer in the supermarket pays a little more for sustainably produced products, such as meadow milk.

5 The Open Soil Index is a standard for measuring soil quality. The tool has been developed in collaboration with agricultural entrepreneurs, soil experts and scientific researchers.

6 With Together Against Food Waste, 61 million kilos of food can be saved annually in Dutch restaurants (equivalent to EUR 582 million euros).

7 Natura 2000 is a European network of protected nature areas. In these Natura 2000 areas, certain animals, plants and their natural habitats are protected to preserve biodiversity (species richness).

Food & Agriculture worldwide:

- Globally, it is imperative that we develop clearer and more detailed insights into the impact F&A value chains are having on climate change. We need to know the future climate-related risks for these sectors and also how emissions can be further reduced. To this end, Rabobank has set up a Banking for Impact on Climate in Agriculture initiative together with other banks. The initiative brings together the World Business Council on Sustainable Development (WBCSD), United Nations Environment Program Finance Initiative (UNEP FI), academia and the financial sector. In addition, Rabobank collaborates with the Food and Agriculture Organization of the UN (FAO) to design and implement measurement systems for greenhouse gas emissions from food.

Small and medium-sized enterprises (SMEs) are an important lending portfolio:

- Making SMEs more sustainable is essential for a future-proof economy and for prosperity and well-being. The sheer number of SMEs, their diversity and the limited resources they have makes it difficult to come up with one-size-fits-all solutions. Therefore strong client relationships and broad knowledge of sustainability/climate challenges and solutions among our own bankers is crucial. Together with partners, banks help SMEs to draw up sustainability plans. For example, Rabobank helps businesses transition into circular enterprises by providing access to a Circular Business Desk and by offering green incentives and earmarked green products. The bank provided a total of EUR 10.1 billion of finance to Dutch sustainable front runners. It has also set up a so called green bank to further support the sustainability transition. Green banks use sustainable deposited savings to provide finance with an interest discount on the basis of a national fiscal green scheme – already provide a current total volume of several billion euros in green loans (RVO Nederland, 2020). The green banks and green funds annually finance approximately EUR 800 million in sustainable projects through this scheme. This is likely to increase sharply in the coming years as a result of all the plans and incentive measures to green the economy. At the same time it is fair to say that the current volumes are still just a drop in the ocean when looking at total lending and the total size of the economy. Therefore, we will need to scale up the number of green projects significantly to achieve more impact together.

Private Investments:

- Banks will increasingly make investment funds sustainable as the default proposition. These funds will be less carbon-intensive and therefore meet higher sustainability criteria than is currently the case with funds worldwide.

We see a growing demand from customers looking for green investment opportunities. Also worth mentioning is the role that the EU Green Taxonomy will play here (see section 4).

The energy sector:
- Banks invest in hydrogen and geothermal energy and in the development of even more renewable energy.
- Banks encourage clients to participate in local energy projects involving solar panels, biomass, geothermal and wind turbines. Rabobank has been a leader in financing wind energy for over 20 years and is currently a top-five wind financier in Europe and a top-10 player in the world.
- The carbon footprint of Rabobank's power generation portfolio is already well under the International Energy Agency's decarbonization pathway. We have the ambition to expand our portfolio in the coming years by specifically targeting companies aiming to transition to more sustainable forms of power generation.

2. Measuring a CO2 (Equivalent) Footprint and Determining Climate Risks and Opportunities

We discern that there are two ways of looking at the impact of climate change with regard to the banking sector: on the one hand a bank's own impact on the climate, and on the other the impact of climate change on the bank through the impact on its customers. Traditionally, a bank's link to climate was seen through the lens of its contribution to climate change (positively and negatively), but in recent years the focus has shifted to the impact of climate on the bank (climate risk) as regulators earmarked climate change as a possible source of systemic risk. One of the very first to point out this systemic risk was Mark Carney, the then governor of the Bank of England, in 2015. When looking at climate change impact we need to be aware of this concept of double materiality. This denotes a significant change in the way that banks are thinking about climate change (Rabobank, 2020).

The method developed by the PCAF[8] has emerged as a leading methodology to measure financed emissions by financial institutions, i.e. the impact of companies on climate. Of course this work does not replace in any way the work of parties such as the Carbon Disclosure Project (CDP) on other emission reporting

8 PCAF, 2017; and annually updated.

methods. The strongpoint of PCAF is the attribution of emissions to assets on a balance sheet.

The Task Force on Climate-related Financial Disclosures (TCFD) guidelines provide a comprehensive framework for the measurement and disclosure of climate-related risks, i.e. the impact of climate on companies. Dutch banks, including ours, support the guidelines of PCAF and the TCFD, and report on them in their annual reports. In UNEP FI TCFD pilots, banks are also working on developing new approaches for estimating physical and transition risks in the portfolio (United Nations Environment Programme Finance Initiative, 2020). In addition, several Dutch banks work, or are starting to work, with the Paris Alignment Capital Transition Assessment (PACTA) method, aligning capex with transition pathways (Dutch Banking Association, 2019).

The financial impact of climate-related risks includes physical and transition risks, both of which ultimately influence our clients' ability to repay their loans. For example, a company may be exposed to a transition risk because environmental legislation is becoming increasingly strict. Or a company could face higher costs if it has to pay more for emission rights.

Four particularly relevant challenges identified by the Working Group on Climate Risks of the Dutch Platform Sustainable Finance, 2020 are:

1. Relevant climate data are in many cases not available, incomplete and / or not at the desired level of granularity. A wide variety of definitions are also used, which hinders consistency and comparability. The ideal solution, together with national governments and the EU, is to enrich, bundle and make relevant climate data public and easily accessible, for example by setting up a new European ESG data register.
2. There is a discrepancy in the time horizon: risks are modelled / estimated by financial institutions with a time horizon corresponding to the average maturity of their portfolios (generally indicative 3–5 years), in accordance with current legal requirements. However, the effects of climate change occur over a much longer time horizon (10 or more years) and are not linear, which means that refinancing risks can be different over time. Uncertainties increase as timelines lengthen, underscoring the need for working with multiple scenarios. In this respect, there is also a difference between physical and transition scenarios: the former are based on climate science, the latter on political and technological choices and innovation breakthroughs.
3. Not all critical climate risks are known at the time of the investment / financing decision. Or the likelihood of such risks cannot be accurately estimated. Think of the loss of biodiversity, effects in ecosystems, tipping points: all this is still poorly understood and can have major consequences. This can lead to an under-estimation of risks.

4. There are still no generally accepted methods for estimating climate-related credit risks. To create some consistency and comparability between financial institutions, guidance from supervisors is needed. In order to make informed choices and correct value assessments, financial institutions and other stakeholders must also be aware of the serious limitations of models. In particular, careful interpretation is required for the evaluation of results from off-the-shelf products.

On the other hand, we believe that there are plenty of opportunities if businesses succeed in developing cleaner technologies than their competitors, and there are savings opportunities for individuals when they manage to reduce their energy use. Examples where we as banks can play a role are:

- Create awareness in the housing market for energy-saving measures and present financing options and returns.
- Finance and facilitate the transition to climate-smart agriculture, financing transitions to regenerative agriculture and investments to reduce emissions and reduce waste.
- Carbon banking – Develop propositions that will enable clients to contact the bank not only for financial transactions but also for voluntary nature-based carbon solution. In 2021 Rabobank launched the Rabo Carbon Bank that enables farmers to transition to carbon farming. Farmers are empowered to adopt regenerative farming practices and the Carbon Bank helps them to make their efforts tangible and verifiable. Then the resulting carbon removals can be sold in form of carbon credits. Next to removing existing GHG emissions from the atmosphere and storing them in soils and trees, Rabo Carbon Bank aims to reduce GHG emissions that enter the atmosphere. The Carbon Bank facilitates large food corporates to achieve scope 3 reduction by setting up projects and by incentivizing farmers and other suppliers upstream to participate. In this way, Rabobank mediates between parties that store CO2 and companies that want to reduce or compensate for their emissions.
- Accelerate the transition to a low-carbon energy system by financing renewable-energy projects, supporting innovation and scaling up low-carbon energy solutions.
- Using sustainable financing schemes and incentives such as green bonds to enable (large) companies to raise finance to green their activities.
- Provide financial solutions -including private equity and venture capital – for disruptive technological innovations for regenerative and renewable technologies.

Opportunities and challenges that we see in terms of return and risk appetite in the financing of climate transitions:

- Banks have a risk profile that seldom really matches the risk profile of many early-stage transitions. We require a relatively large amount of collateral for conventional lending and project investments, partly because of supervisory requirements. Other players, such as venture capitalists or capital market funds can take on more risk. Next to this, governments have tools that can help mitigate some of the top risks, either through guarantees or backstops. These measures ensure that the risk profile is more within the financing capabilities of banks as well.
- Return is the compensation for the risk on a transaction. Sustainability should not only pay off because of its importance to nature, but also generate returns. Research into the relationship between sustainability and return shows that projects with a good sustainability score can also show a good return, or even a better one compared to less sustainable projects (Rockefeller Asset Management, New York University Stern Center for Sustainable Business, 2021). Companies with more sustainable products or services can also improve their competitive advantage.
- Examples of good financing opportunities are the business cases for onshore and offshore wind and solar energy, as well as programs for reducing food waste.

3. Engagement: Stimulating Companies to take the next Step in the Transitions

As banks we can talk about sustainability in the periodic contact we have with our clients. For example, with business clients when they face investment decisions and require credit, or with private clients making choices to invest, save, or to buy a new home. There are many such moments. Our clients naturally make the decision themselves, but we can interpret the financial impact of decisions and, where necessary, pass this on in a risk premium or discount.

Rabobank already engages with business clients (outstanding loans of above EUR 1 million) to assess sustainability risks and opportunities as part of the qualitative credit risk analyses. This is less the case with smaller SMEs, mainly due to a lack of data and practicalities to engage with larger numbers of clients, but we do consider risks at sector level for example.

Earlier we described what we as a bank can offer clients: helping to finance energy-saving projects, encouraging real estate owners to take energy-saving measures, and helping companies that emit a relatively large volume of CO2 to transfer to technologies with a low(er) climate impact or to circular business models. In addition, our focus on climate can also lead to divestment if there is insufficient progress in sustainability performance. In other words, a conversation about (missed) opportunities can lead to the conclusion that there is no longer a match between a client's ambitions and our own principles. Client engagement must also have teeth in order to be effective.

With private clients, our conversations mainly focus on advice about financial products. It is also important and increasingly common to look at climate and sustainability-related aspects and to point out the possibility of more sustainable financial solutions where relevant.

This may sound obvious, but sustainability topics are still far from commonplace in the conversations banks hold with their clients. This will become more and more mainstream, because climate and environmental risks are serious challenges that everyone has to deal with and for which everyone bears their own responsibility. It helps that clients themselves are increasingly interested in having this conversation.

4. Role of Regulations and Government Policy for the Transitions

To make it clear that the climate transition is a necessity and not a choice, we consider it essential that governments take decisive measures to green the economy, backed up by concrete support measures to make the transition. If governments impose legally binding restrictions on emissions, that will have a major impact. The same applies to requirements for setting a minimum percentage of clean energy, how many houses must have a certain energy label at any given time, and so on.[9]

To some degree, these policies can be supported by the use of targeted – and temporary / evolving – subsidies or tax incentives, such as for green loans, for green deposits, investments in solar and wind energy, and for innovation in more carbon-neutral food production. Common standards can also play a supporting role, for example the European taxonomy for sustainable activities[10]. This should provide clarity to European financial institutions about what is and what is not

9 A Dutch example is the government's requirement that from 2023 all offices must have a climate label of at least C.

10 The European taxonomy qualifies an economic activity as 'green' if it makes a significant positive contribution to at least one of the six criteria defined in the taxonomy, while ensuring that there is no significant negative impact on the other criteria.

considered 'sustainable' financing. We believe that the direction the European Commission is taking here is timely and important.

Above all, combating climate change requires a better pricing of greenhouse gas emissions. In Europe this is covered by the EU Emissions Trading System (ETS) mechanism. We need an ETS that truly reflects the societal costs of emissions. For the system to work properly, CO2 rights must be scarce and therefore entail a high price. The 'polluter pays' principle will then work better. An effective price mechanism for CO2 and other greenhouse gases fosters more sustainable choices by producers and consumers. In addition, if done properly, it will reduce the need for complicated coordination measures, extensive controls or the use of subsidies. However, getting it right is not easy: ETS systems are complex and political interference (such as granting businesses too many free emissions rights at the beginning of schemes) hampers their effectiveness.

Zooming in on this topic, emission pricing should help speed up the transition, reduce market distortions and improve predictability. Market participants will take into account expectations about the development of the CO2 price (respective prices of equivalent greenhouse gases) and make their investment and production choices accordingly. This makes it a very important tool for financial institutions to avoid cliff effects as much as possible: sudden write-downs of assets that lead to losses for investors. Because – and certainly just as important – these may lead to social costs and job losses. Early intervention will allow for gradual phase-in, late intervention will increase the likelihood of a disorderly transition. The impact will then be correspondingly greater.

It is good to see the progress the European Commission is making in this respect with the Green Deal package.

One of the many other relevant issues is whether the capital requirements for financial institutions should be adjusted to reflect new insights about climate risks. Central to this is that climate risks can change or influence the probability of default and the loss given default in credit models. A factor co-determining exposure to climate-related risk is the extent to which companies can take measures to increase their resilience to climate change or if they can reduce their climate footprint. Companies doing better than their peers in this regard will represent a different exposure. This should be reflected in the capital requirements and loan provisions. Further work must be done to improve these insights in the coming years. In our view, capital requirements must in any case be based on risk sensitivity and must therefore include climate risk.

5. Conclusion

A climate disaster is looming and companies, citizens, non-governmental organizations, academia, banks and governments must work together to turn this tide. Measuring impact and risks is one of the key challenges and we especially need data at the right level of granularity and more harmonized definitions for what gets measured. We also need to chart the most affected areas and sectors to help guide our climate strategy. Strong financial incentives should then be applied, including CO2 pricing, and clear transition paths developed, to give direction to the change process towards a net zero economy and to make economic sectors and society more resilient to the impact of climate change. We will take our role and responsibility as a bank and will engage with our clients to help them on the road towards a low-carbon society.

References

Dutch Banking Association (2019), *Fifty financial institutions sign up for climate targets.*

Dutch Banking Association (2019), *Measuring climate impact: how do banks do that?*

Dutch Banking Association, *Banks' Climate Commitment 2020, Insight in measurement methods and climate actions of the banking sector.*

European Commission(2020), *EU Taxonomy for Sustainable Activities.*

European Commission (2020), *Farm to Fork Strategy.*

Nutrient management Institute and Wageningen University (2020), *The Open Soil Index 0.3.*

Platform Carbon Accounting Financials (2021), *Next steps: updates from implementing GHG accounting for the financial sector in the Netherlands*, Annual Report 2020.

Rabobank (2020), *Rabobank and Climate Change – Making the change to safeguard our future*

Rockefeller Asset Management, New York University Stern Center for Sustainable Business (2021), *ESG and Financial Performance: Uncovering the Relationship by aggregating Evidence from 1,000 Plus Studies Published between 2015–2021.*

RVO (2020), *National Green Projects Arrangement* ("Groenregeling").

United Nations (2021), *Climate Change NDC Synthesis Report.*

United Nations (2020), *Emission Gap Report 2020.*

United Nations Environment Program Finance Initiative (2020), *various reports.*

Working Group on Climate Risks of the Dutch Sustainable Finance Platform (2020), *Climate risk and the financial sector: sharing of good practices.*

Daniel Mminele

Banking on going green...

COVID-19 has highlighted the interconnectedness between the fragility of our current global socio-economic system and climate change, and the urgent need to accelerate the green transition as part of addressing a global challenge.

The financial sector has an important role to play in enabling the green transition, and it is encouraging to see banks, insurers and investors, etc. increasingly accepting their responsibililty in facilitating and incentivizing a green agenda, as shown by commitments being made and changes being effected to their strategies to align their businesses with the Paris Climate Change Agreement (2015) and the Sustainable Development Goals (2015).

However, significant challenges are confronting the financial sector on its transition journey: No two institutions are the same, and the ability of firms to support the transition is influenced by their macroeconomic environments, the structure and strength of their financial systems, capital markets developments, and also their political environments. This will influence scale, speed and sequencing and thus results in organisations across the globe being on different levels of maturity in this transition journey.

Despite these challenges, progress is being made. In South Africa, several banks, including Absa, are integrating climate change into business practices and corporate governance, by, for example, publishing coal financing standards or policies, and embedding climate considerations into credit frameworks. With its dedicated sustainable finance team, Absa is also looking to increase capital allocation towards financing activities that support environmental protection and inclusive growth in Africa. Corporate behaviour, aligning internal risk processes and credit strategy to climate risk, influencing policy outcomes and building the data, tools and transparency required to embed climate change into markets behaviour are becoming increasingly important steps in demonstrating leadership on climate change.

In managing the green transition, Absa has encountered global as well as region specific challenges: Accuracy and availability of environmental and social data is a challenge, especially for smaller, unlisted companies, hence the need for rigorous due diligence. This is especially important for banks to ensure projects they finance do not harm society and enhance sustainability. Climate change forecasts, while readily available, sometimes lack the granularity required to support decision making in our regions. New skills are required for integrating sustainability into business, which are generally in short supply in Africa. Thus, collaboration across geographies and industries will be vital moving forward.

https://doi.org/10.1515/9783110752892-004

Dialogue, collaboration and resource mobilisation also play a key role in enabling a just transition. It is evident that different levels of development exist within and across countries. As many countries in our region are highly dependent on fossil fuels, too stringent or unduly rushed implementation of current global best practices, without country-specific considerations and clear transition plans, could put their financial sectors and economies at significant risk. These nuances must be considered in addressing climate change, as policy and regulatory decisions can have significant unintended consequences on people's lives and livelihoods, which could ultimately threaten global stability. From a banking sector perspective, regulatory actions will strongly influence how the financial sector responds to the climate challenge, as seen in some developed nations.

Beyond the many challenges, the green transition also provides considerable opportunity for the financial sector. For example, Africa's significant transition requires material investment and effort, which banks such as Absa, are well placed to support as part of our commitment to addressing climate change and sustainable human development. Holistic regulatory and policy certainty, as well as access to pools of global and regional ESG capital, including from Development Finance Institutions, will be key enablers to assist African countries to leapfrog into clean, green technologies and close the growing infrastructure gap on the continent.

Thus, by working together, we can accelerate the transition to a low-carbon economy and contribute to sustainable growth.

Ted Moynihan

How Banks can help Achieve the Paris Agreement

Relationships with Borrowers will be crucial for Decarbonization

Nearly five years after the Paris Agreement, the business world is full of good intentions – but not yet enough action.

The agreement aims to limit global temperature rises to well below 2 °C, and preferably to 1.5 °C, a goal that will need new technology development and fundamental changes in the way corporations operate. Financing these changes will require up enormous amounts of capital in the coming years. The OECD estimates that around USD 6.9 trillion of infrastructure investment is needed each year to 2030 to meet development goals within the goals of the Paris Agreement. To ensure the funds contribute to a reduction in greenhouse gas emissions, banks need to target their lending. That implies incentives, such as favorable terms for borrowers that reduce their carbon footprints and financing that targets programs to help "brown" companies become "green".

This new role for finance raises major questions about the way banks work, their relationships with their clients, and the wider environment of the financial industry. Decarbonization projects will often be long and high-risk and come with uncertain return. Consider, for example, a project to develop commercial airplanes fueled by hydrogen cells. Lending to many such projects will not meet bank loans' traditional profile of risk, return, and duration. Moreover, banks might face tough decisions over how to assess clients' decarbonization programs and what to do if they don't measure up: Cutting a client off would be bad for business and would likely only push the client to another lender with less-stringent standards.

As a result, the shift to green financing is likely only to be effective with changes in bank culture and processes – changes that go beyond regulatory compliance and integrate environmental responsibility into banks' daily processes.

Banks' new Job

The green transition represents a great opportunity for financial institutions to fund corporations that are making an effort to decarbonize. In the automotive sector, for example, the rise of electric cars and car-sharing could change the entire ecosystem of manufacturers and service providers. Existing companies are investing and divesting to adapt, while new enterprises are emerging: There were 138 start-ups of this kind in 2018, collectively worth $46 billion.

https://doi.org/10.1515/9783110752892-005

Sustainable finance ecosystem

Area	Sub-area	Revenue potential
Savings and investing	Impact investing Sustainable investing Integrated ESG investing	$100-150 billion
Financing	Green bonds Green lending Transition finance	
Content and risk transfer	Data and analytics Advisory Insurance and risk transfer	

Fig. 1: The sustainable finance markets represent a $100–150 billion revenue opportunity over the next decade[1]
Source: Oliver Wyman analysis

In some industries, however, executives say they want to take action but are limited in what they can do – either because customers won't bear the costs or because investors want to optimize for short-term returns. To incentivize change, financial firms can steer capital away from the most polluting companies, and toward the environmental leaders. Banks representing 95 percent of all corporate lending to European corporates have ambitions to align their lending with the Paris Agreement. That is, they plan to lend to corporations that are following decarbonization programs that – if companies worldwide followed similar programs – would lead to the achievement of the Paris Agreement targets. Over 70 percent of the biggest asset managers have similar ambitions.

In theory that can mean cutting off lending to borrowers that are not ambitious enough in their plans for change. But such moves could have drastic unintended consequences for people's livelihoods and living standards – especially in developing countries, where power generation often relies on coal, and alternatives will require a lot of time and money. Moreover, bankers warn that abandoning a client would be counterproductive: They would soon find another lender, and a lender that wants to contribute to the green transition will then have lost its influence. Instead, it's more effective to engage with borrowers. At the ILF conference on Green Banking and Green Central Banking the CEO of one major bank said his efforts to influence companies in the food supply chain had led these clients to refer to him as the NGO of the financial sector. But these conversations eventually led such clients to become partners in the green transition – reducing their carbon footprint and increasing the Paris-aligned proportion of the bank's

1 *Climate Change* by Oliver Wyman (2020).

loan portfolio. "I think the best method is to apply the pressure that you can while you're financing these clients," the CEO said. "You have much more leverage when you are in the conversation than when you pull out."

Banks' new Tools

Directing lending towards corporate efforts to decarbonize will need a variety of new products and processes, some of which need much more development.

Green bonds have been a major success story, achieving issuance of $250 billion in 2019, from a standing start 10 years ago.[2] As the market has grown, the set of issuers has expanded beyond sovereigns and development banks into the private sector. Yet the market remains small, and it is skewed towards higher-grade credits. Critically, the issuer base is particularly small in those areas where the largest change is required, such as in emerging markets and in sectors that have the most work to do in order to transition to a lower carbon model.

A major challenge for banks is how to measure a corporate borrower's ambition and efforts to decarbonize. Emissions from a company's fuel combustion (Scope 1) and from purchasing power (Scope 2) are relatively straightforward. But for many companies, the bulk of the emissions they cause occur in their supply chain (through the manufacture and transport of components) or through use of their products (especially for products such as vehicles). These Scope 3 emissions are far harder to establish, and so far less than 35 percent of companies in high-impact sectors are disclosing information on them.

Climate risk will become an integral part of banks' client ratings, but that will only be possible once the bank has the necessary data and analytic skills, said the CEO of one major bank at the conference. "We still have to develop some of these skills for analyzing and pricing this risk," he said. "I think we are still far away from a point where this becomes almost second nature – where, for instance, market discipline takes over and we have sufficient transparency and symmetry of information for pricing."

To understand better the impacts of their clients' activities, some banks have started to use the new EU Taxonomy, which sets performance thresholds for economic activities that make a substantive contribution to environmental objectives. These thresholds help identify which industrial activities are already environmentally friendly and which need to be improved to qualify for green financing.

---

2 *Climate Change* by Oliver Wyman (2020), p. 14.

Outside firms are currently developing ways to capture and analyze data to measure corporations' decarbonization progress and assess progress in delivering against transition goals. This activity might become standardized, as more-rigorous assessments of banks' own climate readiness start to emerge from research firms, and they begin to act a bit like credit ratings. Failure to secure a positive rating – or to show progress in reducing the carbon intensity of the balance sheet – would then potentially be a source of reputation risk for a corporation. "Our ambition is to make sure that we know the CO_2 footprint of our clients," said the CEO of another major bank – "that is, the total CO_2 emission that is attached to the money that goes to the clients that we finance. At some point this needs to be a standard."

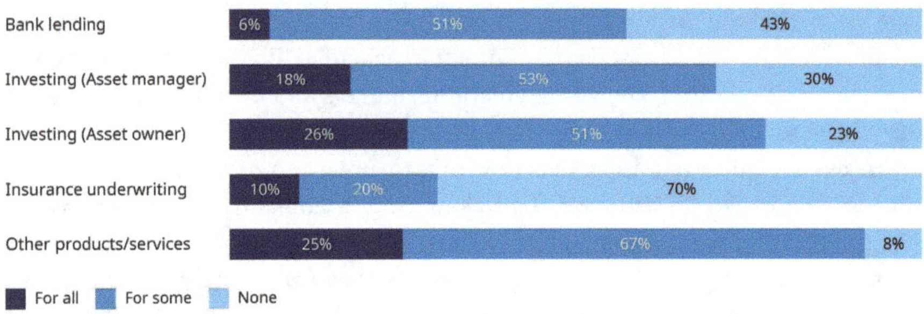

Fig. 2: Share of financial institutions that assess whether clients' and investee's business strategies are aligned to a well-below 2 °C world in 2020[3]
Source: Oliver Wyman analysis, CDP disclosure data

Banks' new Culture

If a bank is going to lead in green finance, its new jobs and processes must be more than just add-ons to its existing business. They must become its core way of doing business. "It is about mainstreaming green elements into general banking principles," as the CEO of one banking group said. "This cannot be a parallel line or sideshow issue."

Some banks have been greening in stages. First, they offered green funds to interested investors. Then they scaled these up to provide financing for major corporate transitions. In the next stage, banks will dedicate their whole balance

3 Running Hot – Accelerating Europe's Path To Paris by Oliver Wyman and CDP (2021), "Other products/services" includes any product held off institutions' balance sheets.

sheet to the green transition, meaning it will involve every client. That does not mean cutting off clients that have failed to reduce their carbon footprint or to come up with a credible plan to reduce it: Part of banks' role will be to generate bridging solutions involving other parties, such as development banks, so that they can provide finance with an acceptable profile of risk, return, and duration. "Now it's not a matter of whether you dedicate some part of your balance sheet towards this transition," said one bank CEO. "It actually is the whole balance sheet that should be put into this transition."

To ensure that the new principles filter throughout the bank, some supervisory boards have given management clear expectations and targets for environmental performance. These can include clear sustainability targets, such as the total loan volume going to transitioning corporations by a particular year. "We have dedicated research teams and aim to be a thought leader to galvanize the industry into action," said the CEO of a major European bank. "With our sustainability governance and strategy, we touch almost every department in our bank including risk and finance. This part of banking must be an integral part of our business. If we don't do this, we are out of business."

The Role of the Public Sector

No matter how banks change the way they work, they will still have to issue loans with a different profile from those they are used to: For the return the loans yield, they are higher risk and last for longer. If banks cannot make loans that fit the right business profile, they will not be able to finance substantial green investment.

One way to ease the transition is public support, when a government or development bank contributes part of an investment or offers guarantees to private investors. This backing can lower risk for a private lender, enhance return for an equity investor, or both. The goal is to enhance the private capital that is seeking a reasonable risk-return ratio. Estimates of the total investment – private and public – needed for the climate transition vary. According to one conference panelist, more than €800 billion in public support will be required over the next 20 years through public-private partnerships globally.

The core competence of development banks is to structure the right incentives to attract private capital – and many of them now have expertise in climate protection and CO_2 reduction. An example of their activity is loan programs to refurbish and modernize the housing stock, or to build energy-efficient new houses. In Germany, one public bank's loans have triggered almost three times the lending from private-sector banks.

Such public aid need not last forever. For example, many offshore wind parks were not viable investments 10 years ago, because they presented far greater technology challenges than onshore: The rotors are much bigger, as are the wind speeds the turbines have to withstand. But the technology has since been mastered. "Today, offshore wind parks in the North Sea are bankable without any public support," said the CEO of one European development bank.

Multilateral and investment banks are widening their range of activities. Some green investment funds are being structured with a focus on Africa: Any serious attempt to limit global warming needs to finance green investment in Africa, a continent with a growing population of 1.3 billion people and great potential for economic growth. In some these funds, development banks will take the first loss, and private capital from asset managers will take the second.

Sustainable finance could be given renewed momentum in the United States, where President Joe Biden has signalled wide-ranging changes over the policies of his predecessor. These include a return to the Paris Agreement might also feature include tax credits and federal funds to encourage investment in low-carbon energy and technologies that enable it.

Regulation has a role too. Financial services firms enjoy a privileged position at the heart of the economy, protected by protective moats of regulation and benefiting from various forms of explicit and implicit government support. One consequence is that policymakers can adjust the regulatory framework governing financial services in pursuit of social and economic goals.

In some jurisdictions already, regulators are actively incorporating climate considerations through a range of other levers. For example, the Prudential Regulation Authority has incorporated sustainability into its senior managers regime. In addition, the European Banking Authority has published a roadmap for incorporating climate and other ESG (environmental, social, and corporate governance) factors into their regulatory framework by 2025.

Conclusion: Climate Action is a collaborative Endeavor

Financing climate change needs a joint effort that brings together private-sector banks, development banks, governments, and investors. The first task for private-sector banks is to focus on the real economy and address the climate risk in their loan portfolios. While that can include financing businesses that emit no CO_2 at all, a greater contribution could come from ensuring that all investments from now on contribute to a substantial reduction in emissions. To do this successfully, banks need to change their goals, develop new skills, and nurture a culture in which a focus on climate is second nature.

Christian Sewing

Green Banking in Practice: How Banks and Corporates will need to work together to finance the Transition to a more sustainable Economy

Introduction

The transition to a green and sustainable future brings numerous challenges – not least the financing volumes required. The European Union alone plans to mobilize one trillion euros of sustainable investments up to 2030. Banks play a crucial role in this transformation through financing, risk management, advisory services and more.

Sustainability will be a deciding factor for the *licence to operate* for our economic system going forward. This is because despite everything, we are late in recognising action needs to be taken, and this challenge is not one that we can leave for the next generation to tackle – as we did in the past. Actually, this topic was at the very top of the agenda once before – in the early 1980s. That was when green parties came onto the scene in many countries. The *Club of Rome* had just published a report that painted a kind of doomsday scenario, and back then the topic was already the focus of some CEOs. Shortly before his assassination Alfred Herrhausen, then Deutsche Bank's CEO, called for the world's great biotopes like the Amazon rainforest to be placed in a trust for all of humanity.

But what happened then? The fall of the Berlin Wall and the collapse of the Soviet Union diverted attention away from this important topic. Effectively we lost 30 years. Now the issue of sustainability has returned with a vengeance. There has been a shift in public opinion symbolised by movements like 'Fridays for Future', and the pandemic has generated a new awareness. More and more people seem to agree with the words made famous by former US President Barack Obama: "We are the first generation to feel the impact of climate change and the last generation who can do something about it."

So a priority has emerged that is here to stay. Across politics and the economy, we will have to deploy our intellectual, technological and financial resources on an unprecedented scale. In order to meet the challenge facing the business world, to also seize it as an opportunity, we would be well advised to collaborate as closely as possible. Thus sustainability and above all the fight against climate change has also become a driving force which will shape banking during the next decade. It will impact how we work, which products we offer – and how we work with our clients.

https://doi.org/10.1515/9783110752892-006

ESG is Gaining Importance

The new societal consensus that increased sustainability is a must, is reflected firstly in the expectations that various stakeholder groups are conveying to us all. For listed companies this starts with investors. In this case we're no longer talking about niche funds – the leading voices come from the elite of global asset managers. As one of the front runners, BlackRock is unequivocally calling for a climate-neutral economy by 2050 – and has already announced concrete actions for this year. For example, they want to publish data about the climate impact of an equity or a fixed income fund, wherever this is possible. And if the world's largest asset manager demands data from listed companies then these firms will quickly demand the corresponding data from their suppliers too. So a new standard will emerge, one that everyone will have to comply with – not just listed companies.

Incidentally, the pressure is coming not only from large institutional investors. Our Wealth Management colleagues report similar demands from conversations with their clients. Especially the current generation of people with inherited wealth often want to manage their assets in a different way to their parents or grandparents – they come with a specific objective of reallocating a considerable share of their portfolio into sustainable investments. The purpose of an investment is becoming increasingly important.

These clients expect us to find these investment opportunities or even to create them ourselves. We are after all a global bank that with its credit portfolio of nearly 450 billion euros can generate precisely those assets that our investors are now demanding.

Last but not least, the seriousness with which we invest into our sustainability efforts will be an important factor in determining how attractive we as an employer will be – as the younger generation cares much more about a sustainable future than the previous ones.

Hence, we are talking about fundamental change for all stakeholders with pressure and opportunities for all stakeholders. Environmental, social and governance issues have moved to the top of the agenda and will stay there. Among the ESG issues, fighting climate change is undoubtedly the highest profile topic. But it is also a matter of environmental protection in general and biodiversity specifically. And it is also about the other two strands of ESG – social issues and good governance.

Ultimately this expectation of investors and other stakeholders is directed not only at us banks – but at the economy as a whole. We banks are only intermediaries between investors and investment opportunities. So if investors want to invest mainly in sustainable assets going forward, then that will have a direct impact on what can be financed in future. Sustainability is not simply some new product – but an issue that will shape our whole value chain and our interaction with clients.

Policymakers and regulators will become driving forces here: sustainability and ESG are now mentioned in almost every meeting with our regulators. Their main focus is on risk management aspects: firstly, about managing credit and market risk correctly – and climate risks are an increasingly important factor in this. And secondly, non-financial risks are becoming just as important. So, in the same way that we banks are required to contribute to the fight against financial crime, in future we will also be instrumental in the fight against climate change. For the financial sector will increasingly become a key lever for governments in the fight to reduce greenhouse emissions – by making it more difficult to finance activities that exacerbate climate change and at the same time promoting climate-friendly investments.

Deutsche Bank's Sustainability Strategy

As a consequence, sustainability will be a key factor in determining how banks develop in the coming years, if not decades. Deutsche Bank may not necessarily have been a pioneer in this field, but we have made great progress – especially over the course of the last 24 months. We defined a comprehensive sustainability strategy which goes far beyond reacting to external pressure; we see sustainability as a great opportunity, which is why we have made it one of our bank's four management priorities – next to client-centricity, technology, and risk management.

When we talk about sustainability at Deutsche Bank, there are four components to it.

- The first component focuses on our own operations: for instance, our business has been carbon neutral since 2012 and our plan is to obtain all our electricity from renewable sources by 2025. Admittedly, in a business where most of our work is done in offices or now even at home, that task is not hard to achieve.
- The second component is our wish to contribute to the public debate around the sustainable transition of the economy not just with our research but also our expertise. Furthermore, we will collaborate closely to develop standards. We should be clear on this: we all urgently need reliable guidance – companies and banks alike. And this guidance must come from governments and regulators.

We can make the biggest impact, though, in our own area of business – in our work with clients. And that is what the other two components of our sustainability strategy are about:

- First, we must control the impact of our business on the environment and society – and we have started to do so. This involves being able to measure the carbon footprint of our loan portfolios. And it also involves formulating internal policies for those areas of business in which we no longer want to engage with or only in a limited scope – like our decision to withdraw from business activities associated with thermal coal mining by 2025. Usually, though, it is not a case of *exit or not exit*; it is not as clear cut as this. It is about initiating gradual change.
- And it is precisely this that is at the centre of the fourth component: we want to finance the economy's transformation, actively shaping it at the same time. We have set ourselves the target of facilitating a total of 200 billion euros of sustainable financing and investments in the ESG space by 2023 – two years earlier than originally planned. In other words, we want to support the transformation of the economy.

That leads to the practical questions: how exactly does sustainability impact our collaboration with companies and other clients?

Our Collaboration with Clients

First, sustainability must be a natural part of our offering. Our account managers will talk to their corporate clients about sustainability the same way they do about loans, or interest rate and currency hedging strategies.

That begins with us having to ask clients questions as we are going to need data. We will have to incorporate climate risks into our risk management practices. We already committed ourselves to measure the carbon footprint of our loan portfolios by 2022. This is the only way for us to show just what kind of an impact we can really have in the fight against climate change.

By extension, though, we have to know the impact our clients have on the climate. In order to measure this, not only will we have to need more information about their operations, we will also increasingly need data from their suppliers and other business partners. So corporates will have to invest in their own ability to collect this kind of data. Banks and other financial intermediaries will not just be able to model all of their assumptions.

Of course, calculating a carbon footprint is not the only thing we will do. We have committed ourselves also to give guidance on how we will gradually reduce this footprint. That is what governments and regulators will eventually expect when the data is available. And more and more investors are going to expect it, too. This transparency will exert pressure on us – and on our clients.

What this boils down to is that, in future, also a carbon budget will determine how we deploy our capital in the interest of our clients. And the larger a loan's carbon footprint is, the more expensive it will be for us as a bank because it will put a larger drain on the carbon budget, meaning we can deploy less of this budget elsewhere – similar to a riskier loan consuming more of our capital as it leads to higher risk-weighted assets. For our corporate clients' business, this means that the more carbon intensive a company's operations are, the more expensive a bank loan will tend to become.

In this context, not just the here and now will be important; it will also very much be about a company's long-term strategy. In future, we will have to examine a company's strategy very closely in order to reduce our own Scope 3 carbon footprint. Transformation plans will therefore be key for our decisions on how much access we are able to grant corporates to equity and debt financing.

The view in this context is a gradual one, i.e. the less carbon intensive, the better the forecast, the easier it will be to provide financing. At the same time, certain standards will also have to be fulfilled. Going forward, the most important standard will be the EU Taxonomy, which continues to evolve. The EU Taxonomy determines which kinds of financing can be classified as "sustainable". It gives guidance on what is green and, in future, what is considered social. This framework is the prerequisite for activities involving green bonds or social bonds that comply with the EU standards. The Taxonomy will also help us in the public discourse about what is considered sustainable, and what is not.

So the Taxonomy will be an important factor for investments as the sustainable investments market is growing fast. In 2020, for example, with a total of 46 billion euros in sustainable financing and investments we comfortably exceeded our initial target by more than 100 percent. And at the end of the second quarter 2021, cumulative ESG financing and investments reached 99 billion euros, close to the bank's full-year interim goal of at least 100 billion euros by end-2021.

This leads to what I believe will be the financial sector's most important task in the years to come – and Deutsche Bank's most important task in particular. In terms of transitioning to a more sustainable economy, first and foremost, we do not want to restrict but to enable. We do not want to simply take financing options away from carbon-intensive industries; we want to help them in their transition. We want to finance the pathway towards a sustainable economy and, with our advice, we want to help shape it as best we can.

This, incidentally, is where the EU Taxonomy needs to be taken to the next level. Currently it stipulates what is green, but does not take the transformation aspect into account. This has to change so the "Transition Taxonomy" which is currently being developed will be crucial.

For this reason, we see strict exclusion criteria like in the case of coal mining as more of an exception. It is generally about supporting the development towards more sustainability. We all know that we cannot just flick a switch and instantly make our economy more climate neutral. It is a journey and we need to pick up the pace.

And we all know that the shift towards a carbon-neutral economy will require massive investments. It is clear that trillions of euros cannot just come from banks. To finance this it is vitally important that we promote the European capital market. It cannot be that 80 percent of company financing is still supplied by banks. We need a broader base for investments, including more venture capital for start-ups.

Loans and bonds will be needed, as will IPOs and capital increases. We have to tap the entire range of financing options. We will also witness mergers and acquisitions, with companies fundamentally altering their business models.

That is why I am convinced that sustainability is a top management concern – at banks and in every large company. Because this megatrend affects a great number of processes in a great number of companies and will impact the very root of our value chains. And because it presents a great opportunity – this transformation needs financing and will create new business models. Just like with digitalisation.

Conclusion

In short: sustainability is a topic of vital importance and is here to stay. We need to move fast – as a bank, as a sector, as an economy and as a society. And we Europeans are pioneers in this respect. While overall, the European market accounts for only about a quarter of all bonds issued worldwide, Europe's share of green bonds is more than half. And if you look at which banks worldwide are bringing the most of these bonds to the market, then in 2020, for example, six of the top 10 came from Europe and four of them from the EU.

This is precisely why I am so convinced that the sustainable transformation is a challenge for Europe – but also an opportunity. The financial sector shares responsibility for whether the sustainable transformation is to succeed and we want to play an active role in shaping it. The better we work together here as an industry, the faster and more successful we will be in this crucial race for mankind and the planet.

II. The Chance for Europe

Werner Hoyer

A monumental Shift to green Finance

The European Investment Bank (EIB) is undergoing a radical transformation, probably the most profound in our more than 60-year history. We are remaking ourselves into “the EU climate bank”. The European Union has set a goal of becoming carbon neutral by 2050, and the EIB’s investment support and guidance will be crucial to that endeavour.

As part of our remaking, we have increased our climate and environment commitments, aligning the EIB Group’s strategy with the overarching goals of the European Green Deal.

The commitments include:

- Significantly increasing our level of support for green investment. By 2025, at least 50 % of our annual lending will be dedicated to climate action and the environment.
- Aiming to support €1 trillion of green investment in the coming decade, which is critical to limit temperature rises.
- Making sure that all our new activities are aligned to the goals and principles of the Paris Agreement.

The context behind these commitments is alarming and clear. The combination of climate change and the destruction of ecosystems poses an increasing risk of environmental collapse with enormous human consequences. As illustrated by the Intergovernmental Panel on Climate Change’s Special Report on Global Warming of 1.5 °C, action in the next decade will determine whether we effectively limit temperature rises and keep the most dire consequences of climate change at bay. To do that, the global community must act decisively to respect the climate goals laid out in the Paris Agreement.

The European Union is stepping up to do its part. Through the European Green Deal, the European Union has become the first region to endorse climate neutrality by 2050, and has committed to building green alliances with partner countries and regions worldwide. The European Commission and the European Parliament have adopted even more ambitious goals for cutting greenhouse gas emissions by 2030 – increasing the target to a 55 % reduction compared to 1990 levels, from the 40 % originally proposed.

https://doi.org/10.1515/9783110752892-007

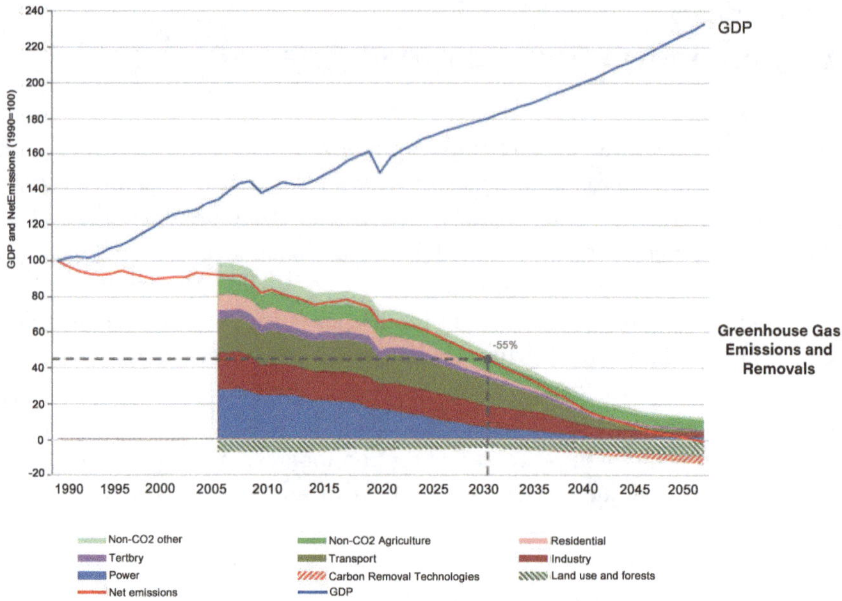

Fig. 1: A pathway to climate neutrality in the European Union

A global problem

Europe, however, is only one part of the equation. After all, it accounts for less than 10 % of global emissions. The rest of the world needs to adopt aggressive mitigation and adaptation policies if we are to avoid the most cataclysmic effects of climate change.

We are already seeing encouraging signs from the United States and China. China recently committed to decarbonise its economy by 2060, while the administration of President Joe Biden has brought the United States back into the Paris Agreement. Countries responsible for producing half of global greenhouse gas emissions (including the European Union) are on a path to cut net emissions to zero.

But what about the other half of the world? These countries, whether in Latin America, Asia or Africa, will be most affected by rising seas and temperatures. They are also home to some of the planet's most precious assets – rain forests, which are rich in biodiversity and provide massive carbon sinks. We need their help in preserving these resources, and with other major issues, such as reducing pollution in our oceans.

Over 840 million people in the world still do not have access to electricity, and many of those people live in Sub-Saharan Africa. Urgent action is needed to provide these communities with electricity, but the source of this electricity must be green.

In short, we need to help these countries adapt to climate change and, at the same time, leapfrog from harmful, fossil-fuel based power generation to more sustainable sources like solar and wind. To do that, development policy and climate policy must be two sides of the same coin.

For that reason, the Bank has proposed overhauling its external lending activity, in partnership with national development banks in the European Union and the European Commission, to help developing countries reshape their economies to rely on more sustainable energy sources.

The EIB currently commits about €7 billion a year to countries beyond the European Union. Over the last five years, 36 % of our finance beyond the European Union was dedicated to climate investments. But we can – and want – to do more in the years to come.

Filling the investment gap

Massive investment is needed if the European Union is to meet its net zero carbon goal. The energy sector alone will need an estimated €330 billion in additional investment annually to reach the 2030 goals.

Like the digital revolution, though, the green revolution will create new markets for goods and services that we can't even begin to imagine. It will change the way we move, what we eat and how we produce the goods we consume. Europe must be ready to seize these new opportunities.

In many ways, we are. Hydrogen is a good example. The majority of the world's new hydrogen projects – 55 % – are in Europe. The enthusiasm for hydrogen comes in part from strong public support. The European Union announced an ambitious Hydrogen Strategy in July 2020, laying out a path forward and setting development priorities for the next decade. Hydrogen is also a core part of the European Green Deal and Europe's efforts to secure its energy future.

While the green transition presents enormous opportunity, the pandemic has weakened European firms' ability to invest the large sums needed. Almost half – 45 % – of the 12 500 firms surveyed in the summer of 2020 for the EIB Economics Department's annual Investment Survey said they planned to cut investment in the next year.

The investment trend is worrying. Europe cannot afford another "lost decade," particularly not a decade as critical as 2020–2030. We need to ensure that the huge resources being mobilised for Europe's pandemic recovery support the green transition and efforts to contain climate change and environmental degradation.

Supporting innovation

The Europe Union has a head start on green innovation. Europe has registered almost 50 % more green patents than the United States. In 2017, it registered 76 % more patents that combined digital and green innovations than the United States – and more than four times as many as China, according to the EIB Investment Report 2020/2021.

Innovative firms in Europe, however, face financing obstacles, and the European Union systematically underinvests in research and development. We still haven't reached the goal of investing 3 % of gross domestic product in R&D set out in the Lisbon agenda over 20 years ago. We also failed on another Lisbon goal: to create the conditions small European firms needs to grow and prosper. Underdeveloped venture capital markets in Europe mean that many firms struggle to attract the investment they need to scale up and make it on their own.

The EIB can make a difference. With the European Commission, we are investing in innovative energy demonstration projects, from a floating windfarm in Portugal to storage solutions in Sweden. These projects will help young firms draw in the investment they need to grow and thrive. In 2020, we committed €26 billion of our own financing toward green projects.

Innovative projects are, by definition, risky. To help absorb that risk, we have a toolbox of financial instruments, including guarantees and equity or quasi-equity products such as venture capital or venture debt, that allow us to mobilise finance for innovation in some frontier areas of the European economy – like the circular economy.

From 2014 to 2019, the EIB provided €2.5 billion to co-finance circular economy projects, and we are standing by to do more. We want to build on that momentum, and have launched a Joint Initiative on Circular Economy with the European Union's largest national promotional banks and institutions, aiming to invest at least €10 billion in the circular economy by 2023.

The Climate Bank Roadmap: Our way forward

Turning the EIB into a key ally in the fight against climate change requires a significant overhaul of how we assess projects, view opportunities and our own inner-workings. In November, we unveiled the Climate Bank Roadmap, our strategy for becoming the green financial partner that Europe needs.

The roadmap ensures that Europe's needs are embedded in coherent policies that support sustainable finance, and that the EIB Group's internal systems and accountability reflect those goals.

Aligning with the Paris Agreement

A core element of the Climate Bank Roadmap is the commitment to ensure "all financing activities are aligned to the goals and principles of the Paris Agreement by the end of 2020." As the EU climate bank, the EIB Group cannot support the Paris Agreement with 50 % of green finance, and then turn around and undermine those goals with the other 50 % of our business.

In short, the EIB Group needs to ensure that all its activities do no significant harm to the Paris Agreement's goals. The new EU Taxonomy for sustainable activities[1] provides a natural reference point, and in the near future should provide specific screening criteria that help us establish whether an activity meets the "no significant harm" criteria. Multilateral development banks' joint efforts to develop a framework for Paris alignment also provide guidance.

To ensure that our individual projects are Paris-aligned, the EIB is also building on the existing tools we use to assess the net benefit to society of a particular project – including how we view the shadow price of carbon, a technical parameter used to estimate the full value to society from saving a tonne of carbon. The economic assessments help us determine whether a project truly benefits society, or whether the hidden costs – environmental or other – actual do more harm than good.

The shadow price of carbon

The shadow price of carbon is particularly important when we assess the economic value of infrastructure projects, such as roads. The prices that the EIB currently uses to assess projects pre-date the Paris Agreement, and do not reflect the European Union's goal of net-zero emissions by 2050, or limiting temperature rises to 1.5 °C.

---

1 The EU Taxonomy is a classification system establishing a list of environmentally sustainable economic activities. The taxonomy is designed to ensure that certain investments support sustainable and environmentally sound practices.

After having reviewed the latest evidence and climate models, the EIB plans to increase the shadow cost of carbon to €250 per tonne by 2030. That price will rise to €800 per tonne by 2050, the deadline for net-zero emissions. These prices closely follow the recommendations of a recent study by France Stratégie, which has been adopted to assess public-sector projects in France.

We will review the prices we use for the shadow cost of carbon on an annual basis and will adjust the cost adjusted accordingly.

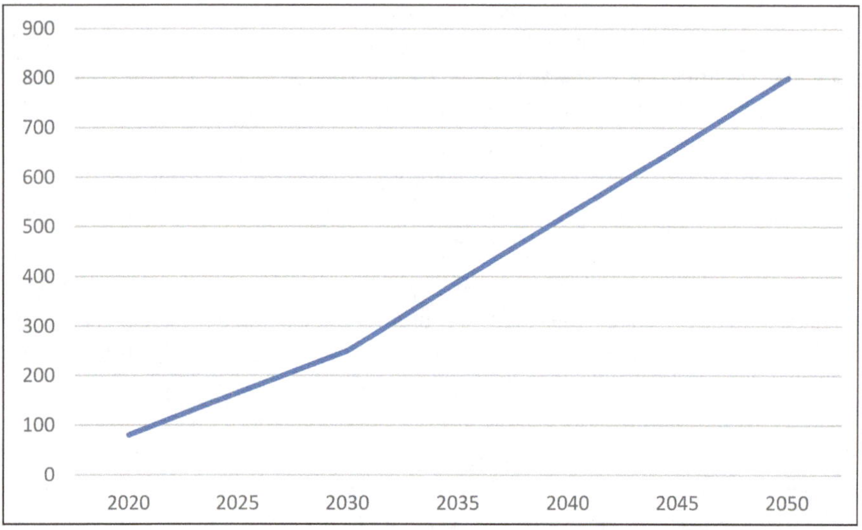

Fig. 2: Proposed EIB shadow cost of carbon 2020 to 2050 (in €_2016 per tonne of CO2e)
Source: EIB

Ensuring a just transition

The discussion on the EIB's climate road map was not always an easy one. Countries and regions will be affected differently by the green transition. We must ensure that our fight against climate change does not leave the most negatively affected regions behind.

Protests like the "yellow vest movement" in France have shown that the best climate action strategy is ineffective if you lose the support of voters in the process.

This is why the EIB is proposing a dedicated energy transition package as part of its climate strategy, which will operate alongside the European Union's Just Transition Mechanism. The Just Transition Mechanism aims to mobilise at least

€150 billion from 2021 to 2027 for the most affected regions to alleviate the social and economic consequences of the green transition.

As Europe moves forward on climate, it is important that no people or places are left behind. Meeting our climate goals requires concerted action among countries, communities and economic sectors, and we must provide the support that regions and communities need to reposition their economies.

Mobilising green finance

The EIB's financing of green projects, like the rest of the EIB's lending, is funded through the issuance of bonds on international capital markets.

As the first issuer of green bonds in 2007, we have been instrumental in the development of green capital markets. In 2018, we also issued one of the first bonds aligned with the United Nations Sustainable Development Goals (SDGs), called the Sustainability Awareness Bond. Funds raised from these sustainability bonds are used to support sustainability objectives, such as water infrastructure, health and education.

For these instruments, we need to be sure that when the label says "green" or "sustainable," the proceeds actually go to green and sustainable investments. Experience on the ground shows that this is not always the case. We still have far too many cases of "green washing."

Neither science nor markets agree on the way forward. This is why we at the EIB very much welcome the initiative of the European Commission to establish the EU Taxonomy for sustainable activities – a common language for sustainable finance – and are actively contributing to its development. The gist of the taxonomy is that it links the sustainability of financial products to the sustainability of the underlying economic activities, and, for an intermediary like the EIB, the sustainability of green bonds with the sustainability of green loans.

The taxonomy provides investors with the comfort of knowing that if they invest in a green bond or a sustainability bond, their investment is linked directly to green and sustainable investment in the real economy. By helping to prevent greenwashing, this vetting makes green finance more attractive to private investors – which is key if we want the green transition to be successful.

Using our heft for climate

While we have work to do to build up Europe's climate bank, we already have a solid foundation. Since 2012, we have provided €197 billion of financing – mobilising over €670 billion of investment – for projects that reduce greenhouse gas emissions and help countries and regions adapt to climate change. The breadth of those activities makes us one of the world's largest providers of finance for climate action and environmental sustainability.

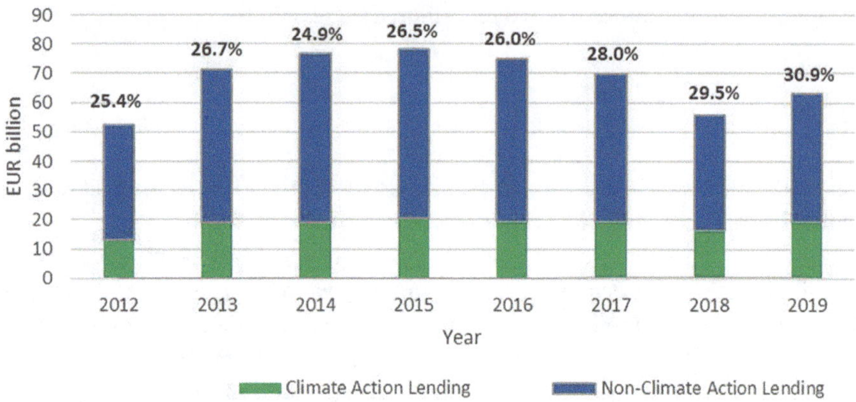

Fig. 3: Climate projects as a share of total EIB lending 2012–2019
Source: EIB

But we want to do more. European countries have started converting their energy networks to renewable power. Falling costs for electric batteries are helping world-leading European automakers pivot to electric vehicles. On a somewhat less glamorous, but equally important note, the technical performance of heat pumps has improved enormously over the decade, allowing electricity to replace carbon-intensive energy sources for heating homes or heat used in industrial processes.

The green transition presents enormous economic opportunities. Focusing Europe's growth on the development of low carbon technologies will make our economies more competitive. Economic growth and green investment are increasingly interlinked.

We need to help the private sector seize those opportunities. Before they put their faith in the green transition, however, businesses need clear regulations, definitions and procedures showing them seriousness of Europe's commitment. They need clarity on carbon prices and other incentives.

Rebuilding economies in a time of crisis takes courage – and solid institutions that are able to lead the way. At the EIB, we are preparing ourselves for the challenge.

Philipp Hildebrand, Jean Boivin, Jessica Tan,
Simona Paravani-Mellinghoff and Ed Fishwick

Climate Change – Turning Investment Risk into Opportunity

Launching our climate-aware Capital Market Assumptions and strategic Portfolios

Summary

- Climate change is real and cannot be ignored by investors. Climate risk is investment risk, yet we see it is as a historic investment opportunity. Our capital market assumptions (CMAs) – a core input to building portfolios – for the first time, explicitly reflect the impact of climate change on the investment landscape. This is one of a set of actions we are taking to prepare investors for the global transition to a net zero emissions economy by 2050 or sooner.
- The commonly held notion that tackling climate change has to come at a net cost to the global economy is wrong, in our view. If no action is taken to combat climate change, the considerable physical damages would imply a lower path of economic growth. Our CMAs reflect our view that the green transition to a low-carbon economy, consistent with the Paris Agreement goals, will deliver an improved outlook for growth and risk assets relative to doing nothing.
- Underpinning the climate-aware CMAs is our view of an orderly transition that successfully limits climate-related damage. The tectonic shift toward sustainability has gathered momentum over the past year following a series of major climate change commitments by corporations, governments and investors alike, bolstering our conviction in an orderly transition to a low-carbon world.
- We see climate change and the green transition as persistent drivers of asset returns, and consequently fundamental to making strategic investment deci-

Note: The authors are, respectively, Vice Chairman, Head-Blackrock Investment Institute, Global Head-Corporate Strategy and Sustainable Investing, Global CIO of Solutions, Multi-Asset Strategies and Solutions and Global Co-Head of Risk & Quantitative Analysis at BlackRock. They thank Elga Bartsch, Debarshi Basu, Anthony Chan, Carole Crozat, Natalie Gill, Paul Henderson, Eric van Nostrand, Christian Olinger, Vivek Paul and Christopher Polk for their assistance in the preparation of this article.

https://doi.org/10.1515/9783110752892-008

sions. Climate change and policies to combat it flow through our CMAs via three main channels: the macroeconomic impact, the repricing of assets to reflect climate risks and exposures and the impact on corporate fundamentals. Macro variables such as GDP would be different in a world that is transitioning to a low-carbon future, meaning traditional risk premia for all asset classes will change. On repricing, we don't believe market prices yet reflect the coming changes, meaning assets poised to benefit from the transition may have a higher return during the transition. Finally, corporate fundamentals – climate change issues impact business models and corporate profitability. We assess the winners and losers at the sector level.
- We focus on the E in ESG. Why? There is now a wide recognition of the importance of climate change for economic and social outcomes and there is consensus on how to measure it – via carbon emissions. There is less consensus on how to define the S (social) and G (governance) dimensions and even less so on how to measure them. Different investors will approach these issues differently underscoring the difficulty in formulating a systematic framework. We see S and G as sources of alpha and so exclude them from our CMAs, which focus on broad market returns, or beta.
- Projections around climate change are highly uncertain due to the complexity of modelling the dynamics between carbon emissions and climate, between climate and economic variables and the myriad dependencies, particularly around mitigation policies. This underscores the importance of explicitly incorporating uncertainty in CMAs.
- Understanding the implications for strategic portfolios warrants taking a more granular view than ever. We now use sectors as the relevant unit of investment analysis. We believe tech and health care are likely to benefit the most from the green transition, whereas energy and utilities may lag. At the broad asset class level, the appeal of developed market equities brightens at the expense of high yield credit and emerging debt due to the higher concentration of carbon intensive sectors that comprise the benchmark indices for the latter.

The green Transition

Climate change and efforts to curb it will have major economic outcomes, not just far into the future but in the next few decades (Dietz et al., 2020). Economic projections that do not take climate change into account are widely relied upon yet are based on an unrealistic future scenario, in our view. We have updated the long-term macroeconomic framework that underpins our CMAs. The upshot: In our view, a green transition to a low-carbon economy, consistent with the Paris Agreement goals, will deliver an improved outlook for growth and risk assets relative to doing nothing. Such an outlook rejects the commonly held notion that tackling climate change has to come at a net cost to society.

We first incorporate climate damages into our economic projections. The economic losses, associated with rising temperatures, build over time and are more pronounced in some regions than others (Burke et al., 2015). Call this the "no-climate-action" scenario – climate damages occur, but no action is taken to combat it. We then consider a second economic scenario, with policies and innovations that could mitigate climate damages – call this the "green transition" scenario. Specifically, in the green transition we consider the actions needed to ensure the Paris Agreement target of limiting temperature rises to below 2 degrees Celsius is achieved. The green transition is our base case for our updated CMAs and strategic asset class preferences.

In our macro model, we combine our long-term growth framework with a detailed energy component with long-term climate dynamics and the repercussions on economic activity. Our model for a green transition combines the economic costs of physical damages related to climate change (Claire et al., 2020), the benefits and costs of energy transition, and other policy changes such as potential spending on green infrastructure. With these in mind, we find the economic outlook is notably brighter under the green scenario versus the no-climate-action scenario. Why? Economic loss due to climate damages can be largely avoided, in our view, by proactive climate policy action that keeps the global temperature change within the margins of the Paris Agreement through a combination of gradually rising carbon taxes and clean energy subsidies (Burke et al., 2018). In our view, the economic benefit of avoiding climate damages through mitigation policies can outweigh the potential economic costs associated with these policies. This conclusion is at odds with the belief that climate change mitigation is a drag on growth – such an interpretation would only be valid if comparing to an unrealistic scenario that ignores climate change altogether.

Globally, we estimate a cumulative loss in economic output of nearly 25 % over the next two decades due to the level of GDP being 2.3 % lower in 20 years' time if no climate change mitigation measures were taken. The charts below show our estimates of the impact on China – an increasingly important pillar of the global economy and one where the impact of climate change is likely to be significant. The left chart shows the potential path of GDP and the right, the potential cumulative impact of three factors – avoidance of climate damage, transition costs, and green infrastructure spending – on GDP by 2040. We acknowledge the risks to the downside in our green transition scenario. Delays in implementing climate policies could result in a "disorderly transition". Policy execution will be key: any shortfalls could undermine the policy predictability and credibility, making the energy transition more costly.

The long-term cumulative economic Impact

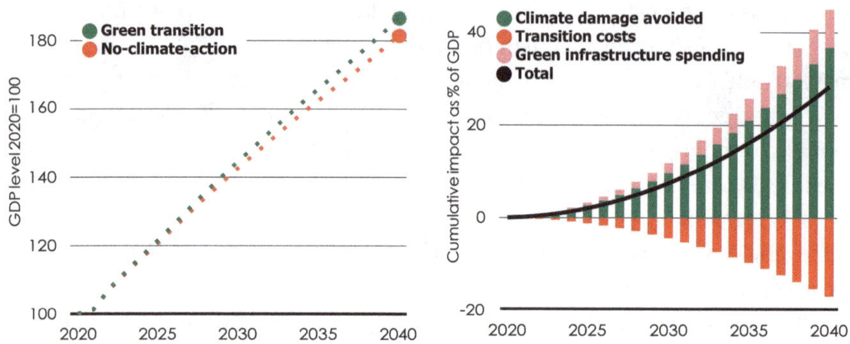

Figure 1: Estimated GDP paths and cumulative impact as a percentage of GDP under two scenarios for China, 2020–40.
Forward looking estimates may not come to pass.
Sources: BlackRock Investment Institute, Banque de France, International Energy Agency, OECD, January 2021. Notes: The chart on the left shows our estimated path for China's GDP over the next 20 years under the two mentioned scenarios. GDP levels are rebased to 100 as of 2020. The chart on the right shows the cumulative impact on long-term GDP under a green transition relative to a no-climate-action scenario. The bars show the overall estimated impact of three factors – avoidance of climate damages (positive), green infrastructure spending (positive) and costs associated with the transition (negative). The black line shows the estimated net impact. Our estimates of the impact under a climate-aware scenario are based on expected changes in energy consumption including composition, relative carbon and renewables pricing and on potential losses due to global warming. Energy consumption is estimated as a function of GDP and the relative price of energy per the Banque de France's working paper no. 759 titled the Long-term growth impact of climate change and policies. GDP losses from global warming are calibrated on analysis of Impact Assessment Models per W. Nordhaus and A. Moffat (2017). We assume green infrastructure spending programs of 1 % of GDP gradually phased out over the next 10 years.

Climate Change impacts all Assets

When evolving our CMAs to account for sustainability, we focus on the "E" in ESG, in particular, we focus on climate change. Why? First, there is wide recognition of the importance of climate change for economic and social outcomes and second, there is consensus on the measurement of an entity's contribution to climate change – via carbon emissions. Carbon emissions are a widely enough adopted indicator of sustainability for investors to the extent that it can be a driver of repricing at the broad market level. We see insights into S (social) and G (governance) issues as potential sources of alpha impacting security selection, rather than as systematic drivers of returns and so exclude them from our CMAs. If consensus around the S and G dimensions grows and availability of consistent and reliable data improves in coming years we would consider incorporating them into our CMA framework.

Macro variables such as GDP would be different in a world that is transitioning to a low carbon future, meaning traditional risk premia for *all* asset classes will change. Macroeconomic variables, valuations across asset classes – equities, credit, government bonds and foreign exchange – and, ultimately, strategic asset class decisions will be impacted. The chart below shows our updated CMAs for selected asset class – the green dots show the mean expected returns in our base case of a green transition and the red dots indicate the expected returns in a no-climate-action scenario. For U.S. equities, our expected returns in a no-climate-action scenario would fall outside the band of uncertainty around our mean estimate, highlighting the potentially large impact from climate change.

Beyond the macro impact, we see the effects playing out through two more channels:

- Repricing: One consequence of shifting societal preferences is that the price investors are willing to pay for assets perceived to be sustainable is changing, driving differentiated returns. This shift means the discount rate we use to value these securities is also changing. Capital flows toward sustainable assets are a symptom of this phenomenon. Our CMAs now directly reflect our estimates of such a premium.
- Fundamentals: This channel could be seen as an extension of the macro one. Some companies and sectors are better positioned than others for a transition to a low carbon economy. Corporate behavior will likely respond by adapting to policy and regulatory changes brought about to combat climate change. Profitability across sectors will be impacted with knock on effects for other variables such as credit default and downgrade assumptions. There will be sectoral winners and losers – underpinning why we believe a sectoral approach to sustainable investing is additive to a regional one.

Uncertainty is a key element of our framework and is built into our CMAs. No one yet knows what a low-carbon world looks like. The transition may play out over several years, if not decades. We will monitor key trends such as capital flows, policy developments and technological advancements – and the way asset prices respond to them – and look to evolve our framework as new information becomes available. Our portfolio construction approach that explicitly accounts for uncertainty and provides a term structure of returns to capture the time varying impact of climate change lends itself well to the structural transformation we see playing out.

A meaningful Impact

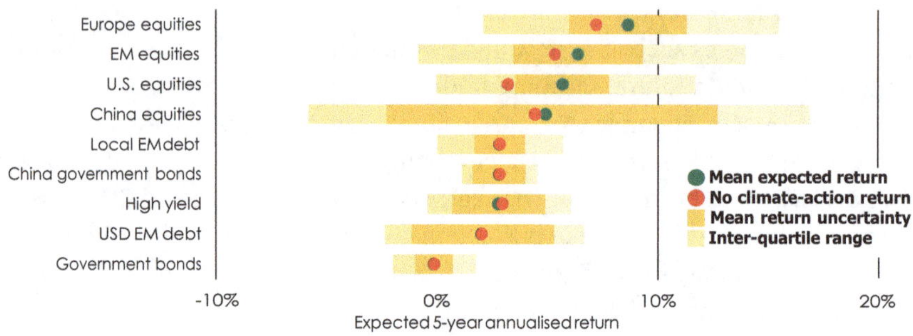

Figure 2: BlackRock capital market assumptions for selected assets, February 2021.
This information is not intended as a recommendation to invest in any particular asset class or strategy or as a promise – or even estimate – of future performance.
Source: BlackRock Investment Institute, February 2021. Data as of 31 December, 2020.
Notes: Return assumptions are total nominal returns. U.S. dollar return expectations for all asset classes are shown in unhedged terms. Our CMAs generate market, or beta, geometric return expectations. Asset return expectations are gross of fees. For representative indices used, see the Assumptions at a glance table. For a full of asset classes we cover, visit our Capital Market Assumptions website at blackrock.com/institutions/en-us/insights/portfolio-design/capital-market-assumptions.There are two sets of bands around our mean return expectation. The darker bands show our estimates of uncertainty in our mean return estimates. The lighter bands are based on the 25th and 75th percentile of expected return outcomes – the interquartile range for more detail read Portfolio perspectives.

The tectonic Shift

The past year has seen a seismic shift in society's resolve to tackle climate change. President Xi Jinping outlined aplanat last year's United Nations General Assembly to make China carbon neutral by 2060 – a significant milestone given the country's growing role in the global economy. U.S. President Joe Biden returned the country to the Parisclimateaccordon the first day of his presidency. Investments made under the EuropeanRecoveryFundto aid the post-Covid economic revival will have to respect emissions thresholds laid out under European Union regulations.

Investors are just starting to respond to the structural shift – suggesting it is not yet fully in the price of assets. The BlackRock 2020 Global Sustainability Survey found that respondents plan to double their sustainable assets under management (AUM) in the next five years – rising from 18 % of AUM on average today to 37 % on average by 2025. Climate change is the most prominent sustainability issue. In our view, changing investor preferences will spur a climate change-led repricing in the cost of capital attached to various assets. We expect changing preferences to drive flows into assets perceived to be more aligned with a low carbon future, spurring a repricing higher for such assets relative to those that are not. The ability to systematically measure carbon emissions, and the broad consensus that carbon footprint matters means it is this measure of E that is likely to drive repricing, in our view. Carbon emissions also indicate the exposure of companies to changing carbon prices, likely a primary policy tool employed to tackle climate change.

We estimate an expected carbon emission intensity by company and then aggregate up the data at the sector and country level to rank markets according to their carbon footprint. The chart below shows the results for U.S. sectors. This analysis drives our estimates for a sector's change in cost of capital that could occur due to climate-driven repricing. We expect more carbon efficient sectors to have falling cost of capital, all else equal, which drives positive returns during the transition. See the Appendix for more detail on the methodology.

There is no precise answer when estimating the change in cost of capital that could occur. We use the carbon efficiency of each sector to estimate the cost of capital (see Appendix for methodology). For the most carbon efficient sector, financials, could fall by 0.4 %, all else equal, and the least efficient, utilities, could rise by 0.5 % over five years. We look to a range of sources, including work from the Cambridge Institute for Sustainability Leadership that showed retail investors would be prepared to sacrifice up to 2.5 % in returns to invest in greener funds. Recent pricing of green bonds – such as the difference in spreads between green and non-green bonds issued by sovereigns – help inform our estimates for credit.

How long before the transition is priced in? Maybe sooner than previously thought given the momentum of global commitments toward carbon neutrality seen just in the past year. The new U.S. administration under President Joe Biden is likely to make climate a major policy focus – potentially hastening the transition. We assume a five-year window for the repricing. This chimes with results from academic research that studies how markets price in predictable but slow-moving shifts in profitability – such as demographics (DellaVigna et al., 2007). Once the repricing phase has passed, this channel is no longer a boon for returns for 'greener' assets. In fact, all else equal, greener assets will have a lower cost of capital, meaning a lower expected return.

The sectoral View

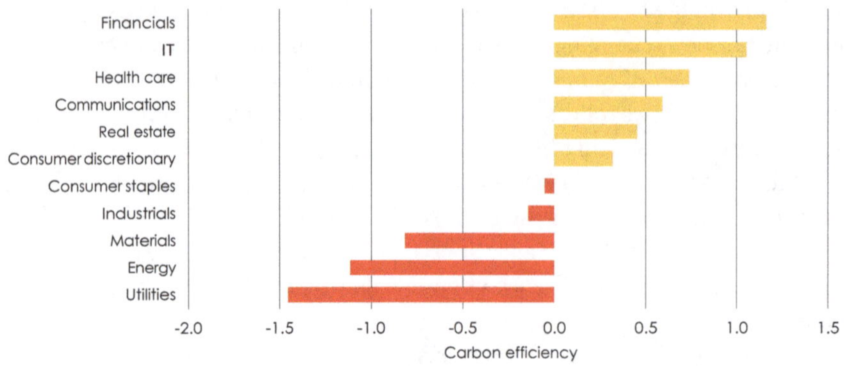

Figure 3: Estimated carbon efficiency for MSCI USA sectors, February 2021.
Indexes are unmanaged and do not account for fees. It is not possible to invest directly in an index. This information is not intended as a recommendation to invest in any particular asset class or strategy or as a promise – or even estimate – of future performance.
Sources: BlackRock Investment Institute with data from Refinitiv Datastream and MSCI, February 2021, Notes: The chart shows the carbon efficiency measured as total carbon emissions relative to the aggregate firm value for the sectors of the MSCI USA index. The carbon efficiency measure is shown in Z-score terms – or in relation to the mean across sectors. Both Scope 1 (direct emissions from owned or controlled sources) and Scope 2 (indirect emissions from electricity purchased) are considered. These can help gauge the exposure of companies to carbon pricing initiatives as part of climate change mitigation policies.

Impact on Corporate Fundamentals

Climate change and the efforts to address it will impact the profitability and growth prospects of companies. This needs to be analyzed beyond the impact on headline GDP growth. First, the transition to a low carbon economy will present opportunities for some industries and challenges for others – through environmental regulation and energy policies, carbon pricing mechanisms and changing consumption patterns. Earnings at the industry or sector level could be meaningfully impacted over the coming decade or as the transition occurs – depending on the speed at which the green transition is achieved.

We estimate corporate earnings consistent with our green transition macroeconomic scenario. To arrive at our estimates, we first assess the sensitivity of earnings to carbon pricing initiatives. We expect carbon pricing initiatives – phasing in materially higher carbon prices – to be a core tenet of climate mitigation policies aimed at achieving the Paris climate goals. The estimated sensitivity of earnings depends on current direct and indirect carbon emissions, expected emission abatement, and the ability of companies to pass through costs. Across sectors, carbon pricing initiatives represent a negative earnings impact of varying size.

The corporate fundamental channel goes beyond this carbon cost – we assess the impact of both transition risks and physical risks for 34 industries. We score these industries on two dimensions – how exposed they are to climate change themes and whether the exposure represents a risk or opportunity. This scoring can differ from the carbon price sensitivity – a company could be a high carbon emitter currently, and so could have high carbon price sensitivity, yet could also be positioned to benefit from the green transition through growing demand for its products. A prime example of such opportunities are chemical companies that manufacture materials for electric vehicle batteries and could potentially be big beneficiaries of a green transition. Conversely, consider an insurance company that has low carbon emissions but whose profits are increasingly at risk from physical climate damages.

The chart below shows the estimated return impact across sectors from both the repricing and fundamental channels. We estimate a 7 % annualized return differential over five years between the energy and technology sectors – a significant difference in a world of low expected returns across asset classes. The energy sector is, unsurprisingly, most heavily impacted: it is a high carbon emitter and is poised for a structural decline in demand, in our view, as adoption of greener energy sources becomes more mainstream. We consider the energy sector as the most negatively impacted sector and a benchmark to measure other sectors against. We acknowledge the high uncertainty around how corporates will respond to the green transition and what the precise impact of changing business models might be for their profitability. Monitoring the sectoral impact will be a key theme in our ongoing research.

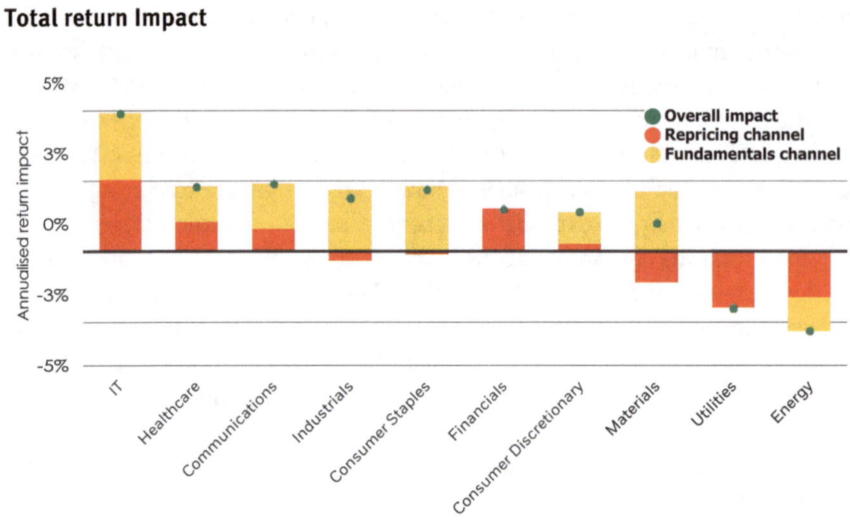

Figure 4: Estimated 5-year expected return differential for MSCI U.S. sectors in green transition vs no-climate-action, Feb 2021.
This information is not intended as a recommendation to invest in any particular asset class or strategy or as a promise – or even estimate – of future performance.
Sources: BlackRock Investment Institute, with data from Refinitiv Datastream and Bloomberg, February 2021.
Notes: The chart shows the difference in five-year U.S. dollar expected returns for the highest sub-category of MSCI USA sectors under two economic scenarios – a green transition and a no- climate-action scenario. The difference in expected return is attributable to repricing – the return impact of changing cost of capital – and fundamentals – or the return impact of changing earnings per share growth.

Portfolio Implications

Tactical, or shorter-term, investment decisions will not be sufficient, in our view, to position for the fundamental reshaping of the global economy we see playing out. Positioning portfolios appropriately requires expressing views at the strategic asset level. Like any investment view, the ultimate implementation and sizing of climate change-led views in portfolios will vary depending on an investor's risk appetite, objectives and eligible universe. Some investors may have to reallocate as much as 10–20 % of existing assets. For others, it will be less. See our investor-specific asset allocation breakdowns for more. Our strategic asset preferences for a hypothetical unconstrained, U.S. dollar investor with a 10-year horizon are shown on the chart below and put our asset class views in a portfolio context. They reflect our views on all drivers of long-term asset returns, from the monetary and fiscal policy revolution to structural trends, such as the U.S.-China rivalry and the polarisation of global growth. The impact of introducing climate change as an additional driver of returns on asset class views is shown on the right.

The most significant impact is a stronger preference for developed market equities at the expense of high yield and emerging market debt. The composition of developed market equity indices better aligns with the climate transition and equities have more ability to capture the upside opportunities from the climate transition. The higher carbon intensity of companies that typically make up high yield and emerging market debt benchmark indices detracts from their expected returns, diminishing their appeal within our overall preferred strategic allocation. Another impact of incorporating climate change in our CMAs – granular investing becomes more prominent in portfolio construction. We believe climate change will drive greater dispersion of returns at a sector level than at the asset class level. We see sectors as the relevant unit of investment analysis and if we allow sector granularity in our portfolio construction, buying assets at the sector level rather than at an index-based regional level, the impacts on strategic asset preferences can be material.

We have a strategic preference for inflation–linked government bonds over nominal government bonds. We see the policy revolution driving higher inflation over the medium-term but expect rising inflation expectations to be reflected more through lower real yields than higher nominal yields, compared to the past. We see the ability of nominal bonds to act as ballasts as diminished, and expect high public debt levels to push yields higher over the strategic horizon. We are strategically underweight credit as we see valuations as expensive on a relative basis relative to equities.

Our preference for a strategic overweight to Chinese assets overall is not diminished – and is, in fact, enhanced for Chinese government bonds given the relatively poorer outlook for comparable assets. The sector composition of mainland Chinese equity indexes differs from the makeup of the broad economy with low exposure to sectors at risk from the green transition such as energy, utilities and materials. More broadly, China's commitment to a net zero economy by 2060 reinforces our views around potential improvements in carbon emission intensity for its companies.

Tilting toward Sustainability

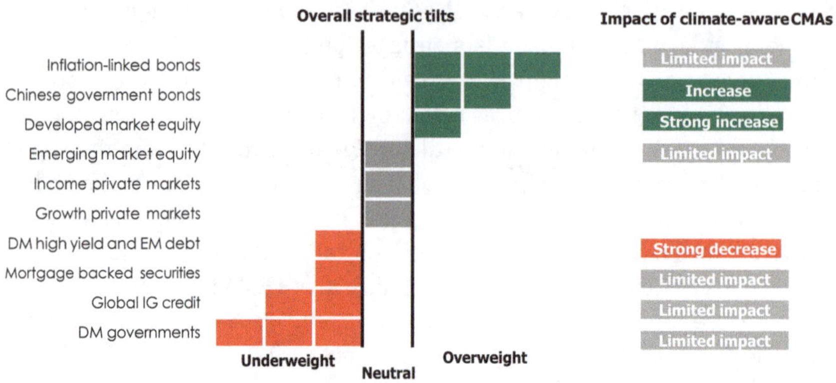

Figure 5: Hypothetical U.S. dollar 10-year strategic allocation vs our equilibrium view, February 2021.
This information is not intended as a recommendation to invest in any particular asset class or strategy or as a promise – or even estimate – of future performance.
Sources: BlackRock Investment Institute, with data from Refinitiv Datastream and Bloomberg, February 2021.
Notes: The chart shows our asset views on a 10-year view from an unconstrained US dollar perspective against a long-term equilibrium allocation described on our capital market assumptions website. The portfolio is illustrative and the allocation above does not represent any existing portfolio, and as such, is not an investible product. The construction of the hypothetical asset allocation is based on criteria applied with the benefit of hindsight and knowledge of factors that may have positively affected it's performance, and cannot account for risk factors that may affect the actual portfolio's performance. The actual performance may vary significantly from our modelled CMAs due to transaction costs, liquidity or other market factors. Indexes are unmanaged, do not account for management fees and one cannot invest directly in an index. See appendix for full list of index proxies.

Appendix

Macroeconomic Model Methodology

We use a long-run model of climate change that allows us to account for the physical damages, energy transition and the impact of public policies and their impact on macro variables, such as level of GDP, in a single, transparent framework. We combine our long-term growth framework with a detailed energy component with long term climate dynamics and the repercussions on economic activity.

We project the impact on GDP level in a macroeconomic climate model for 30 countries/regions using our long-term growth model based on the three factors of production: labor, capital and energy and assume a constant elasticity of substitution – in other words, there is no change in estimated impact if one factor is substituted for the other. We use the Advanced Climate Change Long-term (ACCL) assumptions set out in Banque de France's 2020 paper (Claire et al., 2020) as a starting point for estimates of the impact from climate change. These assumptions use a set of widely accepted calibrations regarding climate sensitivity, carbon emission factors, energy substitutability and efficiency, carbon storage and sequestration and regional attributions of damages in modelling different carbon pricing policies. We further augment these estimates to reflect more recent developments in energy technology based on research from Rhodium Group and Goldman Sachs. The GDP losses from global warming are calibrated on an analysis of Impact Assessment Models by Nordhaus et al (2017). Country-specific energy consumption is estimated as a function of GDP and changes in the relative price of energy (per the Banque de France estimates), while the relative price of energy is computed using the International Energy Agency's (IEA) energy prices (including taxes) and OECD GDP deflators, and projected forward using user-defined carbon and renewables pricing assumptions. Energy consumption is converted into CO2 emissions using IEA data and default emission factors collected from the Covenant of Mayors for Climate and Energy Report. The global stock of CO2 in the atmosphere is converted into a global temperature increase using the greenhouse gas trajectory adopted by the UN Intergovernmental Panel on Climate Change in 2014. The table below shows our assumptions for our two main scenarios: a green transition (our base case) and no-climate-action.

The positive effect of a green transition relative to the no climate action scenario rests on the gradual phasing in of carbon pricing consistent with the Paris Agreement, green infrastructure spending programmes (gradually phased out over ten years) and subsidies on renewable energy. We estimate the net impact of a green transition over the next 20 years to be positive at the global level but with regional divergences. The table shows the specific assumptions we make for each scenario.

Green Transition vs No-Climate-Action Scenario Assumptions

	Green transition	No-climate-action scenario assumptions
Global temperature by 2100	Broadly within that of Paris Agreement at a global temperature increase of 1.9 degrees Celsius in 2100	Materially higher increase in global temperatures of 5.8 degrees Celsius, a more sensitive economic damage function and release of 2 Gigatons from natural carbon sinks to get to climate damages of 27 % by 2100 (consistent with the upper end of the range considered by the Network for Greening the Financial System).
Climate policies assumed within the our adjusted ACCL model	Gradual increase in carbon pricing of 3 % per year and in renewables subsidies of 1 % per year	None
Fiscal policy assumptions beyond the ACCL model	Green infrastructure spending of 5 % of GDP over 10 years, using country specific IMF multipliers, adjusting for historical implementation gaps	None
Updated carbon abatement costs since ACCL model was calibrated	Adding the 20 % reduction in carbon abatement costs as estimated by Goldman Sachs	None

Appendix

Macroeconomic Model Methodology (Continued)

The impact of a green transition over the next years will likely be positive at the global level, in our view, but with regional differences as shown in the chart below.

The long term economic Impact

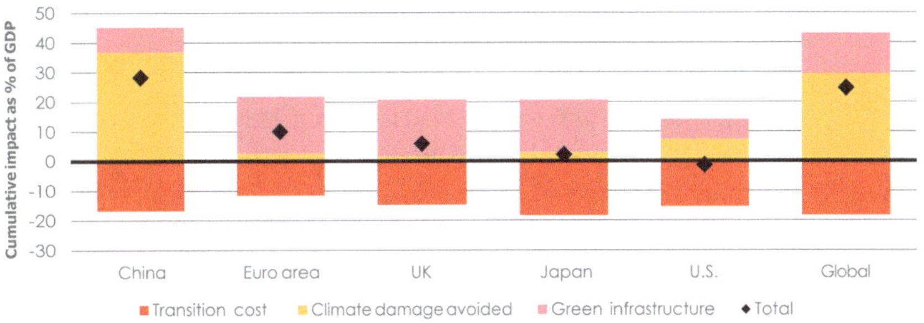

Figure 6: Estimated cumulative GDP impact under green vs no-climate-action scenarios by 2040. This information is not intended as a recommendation to invest in any particular asset class or strategy or as a promise – or even estimate – of future performance.
Sources: BlackRock Investment Institute, with data from Refinitiv Datastream and Bloomberg, February 2021.
Notes: The chart shows our estimate of the long-term economic impact of climate change over the next 20 years in terms of cumulative change in the GDP level versus a no-climate-action scenario, taking the assumptions referenced on page 8 into account.

Our framework, illustrated in the schematic below, outlines how we approach incorporating the implications of climate change and shifting investor sustainability preferences into expected asset class returns and strategic asset allocation.

Three Channels drive the Climate change Impact on Assets

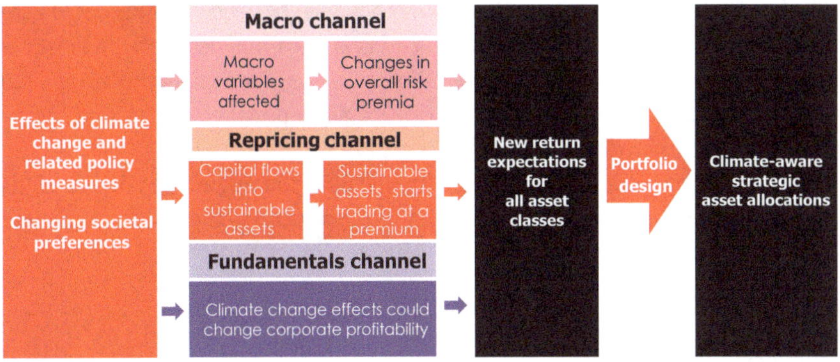

Figure 7: BlackRock framework for climate-aware portfolios. Source: BlackRock Investment Institute, February 2021. Notes: For illustrative purposes only. Subject to change without notice.

Appendix

Repricing Channel

We believe the structural shift toward sustainable investing is not yet priced in. Over coming years we expect assets perceived to be more sustainable to command a premium over less green counterparts, assuming all else is equal. We estimate the impact of this repricing in two stages: first, we arrive at a measure of a company or issuer's carbon footprint and second, use this measure to estimate a change in cost of capital.

We use direct and indirect carbon emissions as our preferred proxy for the cost of capital. Carbon emissions are a consistently and widely reported metric. Broad carbon emissions data across companies is lagged by up to two years, so we estimate the emissions today using the most recent observation and the rate of change over time. We find that future carbon emissions can be estimated up to three years using both the level and trend of today's emissions. We further refine the metric by focusing on carbon emissions *intensity* by measuring emissions against a company's enterprise value – the sum of a firm's market capitalization and debt obligations. Focusing purely on the absolute level of emissions would unfairly penalize large firms. Considering enterprise value also brings debt into the equation, allows us to apply the analysis to both equity and credit. We use z-scores to normalize the data sets to be comparable across sectors and assets classes given the highly skewed nature of carbon metrics. We also scale a sector's carbon intensity score with -3 as the least green to +3 the most green to derive a sustainability premium.

We assume those sectors with highest carbon intensity will experience rising cost of capital and those with lowest intensity will experience falling cost of capital. Based on an estimate of the difference in cost of capital between the most and least carbon efficient companies once climate change impacts are fully priced in, we calibrated the change in cost of capital for all regional equity sectors and regional markets.

Our equity expected returns are estimated using an augmented dividend discount model. The change in cost of capital is introduced to the dividend discount model, to estimate the impact of the 'repricing channel'.

Fundamental Channel

Climate change and the efforts to address it will impact the profitability and growth prospects of companies. We estimate the impact on corporate earnings at the sector level of a green transition. To arrive at our estimates, we first assess the sensitivity of earnings to carbon pricing initiatives, which we expect to be a core tenet of climate mitigation policies. We assume a carbon tax of $125 in 20 years – consistent with our green transition scenario. The impact on each firm's earnings is calculated based on the expected tax on its own emissions (Direct Cost), the increase in its own energy costs (Indirect Cost), the expected passthrough of the tax and the expected abatement of emissions in response to rising carbon cost.

In our fundamental channel, we also take account of the physical and transition risks and opportunities that could impact earnings across 34 industries.

The return estimates are uncertain in nature – quantifying the impact of climate change (through physical and transition risk) is often challenging as there is no historical precedent. We acknowledge certain limitations of our model. We assume that no carbon tax is already priced in and so the introduction of carbon taxes would likely be a drag on prices.

BlackRock's Long-Term Capital Market Assumption Disclosures: This information is not intended as a recommendation to invest in any particular asset class or strategy or product or as a promise of future performance. Note that these asset class assumptions are passive, and do not consider the impact of active management. All estimates in this document are in US dollar terms unless noted otherwise. Given the complex risk-reward trade-offs involved, we advise clients to rely on their own judgment as well as quantitative optimisation approaches in setting strategic allocations to all the asset classes and strategies. References to future returns are not promises or even estimates of actual returns a client portfolio may achieve. Assumptions, opinions and estimates are provided for illustrative purposes only. They should not be relied upon as recommendations to buy or sell securities. Forecasts of financial market trends that are based on current market conditions constitute our judgment and are subject to change without notice. We believe the information provided here is reliable, but do not warrant its accuracy or completeness. If the reader chooses to rely on the information, it is at its own risk. This material has been prepared for information purposes only and is not intended to provide, and should not be relied on for, accounting, legal, or tax advice. The outputs of the assumptions are provided for illustration purposes only and are subject to significant limitations. "Expected" return estimates are subject to uncertainty and error. Expected returns for each asset class can be conditional on economic scenarios; in the event a particular scenario comes to pass, actual returns could be significantly higher or lower than forecasted. Because of the inherent limitations of all models, potential investors should not rely exclusively on the model when making an investment decision. The model cannot account for the impact that economic, market, and other factors may have on the implementation and ongoing management of an actual investment portfolio. Unlike actual portfolio outcomes, the model outcomes do not reflect actual trading, liquidity constraints, fees, expenses, taxes and other factors that could impact future returns.

Index Disclosures: Index returns are for illustrative purposes only and do not represent any actual fund performance. Index performance returns do not reflect any management fees, transaction costs or expenses. Indices are unmanaged and one cannot invest directly in an index.

General Disclosure: This material is intended for information purposes only, and does not constitute investment advice, a recommendation or an offer or solicitation to purchase or sell any securities to any person in any jurisdiction in which an offer, solicitation, purchase or sale would be unlawful under the securities laws of such jurisdiction. The opinions expressed are as of February 2021 and are subject to change without notice. Reliance upon information in this material is at the sole discretion of the reader. Investing involves risks.

In the U.S., this material is intended for Institutional use only, not for public distribution. **In Canada**, this material is intended for permitted clients only. **In EMEA**, until 31 December 2020, issued by BlackRock Investment Management (UK) Limited, authorised and regulated by the Financial Conduct Authority. Registered office: 12 Throgmorton Avenue, London, EC2N 2DL. Tel: + 44 (0)20 7743 3000. Registered in England and Wales No. 2020394, has issued this document for access by Professional Clients only and no other person should rely upon the information contained within it. For your protection telephone calls are usually recorded. Please refer to the Financial Conduct Authority website for a list of authorised activities conducted by BlackRock. From 31 December 2020, in the event the United Kingdom and the European Union do not enter into an arrangement which permits United Kingdom firms to offer and provide financial services into the European Union, the issuer of this material is:(i) BlackRock Investment Management (UK) Limited for all outside of the European Union; and(ii) BlackRock (Netherlands) B.V. for in the European Union, BlackRock (Netherlands) B.V. is authorised and regulated by the Netherlands Authority for the Financial Markets. Registered office Amstelplein 1, 1096 HA, Amsterdam, Tel: 020-549 5200, Tel: 31-20-549-5200. Trade Register No. 17068311 For your protection telephone calls are usually recorded. **In Switzerland**, this document is marketing material. This document shall be exclusively made available to, and directed at, qualified investors as defined in the Swiss Collective Investment Schemes Act of 23 June 2006, as amended.

Appendix

Indexes

European equities: MSCI Europe
EM equities: MSCI Emerging markets index
U.S. equities: MSCI USA
EM debt, local: JPMorgan GBI-EM index
EM debt, USD: JPMorgan EMBI Global Diversified Index
China government bonds: Bloomberg Barclays China Treasury + Policy Bank Total Return Index Global high yield debt: Bloomberg Barclays Global High Yield Index
Global investment grade credit: Bloomberg Barclays Global investment grade credit Global government bonds: Bloomberg Barclays Global Aggregate
Private markets: BlackRock proxy. We use BlackRock proxies for selected private markets because of lack of sufficient data. These proxies represent the mix of risk factor exposures that we believe represents the economic sensitivity of the given asset class.

References

Burke, M., Davis, W. M., & Diffenbaugh, N. S. (2018), Large potential reduction in economic damages under UN mitigation targets. Nature, 557(7706), 549–553

Burke, M., Hsiang S.M,, and Miguel E., (2015), "Global Non-Linear Effect of Temperature on Economic Production." Nature 527 (7577): 235–39

Claire, A.,, Gilbert, C., Valerie, C., Remy, L. (2020), Long-term growth impact of climate change and policies: the Advanced Climate Change Long-term (ACCL) scenario building model, Banque de France WorkingPaperSeriesno.759.

DellaVigna, Stefano, and Joshua M. Pollet. 2007. "Demographics and Industry Returns." American Economic Review, 97 (5): 1667–1702.

Dietz, S., van der Ploeg, R., Rezai, A., Venmans, F., (2020), Are economists getting climate dynamics right and does it matter?, CESifo Working Paper Series 8122.

Goldman Sachs Carbonomics, the economics of net zero carbon. https://www.goldmansachs.com/insights/topics/carbonomics.html

McKibbin, W. J., and Wilcoxen, P.J., (2013), "A Global Approach to Energy and the Environment: The G-Cubed Model."

Chapter 17 in Handbook of Computable General Equilibrium Modelling, 995–1068. North Holland: Elsevier.

Network for Greening the Financial System Climate Scenarios for central banks and supervisors, June 2020

Nordhaus, W.D., and Moffat, A., (2017), "A Survey of Global Impacts of Climate Change: Replication, Survey Methods, and a Statistical Analysis," NBER Working Papers 23646, National Bureau of Economic Research, Inc.
University of Cambridge Institute for Sustainability Leadership (2019). Walking the talk: Understanding consumer demand for sustainable investing. Cambridge, UK: University of Cambridge Institute for Sustainability Leadership.

Patrick Kenadjian

What we meant by "The Chance for Europe": Betting on the Brussels Effect

Introduction

The first panel of the program dealt with the use by financial institutions of their own balance sheets to promote sustainability. The second panel dealt with their ability to mobilize the capital markets. We entitled it "The Chance for Europe" when we started planning the conference in January 2020, because we were thinking of the head start the European Union (EU) had taken over the rest of the world in coming to terms with sustainability in general and climate change in particular. This had seemed to give the EU the potential to set international standards for sustainable activities and to increase the proportion of capital market funded financing of the EU economy, thus giving a boost to its Capital Markets Union (CMU) project.

All of the prerequisites seemed to be there. The EU already had a Non-Financial Reporting Directive (NFRD) and was hard at work on twin regulations, its taxonomy regulation for sustainable activities (the Taxonomy) and a Sustainable Finance Disclosure Regulation (SFDR), which held out the promise of providing a set of mandatory standards to replace the multitude of private sector standards which issuers and financial intermediaries have had to work with. This overabundance of standards caused confusion for investors, needless duplicative work for issuers, and led to the suspicion of greenwashing. The EU was still committed to the CMU, and the majority of sustainable bonds outstanding to date had been issued in Euros and underwritten by European banks.

There was also the precedent of the EU General Data Protection Regulation (GDPR) which had turned into the de facto international data protection standard. As had been the case with privacy, the official United States (US) position on climate issues was either hostile or indifferent, so the road seemed open for the EU to take the lead in another example of what Anu Bradford at Columbia has dubbed "the Brussels Effect.". The demand was also there. Investor interest was driving the demand for sustainable investments, and both governments and private sector issuers were eager to issue sustainability branded instruments to finance needed investment in green, sustainable, or sustainability linked projects. The main problem was the profusion of standards which cried out for unification, and it was unclear how this could be brought about, short of the strong hand of a regulator, which the EU was ready to provide.

https://doi.org/10.1515/9783110752892-009

But by the time we held the conference a year later, on January 25, 2021 things were not looking so simple. The statistics on bond issuances had started to drift away from Euros and European underwriters. The Taxonomy, when published in June 2020, turned out to be a very long and complex document which, at 593 pages was nonetheless incomplete, focusing on green products, but unable to accommodate, in its then form, the crucial issue of what transition activities would be deemed compliant with its rules. These rules were tied to the EU's own climate goals rather than to universal principles. The delegated act which should have covered transition issues attracted some 46,000 comments – serious enough that the Commission had to delay its publication, originally scheduled for year end 2020 – and ask an expert group to advise it on how best to reflect those comments. The proposal for amending the NFRD delivered to the Commission by the European Financial Advisory Group (EFRAG) did not adopt the broadly endorsed suggestions that it be based on the widely accepted approach of the Task Force on Climate-Related Financial Disclosures (TCFD), but instead put forward an intellectually rigorous but highly complex multi-tiered approach with a long implementation period extending to 2024 and beyond.

These complications raised once more two fundamental questions: first, do we need a regulatory solution or can the market solve its own problems? Second, if a regulation is needed, is the EU route too complex and too tied to the EU's own climate goals to serve as an international template?

The consensus among informed observers prior to the delegated act fiasco seemed to be evolving towards answering the first question in favor of a regulatory solution. There were simply too many competing standards creating a cacophony of divergent approaches and evaluations, and each financial institution also seemed attached to its own way of scoring greenness and sustainability. The most referred to set of standards, the TCFD, adopted under the aegis of the Financial Stability Board, appeared to be oft-cited but honored more in the breach than in the observance, at least as far as disclosure of quantitative metrics was concerned, so that even many of its fans had concluded its application needed to be made mandatory by regulation.

But then, in the course of 2020, accelerating in the fall of the year, movement came in the private sector. Five of the most prominent sustainability standard setters (the Five Standard Setters) came together to work out how their standards could be made to work together within the framework of the TCFD recommendations. The IFRS Foundation, which administers the international accounting standards of the same name, offered to create a sustainability standards board (SSB) to devise internationally acceptable standards, incorporating but also further developing the recommendations of the TCFD. The Five Standard Setters offered up their work as a basis for these standards.

While encouraging, this initiative did not initially seem destined for the fast track. But then the International Organization of Securities Commissions (IOSCO) put itself behind the project and set an ambitious timetable for it, with the SSB to be up and running by COP26 in Glasgow this fall, and IOSCO potentially endorsing their standard in early 2022. The US Securities and Exchange Commission (SEC), returning to the climate fight under the new US administration, signaled an interest in an SSB approach and is co-chairing the IOSCO expert group dealing with the IFRS standards.

But why not simply adopt the EU approach? Let us start with the NFRD. It has an almost venerable pedigree, dating back to 2014, but it became effective only in 2018 and was never mandatory. In effect it was no more than a series of suggestions of items that issuers might want to discuss, reinforced by periodic non-binding guidance. So it is itself in need of revision and, if it is revised along the lines suggested by EFRAG, it will be far more complex than it had ever been before and a far cry from the hopes of observers that it could simply incorporate the well-known TCFD standards. Its time line for implementation, as suggested by EFRAG, would also run beyond 2024, and it incorporates the "double materiality" standard introduced by the EU in 2019. This requires reporting both effects on the company and the effects of the company on the environment. The double materiality standard has become common in sustainability reporting, but it is more of a novelty on the international financial reporting scene, so not an easy sell as an international standard.

The Taxonomy itself is also complex and requires the generation of information not currently collected by most issuers concerning the alignment of percentages of income statement line items with the EU's standards, as well as a determination that the activities both do no substantial harm to any of the other enumerated activities and are in conformity with a number of OECD and UN principles. The Taxonomy, as initially enacted, was also incomplete. Its core text covers green products, but it requires delegated acts to cover transition activities, so anything not "deep green", including all those activities which contribute to transforming a business from brown to one of Mark Carney's "Fifty Shades of Green" is not currently covered. A private sector analysis of the financial statements of the members of three European stock indexes (Euro Stoxx 50, CAC 40 and DAX) showed that only 1 to 2% of the activities of the companies that are members of those indexes would be deemed "fully aligned" with the Taxonomy as initially enacted. So the Taxonomy starts to look more like a goal to strive for rather than a tool ready to be used today. While it might have started out as a universal approach to sustainability, it is now looking more like a set of standards more tightly aligned with the EU's own climate goals. That is a fine policy goal in Europe, but it makes the Taxonomy more parochial and less of a logical choice for universal adoption.

As this article was being submitted to the printer, on April 21, 2021, the European Commission (the Commission) published a communication which introduced its response to the failed delegated act under the Taxonomy and what the road map for further action on the NFRD would be. I have not had the chance to view the full documentation, but will refer to what the Commission has said about it.

1. Green, sustainable and sustainability-linked Bonds: From green versus brown to "Fifty Shades of Green"

To put the foregoing in context, a few words about the various kinds of financing involved would probably be useful. These have so far primarily been bonds. In the beginning there were just Green bonds. They served to finance identifiably green projects. And they were good. But there were not enough of them either to meet investor demand or to finance the massive needs of the transition to a world where global warming is well below 2°C. It became clear we needed other kinds of instruments, and the market supplied them in the form of various kinds of sustainable bonds.

Green bonds usually refer to bonds whose proceeds are used by an issuer for specific, demonstrably "green" projects. They generally take the form of Use of Proceeds (UoP) bonds, where the proceeds of the issuance must be used to fund the specific project described in the offering documents. Sustainable and Sustainability-Linked Bonds (SLBs) in contrast focus on financing a transition in a business, leading to a forward-looking sustainability target. The amount of financing available through UoP bonds is inherently limited by the number of projects which can clearly be classified as green. SLBs allow an issuer to finance a broader strategy to transition towards a lower carbon mode of operation – even if it is active in a distinctly non-green sector, for example cement – so long as it selects key performance indicators (KPIs) that conform with a move towards more sustainable operations and agrees to a penalty in the form of a coupon increase for failure to meet these KPIs. See ICMA Sustainability Linked Bond Principles, June 2020.

While Green bonds are not simple structures, their cornerstone, the use of proceeds, is easier to define, evaluate, and monitor than the key elements of SLBs. SLBs involve evaluating and monitoring the strategy involved, the quality of KPIs, the calibration of the related sustainability performance targets (SPTs) which must be ambitious enough that they represent a material improvement in the KPI, (if possible compared to a benchmark or external reference) consistent with the overall strategic sustainability strategy of the issuer and their achievement over a predetermined timeline. The target setting can get quite complex, with a combination of benchmarking approaches, based on the issuer's own performance, that of its peers, and reference to the science, either in terms of scenarios or of absolute levels, such as carbon budgets or official national or local targets. But they do give a greater scope for issuances that can contribute to a transition to a lower carbon economy.

Unfortunately, SLBs also can lend themselves to greenwashing, the practice of dressing up activities and financial instruments to look greener than they are. That issue is a very serious one, but its solution runs through the same path as the solution to the European dilemma: the development of a narrowly defined but widely accepted set of metrics which do not allow the kind of cherry-picking among standards which is so tempting. The temptation is there, and no doubt some issuers and financial intermediaries have succumbed to it, but a more rigorous approach, such as the one set forth by the Climate Bonds Initiative White Paper from September 2020 on financing credible transitions, is also possible. So we should be careful not to let the fear of greenwashing overcome the need to continue to develop solutions that allow the financing of a green transition. Mark Carney, who in his time as Governor of the Bank of England was among the first to sound the alarm about the need for action by the financial sector to combat climate change, has also been among the first to warn against too rigid a "green versus brown" classification and to call for a more flexible "fifty shades of green" approach.

The need for a broader scope of instruments in the sustainability area is clear from the trends in recent issuances as surveyed in Environmental Finance's Sustainable Bonds Insight 2021. The Green bond market grew modestly in 2020 but total sustainable bond issuance almost doubled as sustainability and social bond issuance grew rapidly. This issuance trend has clearly been boosted by the release of new market guidelines, most notably the Sustainability Linked Bond Principles (SLBPs) in June 2020 and the Climate Transition Finance (CTF) Handbook 2020 in December 2020, both administered by the ICMA. But the main driver must be seen as the market's need to move beyond companies and projects which are already viewed as sustainable and to broaden the scope of what can be financed by moving beyond UoP bonds to target linked issues in order to reach a sustainable world. We should keep this need in mind in evaluating existing and proposed standard setting. No matter how intellectually satisfying standards may look, if they cannot enlarge the scope of what can be financed, are they really fit for purpose?

2. Defining "green" and "sustainable"

The OECD, in its 2020 Business and Finance Outlook report phrases the question rather politely: "[c]urrent market practices, from ratings to disclosures and individual metrics, present a fragmented and inconsistent view of ESG risks and performance .... This fragmentation and incompatibility may not serve investors in assessing performance against general ESG goals, or targeted objectives such as enhanced management of climate risks .... Fiduciaries such as asset managers and boards should be managing material ESG risks in a way that supports long-term value creation – but are not necessarily getting the data and information they need to do so." I think it is clear that we should read out the words "may" and "necessarily". Investors are simply not getting the information they need. The CDP March 2021 Report, Running Hot, notes that less than 35 % of European companies disclose meaningful information concerning their Scope 3 emissions, those which occur beyond corporate boundaries in their respective value chains, although the authors estimate these make up the vast majority of these companies' emissions impact as a whole.

One of the CEOs on the first panel at our conference mentioned 30 separate sets of criteria his institution follows in making determinations for ESG and sustainability purposes. The OECD 2020 report, focusing on the environmental aspect of ESG scoring, reporting and measurement, notes the differences in the scope of metrics, measurement and weight of metrics used for environmental scoring. This plethora of standards and approaches presents problems for all participants in ESG financing. Issuers of securities or borrowers of loans are called upon to provide the raw material for these evaluations in different formats and levels of detail. The duplication leads to inconsistencies and extra work. End investors rely on this data to make investment decisions, but are not in a position to compare information provided by company A to intermediary B with that provided by company C to intermediary D. In the middle are financial institutions which stand between the issuers and the investors and must advise both sides, but especially the final investors, to whom they may owe fiduciary or other statutory duties. The situation is all the more difficult because, despite the abundance of information requested and provided, numerous specific points of data and information that institutional investors consider important, including issuers' environmental policies, climate targets, and sufficiently granular data on carbon emissions, turn out to be missing.

In part the financial intermediaries have caused their own problem, as each seems to see a competitive advantage in having its own proprietary formula for evaluating the components of ESG. Nonetheless, the problem is an acute one which needs to be solved on an urgent basis if we are to develop a broad and liquid market for sustainable products. The main competing systems can be divided, for the sale of convenience, into a few broad categories: (i) the recommendations of the Task Force on Climate-Related Financial Disclosures (TCFD) established under the aegis of the Financial Stability Board (FSB), which is probably the most widely cited set of private sector standards, (ii) directives, regulations and guidance in the EU, in particular the NFRD, the Taxonomy, the SFDR and Regulatory Technical Standards (RTS), (iii) various standards developed by non-governmental organizations, including the Global Sustainability Standards Board (GSSB) promoting the Global Reporting Initiative (GRI) on sustainability reporting, the Climate Disclosure Standards Board (CDSB), the CDP (formerly the Carbon Disclosure Project) and the International Integrated Reporting Council (IIRC) which is soon to be merged with the Sustainability Accounting Standards Board (SASB), to form the Value Reporting Foundation, and (iv) a plethora of service providers offering ratings, benchmarking and verification services, the credit rating agencies working on incorporating environmental aspects into their credit rating processes, as well as financial institutions offering a variety of funds and other products labeled as green or sustainable.

Among this alphabet soup of acronyms it is important to distinguish two strands of rules in the EU, the directives and the regulations. The NFRD applies to reporting by large publicly traded companies and by financial institutions. As it is a Directive and not a Regulation, its exact form can vary according to how Member States have elected to implement it. But, as noted above, for the moment its recommendations are not mandatory. The Taxonomy is directed towards issuers subject to the NFRD and imposes new standards for classifying their business activities as green or sustainable, which will also be binding on financial market participants. The SFDR is directed towards reporting to security holders primarily by financial institutions which offer investment products or advice in the EU, including by pension providers and insurance companies. The standards contained in the three do not currently match up.

Thus, the EU's rules are, to varying degrees, legally binding. For the moment, the NFRD contains only guidelines and recommendations. The Taxonomy, although currently incomplete, is a Regulation, enforceable as written, as is the SFDR. The TCFD, GSSB, CSDB, CDP and SASB standards are voluntary. All of these approaches have supporters, but none can claim universality. TCFD, with their FSB pedigree, comes perhaps the closest to having a global reach. But even there, as we will see, the current degree of compliance with their disclosure recommendations.

3. The TCFD: More honored in the Breach?

The most widely cited of international efforts at setting disclosure standards for sustainable reporting is the TCFD created under the auspices of the Financial Stability Board at the behest of the G20 after consultation with industry representatives. Its recommendations were released in mid-2017, endorsed initially by 100 supporters representing a market capitalization of $3.3 trillion. As of June 2020 it had more than 1,300 supporters with a market capitalization of $12 trillion. But, unlike the Commission, the TCFD cannot compel issuers or financial intermediaries to adopt and comply with its recommendations. Its own 2020 Status Report released in October 2020 concludes that voluntary adoption is not moving fast enough or broadly enough, so that greater standardization will have to be driven by international standard setters such as the IFRS or IOSCO.

As Sylvie Goulard writes in her excellent contribution to this book, the TCFD articulates its disclosure recommendations around four pillars: (i) governance around climate issues within the company (management and board's role in processing, managing and overseeing climate-related risks and opportunities), (ii) strategic implications (approach to risks and opportunities, including how they could impact the business model), (iii) climate-related risk management processes (how risks are identified and managed) and (iv) metrics and targets followed by the company to address strategy and risk. A recent academic paper, (Bingler, Kraus and Leippold, March 2, 2021) uses artificial intelligence (a deep neural language model the authors named ClimateBert) to analyze reporting by companies claiming to support and report in accordance with TCFD, starting before TCFD was published in 2017 and continuing through 2020. The authors concluded there was only a negligible increase in sustainability disclosures over the period and that the increases were primarily in qualitative disclosures, those relating to categories (i) and (iii), covering governance and the structure of risk management, rather than in the more quantitative disclosures of categories (ii) and (iv) relating to strategy, and metrics and targets, the areas which, according to the authors, would provide the most essential and material information to stakeholders. The only exception they found was for French companies, whose disclosures in these two areas shot up after France introduced detailed mandatory climate-risk reporting for large financial institutions in Article 173 of the French Energy Transition law. In contrast they observed no similar increase for European companies in general after the NFRD came into effect in 2016. They note that, unlike the French law, the NFRD is non-binding and not prescriptive with respect to the kind of disclosure companies must make under it. Their conclusion is that "the only way out ... is to turn voluntary reporting into regulatory disclosures."

The Climate Disclosure Standards Board (CDSB) came to a similar conclusion on the spotty adoption of TCFD in its December 2020 report on the state of EU environmental disclosure in 2020. They note that while 68 % of Europe's largest companies make reference to TCFD in their disclosures, only 4 % disclose climate risks over short, medium and long-term time horizons and only 18 % provide disclosure on their resilience to different climate scenarios. Only 38 % applied the Commission's double materiality perspective to their environmental disclosures. The CDSB also concluded that the TCFD recommendations should be made mandatory, within the ambit of an amended NFRD. (CDSB 2020) This route was adopted by the UK's Financial Conduct Authority (FCA) in December 2020, effective for accounting periods beginning in 2021, initially for companies with a UK premium listing.

4. Reporting on Sustainability in the EU: The Art of Cherry-Picking

Turning briefly to the state of current reporting in the EU on sustainability issues more generally, both the Alliance for Corporate Transparency (ACT) in its 2019 and 2020 reports, and the European Securities and Markets Authority (ESMA) in its Enforcement and regulatory activities of European enforcers report in 2019 were less than impressed by the level of reporting under the NFRD. In its 2019 report, covering 1000 European companies, ACT found only 13.9 % reported on alignment of their climate targets with the Paris Agreement goals and that three quarters of the companies with the greatest impact on climate reported neither targets nor plans. Fewer than a quarter of companies provided specific information on the climate-related risks they face and only 13.4 % of financial companies provided details on the exposure of their portfolios to the most polluting sectors. While ACT's 2020 report saw overall improvement, they still found that fewer than half of the companies provided quantitative climate targets and only one third included specific risk disclosures.

ESMA's report was more positive, but the TCFD status reports for 2019 and 2020 on climate related financial disclosures concluded they were still insufficient for investors, that more clarity is needed on the potential impact of climate-related issues on companies and, that of companies using scenarios, the majority do not disclose information on the resilience of those strategies. The 2019 study noted that for fiscal year 2019 reporting the average level of disclosure across their eleven recommended disclosures was 40 % for energy companies and 30 % for materials and building companies and that only one in 15 companies reviewed discussed the resilience of its strategy. And we have seen above what ClimateBert made of reporting according to TCFD standards.

5. EU Regulation

Let us now look more closely at the EU's existing initiatives, in particular the NFRD and the Taxonomy as candidates for global application. Putting aside the "not invented here" and "you don't understand our context" obstacles one always encounters in trying to transplant standards from one jurisdiction to another, there are a few particular obstacles here. Standard setting is of course always a tricky business. Standard setters are torn between the aspirational goal of creating a "gold standard" and the practical limitations of what existing systems can cope with in terms of conduct and information. Perhaps nowhere is this tug of war more evident than in dealing with sustainability, given the seriousness and complexity of the issuers involved. At the end of the day, I think it is fair to say the EU has leaned quite heavily towards the "gold standard" end of the spectrum.

5.1 Taking the NFRD back to the Drawing Board: The Lessons not learned from Apollo 13

The NFRD was adopted in 2014, applicable for reporting from 2018 onwards. It mandates all large listed EU companies with more than 500 employees and financial institutions – some 6,000 companies in all at the time of adoption – to disclose information on environmental, social, human rights and anti-corruption matters necessary to understand a company's position, performance development and impacts. A company should report information on its business model, policies and due diligence and the outcomes of these policies, principal risks, and KPIs with respect to environmental and social issues relevant to its business. However, it does not define what specific information and KPIs companies must disclose. The Commission has issued a series of non-binding guidelines in 2017 and 2019 on the disclosure of environmental, social and climate related information and is in the process of formally reviewing the directive

The NFRD needs to be amended in order to work in tandem with the Taxonomy and the SDFR. The European supervisory authorities, ESMA, EBA and EIOPA, recommend that its requirements be made mandatory, apply to a wider group of companies, be audited and be consistent with the SFDR, the Taxonomy and their own prudential disclosure requirements. So, the NFRD has to be filled with more specific, probably mandatory content. The question is how. One approach can be found in the 226 page report from the European Financial Reporting Advisory Group (EFRAG) which was tasked by the Commission with doing the preparatory work on possible non-financial reporting standards. Delivered in February 2021, the report contains 54 proposals built along a complex architecture consisting of three layers of what the authors refer to as sector-agnostic, sector-specific and entity-specific reporting in three reporting areas of strategy, implementation and performance measurement for each of the three topics of environmental, social and governance. Double materiality, consisting of what is material to the reporting entity and of what effects the entity may have on its environment, is at the core of the proposals, with the assessments to be done by the standard setter for the sector-agnostic and sector-specific disclosures and by the reporting entity for entity-specific disclosures. The sustainability reporting needs to be connected with financial reporting through the use of anchor points with the necessary reconciliations or cross-references. The information provided should be both retrospective and forward-looking, and the reporting should go beyond the scope of the reporting entity's own operations to cover its value chain. Implementation will necessarily have to take place in phases.

That is one approach. It is thorough but complicated and rather abstract, and I question how it will work in practice. It is to be phased in over time, but even the first phase, targeted for the end of 2022, strikes me as a challenge, since it is to be made up of two priority conceptual guidelines on double materiality and quality of information, plus cross-cutting 'core' standards covering reporting areas, reporting structure and entity-specific materiality assessment, together with 'core' standards for most sub-topics and 'advanced' standards for some priority sub-topics, such a climate change. I wonder about both its feasibility and how easily it can serve as basis for the "mutually reinforcing cooperation between the EU and international initiatives or fora" the authors envisage for it.

It is what I would call the anti-Apollo 13 approach to problem-solving. You may recall from the film of the same name that after Tom Hanks announces "Houston, we have a problem", Mission Control does not ask the team in Houston to go back to the drawing board for a theoretical solution, but rather dumps on the table everything the crew has available to it in the capsule to fix the problem and asks the team, focusing on the elements at hand, to come up with a solution. Applied to the NFRD, the Apollo 13 alternative approach would be to start with something that already exists, for example the TCFD and to build on that, as the UK is now doing, and as the CDFB recommended in its December 2020 report on the state of environmental reporting in Europe. Building on already accepted principles would surely gather more momentum internationally than starting afresh with such a complex construct and be achievable on a shorter time scale.

However, in its April 2021 Communication, the Commission indicated EFRAG would be in charge of writing a new Corporate Sustainability Reporting Directive (CSRD) proposal. The contents were not specified, but it is probably safe to assume it will follow EFRAG's advice to the Commission. It is to deliver a first draft by mid-2022. Nevertheless, both the Commission's communication (the Communication) and its accompanying Questions and Answers paper on CSRD mention that EFRAG should be looking to the work of the IFRS and the Five Standard Setters with a view to contributing to standardization initiatives at the global level, so maybe we will see some changes in approach.

In the meantime, the existing recommendations of the NFRD are not being followed by the majority of companies to whom it applies, and its future shape is uncertain. So it does not seem to be a model ready to be offered up to the world for emulation.

5.2 The Taxonomy: The 593 Page Gorilla

Turning to the Taxonomy, let me first refer you to the extremely lucid explanation of its overall structure contained in the excellent article in this book by Matthias Kopp and Valentin von Massow, before noting that there are also a number of issues in turning those into a global standard. For one thing, despite having come into force in July 2020, it is far from complete. It excludes for the moment certain sectors which do not have their own NACE industrial classification codes, such as buildings, and was conceived primarily as a sorting mechanism to distinguish between economic activities which substantially contribute to at least one of six defined environmental objectives, do no significant harm (DNSH) to any of the other objectives and comply with minimum safeguards, such as the OECD Guidelines on Multinational Enterprises and the UN Guiding Principles on Business and Human Rights. It requires issuers to report on the proportion of their turnover, capital expenditure and operating costs which are aligned in the Taxonomy. The Taxonomy's rules relating to recognition of capital and operating expenditures and resulting turnover are quite complex and must be analyzed at the asset, project and company levels and provide for different disclosure methodologies for equities and fixed income securities. These rules also raise the question of the need for external verification.

The Taxonomy, by its terms, does not purport to affect issuer operations outside the EU. Nor, in my view, should it because, the closer one examines it, the clearer it becomes that, while it may have started out as a project of universal applicability, it is now a very European project. Activities can be classified as sustainable to the extent they are aligned with the EU's 2030 and 2050 sustainability goals, both in terms of overall mitigation of climate change, e.g. a 55 % versus a 50 % or lower reduction of greenhouse gas emissions, against 1990 levels, and in terms of the policy compromises leading to the inclusion or exclusion of categories of politically sensitive activities such as nuclear power and natural gas. The political compromises that result in including or excluding these activities simply cannot be seen as of universal applicability. Nor can the EU's ambitious overall climate targets, in particular the 55 % reduction goal, be expected to be taken over by the rest of the world. I am not an expert in the inner workings of the Taxonomy. Thus I cannot say for sure how easy or hard it would be to untangle these goals or even to compare the goal of a 55 % reduction against 1990 (EU) to a 40 % reduction against 2005 (Japan) from its technical provisions in order to apply them outside the EU. But I fear it will not be straightforward. The EU's goal is a worthy one, but it is also now a more local one, tailored to the EU and its Member States who emit, in total, 8.4 % of the world's greenhouse gasses. A solution of broader applicability needs to be found for the other 91.6 %.

The Taxonomy has also been criticized for being overly focused on drawing lines between green and non-green, and thus lacking the flexibility to deal with the growing need for investment outside of issuances to finance a demonstrably green project – for example, to finance transition and sustainability-linked bonds. This complaint sounds odd because the Taxonomy explicitly covers mitigation and adaptation activities. Mitigation activities are intended "[t]o establish transition pathways for heavily emitting sectors for which low carbon solutions are unavailable" so long as the activity does not result in a lock-in of assets incompatible with the Taxonomy's six goals and ensures environmental performance well above the sector average. Adaptation activities cover so-called "enabling activities" which include those which do not lead to a lock-in of assets that undermine long-term goals, considering the economic lifetime of the assets and have a substantial positive environmental impact on the basis of life-cycle consideration. So, is the criticism unwarranted? Actually it is warranted, and the reasons lie in the Taxonomy's unfinished state. There is currently a Usability Guide on the EU Green Bond Standard put out by the TEG in March 2020 which focuses on the UoP approach for Green bonds. What does not yet exist are the delegated acts which are needed to implement those parts of the Taxonomy relating to transitional activities. The first of these should have been adopted by December 31, 2020, but after receiving 46,591 answers to its consultation on it, the Commission has delayed its adoption. So, at the time I write, those activities cannot, as practical matter, be counted.

The Commission was acutely aware of the problem and in January 2021 asked its expert group, the Platform on Sustainable Finance, to recommend a set of solutions which would allow the Taxonomy to provide greater support for attracting capital to transition activities. The Platform reported back promptly in March 2021 with some helpful suggestions which should result in improvements, and, on April 21, 2021, the Commission did publish a revised delegated act. In its Communication the Commission said it had reflected some of the comments received, especially those related to transition issues. It also assured us that the delegated act would be a living document, subject to further amendment as required by science or reality. I have not had the time to review the changes aimed at making the Taxonomy "more usable by economic factors" or the changes "simplifying criteria, reducing complexity and overall burden and, where appropriate, adjustments to make them more specific and flexible", but it is heartening that the Commission has clearly read and taken to heart the ISS ESG report discussed below.

Perhaps less heartening is that a number of delicate issues such as nuclear power, gas, and agriculture are being left to later delegated acts, while bioenergy and forestry found their way into the text. The delegated act is to be adopted at the end of a scrutiny period (four months, extendible for another two months). The Commission also seems to recognize that the Taxonomy, as is, will not be able to be applied globally and refers specifically in the Communication to cooperation with China on a Common Ground Taxonomy to be developed under the aegis of the International Platform on Sustainable Finance (IPSF) to which the Taxonomy would contribute.

Perhaps the best summary of the problems with the Taxonomy I have read comes from an article dated March 18, 2021, by Huw van Steenis, Chairman of sustainable finance at UBS and formally senior advisor to Mark Carney at the Bank of England, entitled "Climate Change Won't be Stopped by 593 pages of Green Tape". The reference to 593 pages is to the length of the Technical Annex to the Taxonomy. The author makes three main points. First, the Taxonomy is too binary in supporting only what is the purest shade of green. According to his analysis, almost all European Green bonds issued under the private sector standards of the International Capital Markets Association ("ICMA") and the Climate Bond Initiative would fail the Taxonomy standards, potentially closing the Green bond market at a stroke. Second, he finds the methodology, by turns, too strict and too broad, citing a study of the Euro Stoxx 50 index companies by ISS ESG which found that while a fifth of their revenues are broadly aligned with the Taxonomy's principles, only 2% could be considered as strictly aligned. He notes that wind is in but hydropower is not. Third, there is no category for firms in transition. He sums up by saying "Brussels has gotten bogged down in the details of a noble, but self-defeating desire to create an exhaustive, one-size-fits all solution". He concludes that, as a result, "the Taxonomy is not going global in the way Brussels had hoped". He urges that, instead the EU should build on existing frameworks, in particular, the TCFD. In that he joins the recommendation of the CDFB and the direction taken by the UK FCA.

The ISS ESG Study he refers to is the European Sustainable Finance Survey 2020 which it conducted jointly with the think tank adelphi. It contains some very illuminating information, based both on market analysis and on in depth questionnaires from 84 listed European companies. Its market analysis leads the authors to conclude only 1 % of the revenues of the companies listed on Germany's blue-chip DAX index would qualify as fully aligned with the Taxonomy and thus as sustainable under the proposed rules, despite those companies deriving over 20 % of their revenues from Taxonomy relevant activities. This number grows to 2 % for the revenues of the companies included in the French CAC 40 and Euro Stoxx 50 indices. The results of the questionnaires are well worth reading in their entirety, but I would like to select a few points. The first relates to transition activities. It appears that the Taxonomy's quantitative emission intensity thresholds are set at a level such that only a fraction of transition activities can meet them. The second relates to the DNSH test. It appears that half of revenues that otherwise substantially contribute to climate change mitigation or adaptation do not qualify, because they fail to meet the DNSH criteria. The third relates to research and development activities for which there is apparently no room under the Taxonomy. The last point relates to reporting. The calculations required to report alignment with the Taxonomy do not align with current company reporting of KPIs under existing standards, so many companies are simply waiting for them to be finalized before starting to align with them. This means it is possible that a higher percentage of their revenues would qualify, but also that companies are unprepared to comply. The revised delegated act presented on April 21, 2021 may change this.

The European Parliament must still approve delegated acts. Seventy-one votes are required to approve or reject them, and 65 MEPs had already expressed opposition to them in their prior form, leading to the danger that the Parliament could "nip the Taxonomy in the bud" as one Parliamentary source was quoted by the FT as saying. This may explain why, as noted above, the Commission opted to postpone a decision on some of the most delicate political/policy questions concerning nuclear power, gas and agriculture to later delegated acts, calculating that with these issues stripped out, they increased the chances of getting the bulk of the Taxonomy's technical standards approved by the European Parliament – thus hopefully solving many of the practical issues concerning the ability of the Taxonomy to accommodate transition activities.

5.3 The SDFR and the Brussels Effect

The EU has another card up its sleeve. Its rules on sustainability apply not only to EU issuers, but also to any financial advisor which sells or advises on financial products sold in the EU under the Sustainable Financial Disclosure Regulation (SDFR). The SDFR applies from March 10, 2021 and requires disclosure both at the firm and at the product level from any international fund manager active in the EU in compliance with EU categories, including the Taxonomy.

This can be seen as a variation on the GDPR strategy of catching the big international fish and requiring them to play by local rules if they want to stay in the pond. Once their systems are in place to comply with the Taxonomy, the financial intermediaries can become allies in its propagation beyond the EU's borders. This can be analysed as a manifestation of what Professor Bradford has termed the Brussels Effect in her brilliant book of the same name. The theory is that the EU through its own standard setting in certain areas, including privacy and environmental protection, can influence conduct worldwide through decisions of the private sector where access to the EU market is important and can be controlled and a single set of standards worldwide is easier than trying to administer separate standards. This is in particular the case where the rules apply to inelastic targets such as consumers rather than more mobile targets such as capital and the product or service is indivisible, legally, technically or economically.

The Brussels Effect worked with the platform operators in the privacy sphere, but a close examination of Professor Bradford's criteria for its effectiveness would lead to a number of doubts as to its applications to standard setting in the sustainability area. One difference is particularly important for me. In privacy, the decision was solely in the hands of the platforms to adapt their policies to comply or not. In sustainability, the financial intermediaries are dependent on the companies they invest in to provide them the needed information on their operations outside the EU. The intermediaries will clearly be incentivized to do so since, if they are unable to classify an investment as Taxonomy compliant, this will negatively affect the green rating of their own products and portfolios which include the asset. The effects on the intermediaries may be even greater if they are called upon to include the effects of their portfolios as part of their own "Scope 3" reporting, as the recent CDP Financial Services Disclosure Report 2020 suggests they ought to do. Whether companies outside the EU can be convinced to report along the lines of the Taxonomy will depend on how difficult that reporting is and whether a broadly accepted alternative system is available, which might be more user-friendly. We have seen that the Taxonomy contains a novel approach, requiring the collection of information customized to EU climate policies, which non-EU companies may be hesitant to start generating.

6. The IFRS and IOSCO to the Rescue?

And there may soon be at least one other proposed solution which might be broadly acceptable. A new entry in the standard setting sweepstakes is the 2020 initiative by the IFRS Foundation, which oversees the international accounting standards of the same name, soliciting comments on whether the Foundation should sponsor a Sustainability Standards Board (SSB) with a mandate to become a standard setter to achieve coherence and comparability in the area. Given that the IFRS principles are used for the preparation of financial statements around the world (with the exception of the US) tasking the Foundation with the development of consistent and comparable sustainability related reporting might be the best solution for developing a globally acceptable set of reporting standards. The stars seem to be aligning around the proposal. It has been endorsed by the International Organization of Securities Commissions (IOSCO). At the end of 2020 the group of prominent standard setters I referred to above as the Five Standard Setters, made up of the CDSB, the CDP, the GRI, the International Integrated Reporting Council (IIRC) and the SASB, who have been working together with the encouragement of the World Economic Forum (WEF) on a vision for a comprehensive reporting system, produced a report on how current frameworks and standards, including the recommendations of the TCFD, could be used to provide the basis for global standards for sustainability-related financial disclosure. They have offered their work up to the IFRS as input for their project.

Their report, dated December 2020, entitled "Reporting on enterprise value", pulls together the various strands of reporting its contributing institutions had previously developed. The report suggests that these various approaches can be understood as a set of concentric lenses starting with the widest aperture of sustainability and ending up with the narrowest focus on monetary amounts recognized in the financial statements. For example, starting with carbon emissions which enter the widest lens when society becomes aware of global warming, moving to the middle lens as investors start to factor net zero transition into capital market pricing, and ending up with the narrowest lens as financial consequences are felt in net asset values. A key concept is the interoperability between the various focuses of reporting.

The report includes a prototype disclosure standard to show how their conceptual framework can be made to fit in with the IASB's conceptual framework for financial reporting and the TCFD framework. The IFRS Foundation has indicated a willingness to consider their input. While we are far from having a unified product, the IFRS could provide the "unifying force" that finally makes universal ESG standards a reality, according to the analysis of the FT Moral Money blog published March 10, 2021. The WEF's International Business Council (IBC) has announced plans to mobilize CEO support for the SSB and for a "building block" approach to global sustainability. The building blocks would comprise a set of "stakeholder capitalism metrics" developed by the Big Four accounting firms and the IBC, including 21 core metrics and 34 expanded metrics, drawn largely from existing standards. In January 2021 60 large multinationals pledged to start reporting those metrics.

There are still a number of significant issues to be resolved to make the IFRS project a reality. First is the number of the parties involved, which can be expected to slow down the process. But here IOSCO seems to be setting a very brisk pace. Second is the question of whether to focus first on the environmental pillar, which is the IFRS's preference, or go towards a broader range of ESG and sustainability issues. The decision seems to have been made to focus on the former. Third is the definition of materiality. The IFRS's approach is to use an enterprise focused standard of what is material to the reporting entity, whereas the Commission has endorsed the concept of "double materiality" mentioned above, which also includes the external impact of the reporting entity on the environment. The Commission's position was supported by a number of the comments submitted to the IFRS Foundation by European entities. The external impact aspect of double materiality comes from a number of sustainability reporting initiatives, such as the GRI, and was first introduced in 2019 by the Commission in its second set of non-binding guidelines on the NFRD. Double materiality is also firmly embedded in the intellectual foundations of the Taxonomy, so the key will be how to resolve this issue.

The approach taken by the Five Standard Setters is to focus on the concept of enterprise value and the broader scope of factors which over a longer time span can affect a company's value, both directly and indirectly. These factors evolve over time as the environment in which the company operates and the priorities of its stakeholders change. Thus, the Five Standard Setters are in effect shifting the focus from outwards directed sustainability reporting to sustainability related financial reporting for enterprises of information relevant to its stakeholders. To the extent these stakeholders find sustainability is material to their decisions, it will also be material to the companies involved. As Ashley Alder, Chief Executive Officer of the Hong Kong Securities and Futures Commission and of IOSCO, stated in a speech on April 15, 2021, "enterprise value and double materiality are complementary concepts and will become even more so as investors demand more information about the material impact companies' activities have on the environment." Alder 2021. This is a promising approach which fits in with current work being done more broadly on the concept of dynamic materiality in the ESG context. See Truvalue Labs, Dynamic Materiality™ Measuring What Matters (January 2020). This may be the key to the IFRS/IOSCO project moving to the pole position on a broadly acceptable system of sustainability linked financial reporting.

7. The Limitations of the European Capital Markets

The issues discussed above are common to all markets for green and sustainable products, but the EU's capital markets suffer from additional handicaps identified more than a decade ago in the wake of the great financial crisis, and which are still largely with us. The Final Report of the High Level Forum (HLF) on the Capital Markets Union published in June 2020 opened with the sober assessment that "Europe has for decades struggled to make its capital markets work as one and to a large degree still has 27 capital markets, some fairly large, and quite a number rather small."

The European Capital Markets Institute (ECMI), in its November 2020 Policy Brief no. 28 entitled "Europe's capital markets puzzle", details the stark comparisons with the US. On the equity market side, the US capital market, as measured by the Bloomberg MSGI equity market index, has advanced enormously over the past five years, while Europe has remained flat. The attractiveness of the equity markets in Europe remains low, at approximately half the size of that of the US. On the debt securities markets, the European sector is about half the size of the US, with €19.5 trillion securities outstanding in Europe, compared to €36.6 trillion in the US in 2019, and debt securities issued by governments and financial institutions make up 89 % of the market in Europe, while corporate debt amounts to only 11 %, as compared to almost 31 % in the US. The gap in funding for SMEs is even larger, with average annual risk capital investment in the US over the period 2015–18 almost nine times as high as the amount invested in the EU-27, with US pre-IPO capital representing 1.2 % of GDP, compared to 0.14 % in the EU-27. Finally, while firm numbers are hard to obtain, the authors estimate that only 1 % of financial services provision in Europe is cross-border.

The Europe Regulatory Update published by Eurofi in September 2020 in its article entitled "CMU 2.0: latest proposals and next steps for relaunching the CMU in the COVID context" further notes that the EU-27 average stock market capitalization is still much lower than that of the US and UK (58 % of GDP in EU-27 with many countries having practically non-existent capital markets, compared to 115 % in the UK and close to 150 % in the US), and the share of listed securities remains limited in the funding structure of EU non-financial companies (28 % compared to 47 % in the UK and 69 % in the US). The article also notes the persistent home bias in investments and that cross-border capital flows have not recovered their pre-2008 crisis levels. It also details the timetable(s) for the reforms to the CMU contained in the HLF final report, some of which extend to 2028, so to the end of this crucial decade in which we must take control of climate change.

This is a sobering assessment of the results of the Capital Markets Union project started in 2014 to which the ILF devoted a conference which Andreas Dombret and I co-chaired in 2015. At the time we questioned whether it was a viable concept and a real goal. We concluded that it was an eminently worthwhile goal, but feared it would not be achieved. I am afraid we were right. The authors of the ECMI article view the Investment Firm Regime and the European Supervisory Authorities (ESAs) as the two main achievements of CMU 1.0. Evaluating the CMU 2.0 Action Plan, made up of 16 actions, including adaptation to the green recovery and digitalization, more disclosure and better access to finance for SMEs, they view none of them as controversial or requiring big changes, with the exception of a proposal for an EU-wide system for withholding tax relief at source, but observe that this proposal would require unanimity in the EU Council, since it concerns tax harmonization. I found the same lack of ambition at the core of CMU 1.0 in my 2015 article on it in our book on the European Capital Markets Union.

The authors of the ECMI article conclude that "[s]ix years after the start of CMU, Europe has moved backwards rather than forwards towards a more balanced financial system. Fragmentation has led to smaller and disconnected liquidity pools with less efficient and more volatile pricing. Market financing is not advancing." The European Court of Auditors delivered a special report on CMU 1.0 which concluded "the results are still to come." The ECOFIN December 2020 conclusions pushed back the most ambitious proposals of CMU 2.0, relating to insolvency and withholding tax regimes, back to the "medium term." So, here again the EU is moving more slowly than one would wish.

8. The US returns to the Table

Good news has come from outside the EU. The new administration in the US which took office on January 20, 2021 has meant a return of the US to the table on issues of climate change and sustainability. US financial intermediaries had already been present in the ranks of those requiring additional disclosure, but until recently had to some extent been stymied by initiatives taken by the prior administration to limit the extent to which fiduciaries subject to the rules of the US Department of Labor (DOL) under the Employee Retirement Income Security Act (ERISA) could take non-financial goals, such as sustainability, into consideration in making investment decisions. Those rules are likely to be ultimately relaxed under the new Biden administration, which has already indicated an intention to review them, and the DOL has announced that it will not enforce them pending a fuller review. Although the DOL rules applied directly only to a portion of the investment plans in the US, they were clearly intended to have a chilling effect on fiduciaries taking ESG factors into consideration in evaluating investments, as the DOL acknowledged in its statement.

On March 15, 2021, Allison Herren Lee, Acting Chair of the SEC, pending the confirmation of Gary Gensler as Chair, following the recommendation made by the Investor-as-Owner Subcommittee of the SEC Investor Advisory Committee in December 2020 that the SEC adopt standards for the disclosure of material ESG risks, announced a request for comments due within 90 days on how the SEC should approach disclosure concerning climate change and, more broadly, other ESG matters. From the request it is clear that the SEC is inclined to tackle climate first. It contained 15 questions covering the kinds of information required: whether the SEC should develop its own standards or allow private groups to develop standards, subject to minimum disclosure standards the SEC would set; whether there should be separate industry-specific standards; whether the SEC should draw on existing frameworks, including the TCFD, the SASB and the CDSB; whether disclosures should be mandatory; whether a single set of global standards would be preferable, with or without mandatory compliance; what level of assurance, including certification by corporate officers, should climate disclosure be subject to; and whether management should be required to provide an analysis of climate disclosure similar to the required analysis of financial condition and results of operations?

A first panel of SEC Commission members and industry representatives met to discuss the issues on March 19, 2021. The meeting revealed that there was currently no broad agreement on whether to adopt ESG rules. Republican members of the Congress have already expressed opposition to them. Thus, while the US appears to be moving in the right direction, it is unclear whether it will take a leading role in the field. Gary Gensler, the new Chair, proved during his tenure as Chairman of the Commodities Futures Trading Commission, that he is capable of decisive and speedy action, but he has a lot on his plate. Nevertheless, the SEC can at least play a positive role in supporting the IFRS/IOSCO initiative. In a separate presentation Ms. Lee made on March 15, she expressed support for IOSCO's endorsement of an SSB at the international level and for international cooperation on climate issues, bilaterally and through IOSCO and the FSB. In particular, she expressed support for an SSB and raised the question of whether the US should also have a domestic standard setter, similar to the Financial Accounting Standards Board under SEC oversight.

Even before the change of US administration, Environmental Finance's Sustainable Bonds Insight 2021 report shows that while only six of the top 15 lead managers for green, social, sustainability and sustainability-linked bonds overall in 2020 were North American (five US and one Canadian), and green and social bonds in particular were still firmly in European lead managers' hands in 2020 by a margin of two to one, 60 % of lead managers for the rapidly growing sustainability bond segment were non-European, up from 40 % in 2019. The Euro still led as the currency for overall sustainable bond issuances – in fact its market share increased from just under 45 % in 2019 to almost 49 % in 2020 – but the dollar's share of issuances also increased from just under 32 % to over 35 %. And for the fourth consecutive year the US and France were two of the three biggest issuing countries of Green bonds in 2020. The US, Netherlands and France were the biggest issuing countries in the sustainability bond market, with the US leading by a wide margin in 2020.

9. Conclusion

I believe the EU has implicitly been betting on the Brussels Effect here, hoping that its experience with the GDPR, where the EU forged ahead alone and the GDPR became, de facto, the global data privacy standard, could be duplicated in the sustainability arena. If the EU built the Taxonomy, the expectation was that the world would follow its lead. I think that outcome is less likely to happen today than it was a year ago and, if I read the Commission's April 21 Communication correctly, I believe the Commission has come to realize that as well. The EU opted to start with an aspirational "gold standard" approach and then to tailor the Taxonomy to its political and policy goals, both of which are perfectly understandable but have the potential to diminish its chances to serve as a universal model. It is to be hoped that the revised delegated act will succeed in making it work for transition activities and will be approved by the European Parliament. Beyond that, some of its metrics may not work for countries which have decided on a different speed or pathway for carbon reduction or disagree with some of its policy decisions. On the NFRD front it looks like it is opting for originality and complexity over trying to adapt the TCFD framework. I fear these decisions can only slow down the process of developing uniform rules which could be widely adopted outside the EU. Although, ultimately, some classification system like the Taxonomy will have to underpin any disclosure system, the solution may well have to involve either a Common Group Taxonomy under the auspices of a group like the IPSF or an IFRS SSB structure, as the Commission appears to be implicitly recognizing in the Communication. And so, I would hesitate to bet on the Brussels Effect in the sustainability standards area.

These decisions have left a path open to an alternative set of standards which the IFRS and IOSCO may be able to use to develop what they can present as a truly global standard, compatible with both international financial accounting standards and the most widely respected sustainability-related reporting system, the TCFD. Their project comes across as less prescriptive and more likely to facilitate the financing of transition activities, thus more pragmatic, open and exportable than the EU project. Success is not assured, but if, together, they can come up with a solution that IOSCO can recommend internationally and one which the US can live with, they could have a formula appealing to the rest of the world.

References

adelphi, ISS ESG (2020), European Sustainable Finance Survey, 2020
Ashley Alder, Speech at the Eurofi High Level Seminar 2021, Corporate sustainability standards: The way forward, April 15, 2021
Alliance for Corporate Transparency, Research Reports 2019 (May 2020) and 2020 (March 2021)
Bingler, Kraus & Leippold, Cheap Talk and Cherry-Picking: What Climate Bert has to say on Corporate Climate Risk Disclosures, March 2, 2021
Anu Bradford, The Brussels Effect: How the European Union Rules the World, Oxford University Press, 2020
Carbon Pricing Leadership Coalition (2017), Report of the High-Level Commission on Carbon Pricing, May 29, 2017
CDP (2020) Financial Services Disclosure Report 2020, The Time to Green Finance 2020
CDP (2021) Report, Running Hot, Accelerating Europe's Path to Paris, written by Oliver Wyman, March 2021
CDP, CDSB, GRI, Integrated Reporting, SASB (2020), Reporting on enterprise value, December 2020
Climate Bonds Initiative (2020), Climate Bonds White Paper, Financing credible transitions, September 2020,
Climate Disclosure Standards Board (2020), The State of EU environmental disclosure in 2020
Climate Policy Institute and International Renewable Energy Agency (2020), Global Landscape of Renewable Energy Finance 2020
Andreas Dombret and Patrick S. Kenadjian (Eds), The European Capital Markets Union, A viable concept and a real goal? De Gruyter Berlin, 2015
Environmental Finance (2021), Sustainable Bonds Insight 2021
Eurofi, CMU 2.0: Latest proposals and next steps for relaunching the CMU in the COVID context, European Regulatory Update, September 2020
European Commission, Communication from the Commission to the European Council, the European Economic and Social Committee and the Committee of the Regions, EU Taxonomy, Corporate Sustainability Reporting, Sustainability Preferences and Fiduciary Duties: Directing Finance towards the European Green Deal, April 21, 2021
European Commission, Questions and Answers: Taxonomy, Climate Delegated Act and Amendments to Delegated Acts on fiduciary duties, investment and insurance advice, April 21, 2021
European Commission, Questions and Answers: Corporate Sustainability Reporting Directive proposal, April 21, 2021
European Financial Reporting Advisory Group (2021), Final Report, Proposals for a Relevant and Dynamic EU Sustainability Reporting Standard-Setting, February 2021
European Investment Bank, Investment Report 2020/2021, (2021) Building a smart and green Europe in the COVID-19 era, January 2021
EU Technical Expert Group on Sustainable Finance, Taxonomy: Final Report, March 2020

Financial Conduct Authority, Policy Statement PS20/17, Proposals to enhance climate-related disclosures by listed issuers and clarification of existing disclosure obligations, December 2020
Group of Thirty (2020), Mainstreaming the Transition to a Net-Zero Economy, October 2020
High Level Forum on the Capital Markets Union, Final Report, A New Vision for Europe's Capital Markets, June 2020
ICMA (2020), Sustainability-Linked Bond Principles, June 2020
Karel Lannoo and Apostolos Thomadakis, European Capital Markets Institute (2020), Europe's capital markets puzzle, Policy Brief no. 28, November 2020
OECD (2020), Business and Finance Outlook Sustainable and Resilient Finance, September 2020
Task Force on Climate related Financial Disclosures (TCFD), 2020 Status Report, October 2020
TCFD, 2019 Status Report, June 2019
Huw van Steenis, Climate Change Won't be Stopped by 593 Pages of Green Tape, Bloomberg Quint, March 18, 2021
Truevalue Labs, Dynamic Materiality™: Measuring What Matters, SSRN-id3521035, January 17, 2020

Günther Thallinger

Climate Change: Boon and Bane for long-term Investors

Climate change is the defining risk of the 21st century, set to impact societies and economies, and therefore business models. Investors have either to act or be forced to react, since investment defines ownership, which comes with responsibility. Not surprisingly, momentum and interest around sustainably-responsible investing has surged over the past two decades, and the demand has to a certain extent been met with efforts such as green bonds and sustainable asset management strategies.

However, given the significant impact the financial industry is positioned to deliver, there is room to do much, much more. To drive real-world change and move to net-zero, asset owners must measure climate impact across their portfolios, integrate climate impact into their portfolio steering and decision-making, and work with asset owners and at the individual asset level to develop entire portfolios in a sustainable direction.

And there is a ticking clock: The planet's so-called "carbon budget" describes the supportable amount of greenhouse gases (GHGs) that can be emitted in total, before rising temperatures trigger catastrophic climate changes. The temperature increase is roughly proportionate to the total level of GHG emitted, and currently, even if all proposed measures are adopted, we are set to exhaust the budget by the mid-2030s.

While humanity still has power over the extent to which we overshoot the carbon budget, it is clear that at least some level of adaptation is inevitable. The further we overshoot 1.5 °C, the greater the extent to which we will be forced to adapt. Asset owners have a responsibility to avoid the downside risks of this change, but also an opportunity to drive the reduction of climate impact. Science tells us this decade is critical for action, and as investors, it would seem this is our last chance to change. The situation can be pithily expressed: "change or be changed".

Such transformation is also expected of us by our key stakeholder groups; clients, shareholders and governments. Clients increasingly seek to transition their lifestyles in a sustainable direction. They understand that while their individual impact may be limited, it will be amplified by selecting financial products that foster sustainability, rather than adding to the issue. Hence, green-labelled investment products show high growth across most markets.

https://doi.org/10.1515/9783110752892-010

Shareholders demand that sustainability be integrated into portfolios, to secure against the downside risks of a changing climate, and to create growth opportunities.

Most governments have joined the Paris Agreement, and explicitly appealed for investor support since without this cooperation, they will be hampered in reaching their commitment targets. Regulators are currently considering ways to mandate a greater focus on sustainability, so if the financial industry does not move to markedly reduce climate impact, policymakers will find their hands forced. Increased regulation should be expected in any case; it can play a role in ensuring a just transition, a "fair" burden sharing across societies, across regions and considering the developmental phase of economies.

At the same time, investment markets present perhaps the biggest opportunity for decades. Transitioning economies from "brown to green" is the work of the coming era, and amounts to a green economic-industrial revolution ripe with investment opportunities: food and agriculture, buildings and cities, transport and industrial processing will change. Another important change lever is education, with the power to shift behaviors and introduce new capabilities. However, long-term investors, already struggling with high operating requirements and targets amid economic challenges, are not well placed to tackle this.

Energy consumption is at unsustainably high levels. Working towards developments that can reduce demand and increase efficiency is crucial, not only across all industry sectors but also from a societal perspective. While energy is at the heart of the transformation, in some sectors the technology to enable significant GHG reductions either does not yet exist or is not yet economically viable. Long-term oriented investors are well placed to work with companies and alongside governments and (development) banks to help finance research and development.

The Asset Owner Alliance and Climate Scenarios

At the UN Climate Week in 2019, the UN-convened Net Zero Asset Owner Alliance (The Alliance) was officially launched. The Alliance takes a radical and science-based approach to greening the economy; members have pledged to facilitate world decarbonization by making their own portfolios net zero by 2050. By that date, member portfolios will primarily consist of assets whose activities do not cause greenhouse gas emissions, a minimal amount of assets with some emissions, and a third group of assets that act as carbon sinks.

The Alliance began with 12 founding members, has expanded to 46 with over USD6.7 trillion assets under management across 14 countries and 4 continents as at July 2021. The steering group is led by the United Nations Environment Programme Finance Initiative (UNEP FI) and the Principles for Responsible Investment (PRI), and the Alliance has been supported from the beginning by the Worldwide Fund For Nature (WWF) and Global Optimism. The founding principle for the Alliance is that climate action must be immediate, and is best achieved via direct integration into the investment decision-making process. Thus the Alliance is led by asset owners themselves. Work is starting with portfolio change and only secondly on calls to action, recommendations and reports.

More critical than abstract long-term goals are the interim targets the Alliance has set: members will deliver on measurable, science-based targets by 2025 – making them the first group of private sector global players to do so. Every five years new targets are set, communicated and worked towards. Why are these interim targets of vital importance, and what input is used to inform them?

Climate scenarios such as those published by The Intergovernmental Panel on Climate Change (IPCC) are crucial for understanding climate risk and its implicit financial risk. The objective is to limit warming to within 1.5 °C, and scenarios range from 'no overshoot' of this limit (known as Pathways 1–3, or P1–3) to 'high overshoot' (P4). High overshoot sees warming temporarily reaching the catastrophic levels of 1.7 °C or 2 °C, before stabilising at 1.5 °C by the end of century.

For most, there is a desire to avoid a high overshoot scenario, as it relies on technologies not proven and not yet economically viable to remove carbon dioxide directly from the atmosphere and bring temperatures back down. High overshoot scenarios also imply a massive risk for mankind, our planet and our economies. Even if the overshoot could be reversed, it is unclear how long that would take and what devastation would occur in the meantime. Overshoot scenarios can also be used to justify a lack of immediate action, and can even lead to accusations of greenwashing against those investors who claim compliance with net-zero pathways, but rely on scenarios such as P4.

Investors with a net zero ambition in line with the 1.5 °C limit must therefore understand and rely on scenarios P1-P3, including their implications on technology, demand and investment needs. Unfortunately, in most cases the scientific models are not granular enough to inform investors on what is needed short- and mid-term, by economic sector and by region, to act. Since the Alliance set targets every five years, the climate models also need to report pathways in five year steps, reflecting short- and mid-term decarbonization needs, which can feed into the asset owners' target setting.

A globally-integrated model, translated into investors' language, breaking broader sectors into the same financial sectors commonly used for investment portfolio steering would enable consistent reporting of scope 1–3 emissions, across all regions and reflecting global economic sector cross-linkage. Model outcomes could then be used to benchmark the decarbonization of the financial sectors within investor portfolios.

In spring 2020, the Alliance commissioned the translation of the One Earth Climate Model (OECM) into financial sectors as described above, enabling reporting on the reduction needs of carbon emissions, carbon intensities and energy intensities in each hard-to-abate sector. In 2021, this model is being further developed to enable scope 3 reporting on all relevant financial sectors, while showing cross-sectoral and regional interdependencies. While work is currently based on the OECM, the Alliance is open to integrating other models, and will continue to seek out the best ones as they evolve.

The Alliance believes starting work on portfolios right now with the soundest scientific methods available is the only reasonable course of action. By pooling members' substantial resources and wielding their combined financial heft, the Alliance's impact is broad and far reaching. The overall approach to net zero 2050 is manifold and interlinked, encompassing several aims across four areas: sub-portfolio targets (at asset class level), sector targets, engagement targets and financing targets. By agreeing to follow through on interim targets, every Alliance member must enhance their investment process such that all decision-making reflects emission effects.

The Alliance has also committed to unprecedented transparency, reporting annually on target progress, similar to the way in which financial KPIs are disclosed. The means for setting and achieving the interim targets is outlined in the Alliance 2025 Target Setting Protocol (TSP), which was jointly developed by Alliance experts, the UN and PRI, climate think tanks and scientific institutes. It was finalized based on public comment. The TSP balances scientific ambition, active owner engagement, and divestment constraints and covers:

Sub-Portfolio Targets

The TSP sets targets for Alliance members' scope 3 emissions, or "portfolio emissions", where sufficient data coverage and credible methods allow. By 2025, members must reduce portfolio emissions by between 16–29 %, from a 2019 baseline, beginning with selected asset classes: listed equity, corporate bonds and real estate assets.

The Protocol goes further and encourages members to set net-zero targets not only on their scope 1 and 2 emissions, but also ideally also those of their underlying holdings in high-emission sectors such as steel, utilities or aviation. The pathway to achieving the reductions is up to individual members to decide, taking into account economic impact and any other constraints.

Sector Targets

The TSP initially sets targets for the high-emission sectors of transport, steel manufacturing, utilities and oil and gas, and will expand the list in future. Sector targets were set after exploring and referencing several scientific pathway models that adhere to the 1.5 °C carbon budget, including the OECM, Investor Leadership Pathways and the Cambridge E3ME. The targets will be tracked using a representative non-managed portfolio of the highest emitters from each sector.

If an Alliance member's portfolio significantly comprises assets in the energy, transport or steel sectors, reduction targets must be set for these. Sector targets also inform Alliance members' stewardship, policy and allocation activities.

Engagement Targets

Engagement with the individual corporations in Alliance member portfolios is an integral part of the drive to net-zero. This work seeks to develop existing assets in a sustainable direction, and while it is currently time-consuming and labor intensive, there is much to be gained from it. By identifying those companies with the highest emission rates where no transition targets have already been committed to, members work with their assets to set action targets. Engagement is expected to be one of the most impactful measures undertaken. The Alliance will also work closely with initiatives such as Climate Action 100+.

Financing Transition Targets

Alliance members are encouraged to contribute to the creation of a green economy by increasing the scope, pace and reach of net-zero compatible technologies. Strategically, this will be achieved by enhancing investment into those activities that mitigate climate change, or are climate-positive, such as green buildings, renewable energy in emerging markets and sustainable forestry and agriculture. This work won't be done alone – blended finance vehicles and collaboration with development banks and other partners will amplify efforts.

The Power of Engagement

How are portfolios best developed, and what are the asset-level measures needed to achieve these targets? Company engagement is not the only way, but it is key. A growing body of research shows that investments with a sustainability focus frequently outperform those without, and additionally are often better at avoiding risks.

Investors have both the responsibility and the power to support the transition to sustainable capitalism. Sustainability can and should be integrated into portfolio steering, regardless of the size or the breadth of an asset owner's investments. While investment in dedicated green assets plays a part, more important and impactful is the work of turning each and every portfolio asset green.

Currently, the best approach for achieving this is via engagement – the Alliance targets for which are outlined above. Engagement is likely to constitute the majority of the work done in driving the transition; it creates huge impact from many perspectives. Firstly, investors are perfectly positioned to provide direction to asset managers, who often seek and welcome more input from asset owners on climate topics. Investors also play an important role supporting their assets, should they receive feedback on ambitious climate commitments. Engagement broadens the scope of asset owner influence beyond their own corporate conversations, helping to drive systemic change. Additionally, if policy and regulation shifts, early engagement can help ensure that assets are well-placed for compliance. And finally, in the case of insurers, engagement works to protect their core business, as climate change goes to the very heart of insurability.

Engagement currently works as follows: using publicly available data, investors analyze the company from the outside in (ideally using criteria encompassing the UN Sustainable Development Goals (SDGs)) to define development needs, then start a conversation with the company to either establish or mature their path to sustainability while also gaining a deeper understanding of risk and return. Companies are often responsive to these dialogues since investors may eventually use shareholder action, however the approach is too labor intensive to be scalable. Often the company is fielding simultaneous requests from other investment partners, banks, insurers or NGOs, making the process lengthy and overwhelming.

Right now, the development process relies on either self-reported or publicly available data, which is often patchy, unreliable and not standardized. From an investor perspective, the "raw material" that engagement runs upon – climate impact and climate risk reporting – should be raised to the same standard as financial reporting. This would take engagement to the next level. To achieve this, the Alliance proposes that governments make this reporting mandatory and auditable, and suggest expanding the standard created by the Task Force on Climate-Related Financial Disclosures (TCFD), or the EU Sustainable Finance Disclosure Regulation.

Engagement is expected to avoid the need for large-scale divesting, with the exception of cases where there is no way or willingness to change – as with coal production and use. In such cases, investors will need to grapple increasingly with stranded assets, including assets in technologies that may vanish in the near or mid-term. Stranded assets need to be well-understood, as today's energy infrastructures alone are set to emit more than double the remaining carbon budget (needed to keep to 1.5 °C) over their currently-assumed lifetime.

While policy factors may be beyond individual Alliance members' control, advocating for change at policy level is a powerful tool that can accelerate real world change. Initial focus areas include embedding net-zero by 2050 in the post-COVID-19 economic recovery framework; Nationally Determined Contributions of the Paris Agreement; sector policies and promoting mandatory climate reporting and business transition plans.

The COVID-19 crisis has afforded societies an opportunity to transition to a new, more sustainable normal. Policy discussions around economic and social recovery should focus on embedding net-zero into the framework, both to equip us for future crises and ensure a new direction. Recovery measures should aim to halve emissions by 2030, consistent with the Paris Agreement; long-term investors should look to support government R&D and infrastructure spending into green initiatives; and a portion of the recovery funds should be dedicated to supporting the transition in emerging economies.

Challenges and Tools

It is clear that any transition will need to be just. That costs and benefits must be fairly distributed among nations and citizens, that workers in industries to be phased out must not be left to secure their own livelihoods, that stability is ensured during any restructuring.

Various climate models, notably the OECM, have plotted rigorous and realistic paths to keeping within the 1.5 °C limit, in ways that preserve and even create jobs, revolutionize renewables while repurposing existing infrastructures, and do so within a single generation.

Many models rely on carbon pricing as a cornerstone of the transition. The efficacy of trading schemes can be witnessed in Europe, where the EU Emissions Trading Scheme (ETS) has resulted in halved emissions from the utilities sector since its launch. Conversely, some of the biggest industrial carbon producers receive their permits free under the ETS in order to discourage offshoring – and there has been little change to their output. Pricing presents many other challenges:

- Currently, the cost of each carbon ton is so low that it is questionable whether it is truly effective
- Pricing schemes covered only around 20 percent of global emissions, as of 2019

- Voluntary carbon markets, where companies purchase carbon credits that purport to offset their emissions, are currently fractured and lack transparency or standardized control
- A reliance on arbitrage hampers long term investments into emissions reductions and results in little to no net carbon reduction: if a high-emissions company purchases "pollution permits" from a low-emissions company that would anyway not have used them, the high-emissions company avoids the work of reducing their climate impact, and overall emissions remain steady.

A global carbon price would be the ideal way to ensure the economic viability of more sustainable production approaches. However, given the current fractured state of carbon markets – some countries run multiple concurrent internal markets – it is more reasonable to aim first for regional pricing. And carbon pricing, when social adjustments are factored in, can also help play a role in a just transition. Social adjustments can ensure the price burden does not fall equally upon those earning minimum wage as the super-rich, just as it cannot equally fall upon developing and wealthy nations.

One area where savings could be realized and put toward effective carbon pricing models is fossil fuel subsidies, which also present a significant hinderance to shifting portfolios to net zero. Each year, trillions of dollars are poured into propping up the oil, coal, natural gas and utilities industries around the globe.

These astronomical sums create a disconnect between government transition aims and real world practice. They foster an unfair playing field where more sustainable business processes struggle to be competitive against the industries powered by these subsidies. At the investor level, they have made it easy to argue that factoring sustainability into portfolio steering comes at the cost of investment opportunities and return. In the short term, it is true that divesting from coal presents certain limits. But for long-term investors, it is clear that this behavior improves risk and return, while also creating opportunities.

The Alliance calls on governments to recognize that Paris Agreement commitments and fossil fuel subsidies cannot coexist. The savings generated from removing these subsidies, when diverted, would significantly advance the transition. Additionally, governments should ensure that stimulus funds committed to COVID-19 recovery are not funneled into keeping fossil fuel industries afloat.

A Call for Commitment

Momentum for asset owners to change is high and mounting, with retail and institutional customers increasingly demanding climate-friendly products and solutions. Corporates are moving, urged on by a growing chorus of employees and clients. Governments are leading, with the need to translate Paris Agreement commitments into real change. The UN Race to Zero campaign is bringing together a global coalition committed to building a resilient zero carbon economy. We call upon investors to make the commitment to transitioning, and to join the Net-Zero Asset Owner Alliance.

There is much talk about sustainable capitalism, often hand-in-hand with speculation on how it can be achieved. The Alliance believes that by changing investment decision-making to make sustainability factors as fundamental as economic decision criteria, we can concretely contribute to the evolution to sustainable capitalism.

The Alliance may have been the source of inspiration for other initiatives, such as a the Net Zero Asset Manager Alliance, launched in December 2020, or the Net-Zero Underwriting Alliance, launched in January 2021, however it remains, in the words of UN Secretary General Antonio Guterres, the "gold standard" for net zero commitments. The financial net zero industry needs to build a strong network to ensure common asks and consistency. A large net zero financial community that includes banks, asset owners, asset managers, the underwriting side and other groups will be able to support the real economy transitioning as the financing flows will be decisive for a resilient global economy. This will spur economic growth to the benefit of our planet and future generations.

Asset owners have both the power and accountability for being at the vanguard of change. Currently, the most difficult work to be done is the engagement with individual assets. Beyond this, what is needed to drive change is a shift in overall approach: for climate-impact measurement to become integral to portfolio steering, for targets to be set and communicated, for sustainability reporting to become mandatory, standardized and auditable.

In parallel, industry needs a combined approach to tackling high-emissions sectors, and can gain much from joint research and financing. The Alliance invites institutional investors to join in supporting not only companies but entire markets as they transition. Alliance numbers are growing steadily, and key partnerships and associations continue to be forged. Supporters include the International Endowments Network (IEN), the Dutch Association of Investors for Sustainable Development (VDBO), and the German Insurance Association (GDV), which represents 460 private insurance companies and EUR 1.7 trillion in assets. The commitments made and targets set by Alliance members now are laying the groundwork for long-term implementation.

Expanding the Alliance will come with challenges as we become more diverse, but bringing more members on board is critical to expanding our impact. Growing especially in regions outside of Europe to become a real global initiative will be decisive; a truly global community of investors will have much more impact in facing this global task. By pooling our resources, merging our expertise and advocacy, we become a key force that can not only foster the transition to a carbon-neutral economy but create major economic opportunities at the same time.

III. The Role of Government Authorities

John Berrigan

The Future of Sustainable Finance: A target-oriented and ambitious Agenda for Transition

Massive investments are needed to meet the objectives of the Paris Agreement and the UN 2030 Agenda on sustainable development goals (SDGs). In this context, the European Green Deal sets out the Commission's strategic growth agenda for Europe to become the first climate-neutral continent by 2050.

The Covid outbreak and its consequences have revealed the vulnerability of our economies, reflecting past failures to focus on sustainability in value chains and financial circuits. The post-Covid recovery will be an opportunity to reform our business models and financial systems in order to finance green, resilient, and equitable economic development, while transitioning towards a carbon-neutral economy. Our aim should not be to return to "business as usual", but rather to "build back better", and achieve long-term sustainability. The economic recovery and the European Green Deal must be mutually supporting in catalysing the green transition.

While public investment has an important role to play in the transition process, unprecedented amounts of private capital must be mobilized to achieve zero emissions and reach the environmental targets. This is the rationale underlying the EU framework for sustainable finance. Ambitious initiatives are needed to put that framework in place and so enable private capital flow towards sustainable projects and activities. The EU Climate Taxonomy, by translating the EU's green objectives into criteria for investment purposes, perfectly fits this purpose; it gives an analytical grid for investors and businesses to take informed decisions and pursue reasoned strategies to grow sustainably. The recently adopted Delegated Act for climate change adaptation and mitigation objectives sets out the technical screening criteria for identifying those activities that make a substantial contribution to these climate objectives[1]. Thanks to these criteria, the EU Taxonomy will help compare the level of greenness across various investments, and it can therefore guide market participants in their investment decisions.

---

1 A second delegated act defining activities that make a substantial contribution to the other four environmental objectives, namely protection of water resources, biodiversity and ecosystems, circular economy and prevention of pollution, will be elaborated once the Platform on Sustainable Finance submits its technical input in autumn 2021.

https://doi.org/10.1515/9783110752892-011

The EU Taxonomy provides a reference point for companies to improve their overall environmental performance, either by upgrading their technology or by developing new, greener activities. This will also allow them to report on their environmental performance and thereby attract investors. The EU Taxonomy supports companies in their transition and provides incentives for them to increase gradually their share of green economic activities and attract new and different types of investors. Moreover, information on environmental performance activity by activity will provide powerful incentives for companies to design and implement transition plans in line with the EU Taxonomy criteria and the EU climate targets set out in the EU Green Deal. The EU Taxonomy also allows companies that are not able to reduce their emissions levels in line with those objectives, to manage their transition towards more environment-friendly economic activities.

Another central element of the European Green Deal is the strengthening of EU's corporate sustainability reporting rules. The exponential growth in the demand for sustainability information and the need for consistency in the framework for sustainable finance, in particular the Taxonomy Regulation and the Sustainable Finance Disclosure Regulation (SFDR), called for a revision of the Non-Financial Reporting Directive (NFRD). The recently published proposal for a Corporate Sustainability Reporting Directive aims to improve the environmental, social and governance (ESG) information that companies report, enabling investors and asset managers to better assess sustainability risks and opportunities. Furthermore, a separate delegated act[2] will specify the key performance indicators that companies falling under the scope of the NFRD will be required to disclose, in particular the share of their turnover and capital expenditures that are aligned with the EU Climate Taxonomy. Those two initiatives are important milestones, as they will enable investors and financial intermediaries to assess sustainability information, so that end investors benefit from reliable and trustworthy information in line with the requirements of the SFDR. This allows the EU sustainable finance framework to cover the full financial value chain, from businesses investing in sustainable projects to consumers managing their savings.

The European Commission is thus implementing its 2018 Action Plan on financing sustainable growth in a comprehensive fashion. It will now explore in its recent strategy for sustainable finance how to provide further incentives for com-

2 Article 8(4) of the Taxonomy Regulation requires "the European Commission to adopt a delegated act specifying the content and presentation of the information to be disclosed pursuant to Article 8(1), including the methodology to be used, taking into account the specificities of both financial and nonfinancial undertakings and the technical screening criteria established pursuant to the Taxonomy Regulation".

panies to transition away from unsustainable activities, to make the EU Climate Taxonomy even more inclusive and provide transitional solutions to all economic operators. Second, the strategy will seek to increase the resilience of the financial system to climate and environmental risks. Financial institutions should already now take all the necessary steps to reduce their exposure to sustainability risks, including transition and physical risks. This represents one of the biggest challenges, but also the most impactful action, in order to make the EU's climate ambitions concrete and to enhance a more resilient economy.

To make sure that the financial sector supports businesses on their transition towards sustainability, regulators need to set clear targets, indicate the direction of travel and provide the private sector with a credible and usable toolbox. The Taxonomy Regulation, the Sustainable Finance Disclosure Regulation and the Benchmark Regulation, now complemented by the Corporate Sustainability Reporting Directive, constitute the backbone of this ambitious agenda. They increase transparency and provide investors and businesses with tools to identify sustainable opportunities. This sustainable finance ecosystem is a powerful enabling toolbox for companies, investors and financial intermediaries seeking to develop a sustainable business model. Financing the transition towards the EU climate targets is essential and, under the EU's sustainable development agenda and the EU Climate Strategy, it will help connect finance with the needs of the real economy.

Wim Mijs

Financing Transition

Introduction

There is little, if nothing, that was not said or written on climate change yet. Although scientists have been providing evidence for decades, little has moved since the major Earth summit of Rio in 1992.

Good news for environmental scientists and activists. Bankers are joining at large. At least in Europe. The European Union (EU) is now fighting the climate emergency from a different angle. While financial interest may have for decades stayed on the wrong side of the battle, money can now be the turning point.

The European Green Deal[1] – Europe's "man on the moon" moment – as labelled by European Commission's President Ursula von der Leyen will require 1 trillion euro to realize.

Public money alone would by a large margin fall short of achieving its envisaged objectives. Private investments will have to complement public finance. Over €1 trillion in financing via (syndicated) bank loans has been agreed in 2020[2] and hence there is clearly sufficient financing available. This is not about the shortage of finance but about its allocation. It is increasingly understood that the decisions banks and their clients make today will steer the economy for years to come and define the societies and the quality of the environment for future generations.

Major European banks are competing in announcing their commitments to align their financing activities with the Paris Agreement or the SDGs[3] as ESG awareness grows in the corporate, retail and investment universe. European banks are among the world's leaders on sustainability. During 2020 alone, the ten largest banks committed to providing nearly $1.5tn of green finance by 2030[4]. Banks understand that the sustainability agenda provides new business opportunities, allows them to connect financial and societal objectives, regain trust and provides them with a competitive advantage.

1 A European Green Deal | European Commission (europa.eu).
2 Platform on Sustainable Finance report on transition finance – March 2021 | European Commission (europa.eu).
3 For example, by signing the Principles for Responsible Banking, or joining the CCCA.
4 EY Sustainable Finance Index.

https://doi.org/10.1515/9783110752892-012

One would argue that portraying banks as the "good guys" is too farfetched. Like companies that are at different stages of their transitional journey, many banks still have a long way to go. Embracing sustainability means no more "business as usual" and requires innovative thinking, strategic changes, compromises to be made at all levels. Support from the highest levels of management is also crucial. However, the drive is not entirely voluntary in all cases.

Policy makers often lack the courage to introduce direct and impactful measures in corporate sectors or fiscal areas such as raising carbon price or restricting undesirable activities directly. Requesting financial institutions to increase disclosure on their financing activities, pushing for recognition of ESG risks in the risk management processes and leaving the decisions on whether and under what conditions to continue financing certain business activities is a cleverly designed regulatory framework to achieve the EU policy objectives without much political or public backlash.

Sustainable finance is one of the fastest developing regulatory and market areas in Europe that will not only be a "game changer" in the financial sector but also impact companies, although through the "back door".

Yet, the transition is not a responsibility of the financial sector alone. The EU and national governments do have a key role in facilitating the transition by setting up clear transition paths, pricing negative externalities and providing incentives such as fiscal measures. This will allow banks to better support their clients in their efforts towards the transformation of the economy and thereby increasing the bankability of sustainable economic activities. Also, while transparency on financial institutions activities is envisaged in the upcoming regulatory framework, governments and central banks are neither covered by the Taxonomy regulation nor are subject to disclosure obligations under the Non-Financial Reporting Directive, resulting in the exemption of sovereign bonds portfolios from transparency requirements (with the exemption of municipalities for house financing that will be covered).

Everyone can agree that financing the right thing is the right thing to do. But how do we agree on what is right? Few would have ever imagined that a public consultation of the European Commission defining which economic activities can be considered environmentally (climate) sustainable for financing and investment purposes would attract 46 thousand responses from a large variety of stakeholders. A lot is at stake.

Financing the Green

It is important to understand what the EU Taxonomy is. It is the backbone of the EU Commission's Action Plan on Sustainable Finance. A classification scheme that aims to provide clear and science based definitions of what economic activities could be considered environmentally sustainable ("green"). It is equally important to also understand what it is not.

It is not a mandatory list of activities in which to invest. It also does not suggest that what is not considered as Taxonomy aligned is unsustainable. Also, while it defines what is "green", it does not define what is "greening". It has been designed to identify and target activities with substantial positive contribution to environmental objectives, thus the thresholds to define "what is green" are very demanding and in several instances go beyond the existing sectoral legislation-which is expected to be revised over time.

There are three main features on which the EU Taxonomy is built:

1. Activity based (as opposed to defining sustainable companies, projects, or business models)
2. Substantial positive contribution to one of the environmental objectives (as opposed to any contribution)
3. No significant harm to other environmental objectives and respect of minimum social safeguards[5]

Labelled initially as a "dictionary and disclosure tool" to provide clarity mainly for investors disclosure purposes, with time, the EU Taxonomy is growing both in scope and ambition as a tool to deliver on the European Green Deal.

In fact, anyone can use the EU Taxonomy for many different purposes. The EU Taxonomy is for example envisaged to be used for the future EU Green Bond Standard, for labeling schemes both at national and EU level such as the EU Ecolabel, but also in the EU and national financial support schemes. Promotional banks, be it the European Investment Bank or at national level, will likely reference the EU Taxonomy framework to support green investment or financing of green projects under the Invest EU Programme. It is also expected that future incentives to support green finance will be linked to the EU Taxonomy. The EU Taxonomy can also be used by companies to guide their transition plans and for communication purposes. Both financial and non-financial companies can also use the Taxonomy criteria for target setting in line with the EU's ambitions.

5 OECD Due diligence Guidance and ILO Convention.

The EU Taxonomy Regulation also envisages mandatory uses of the taxonomy mainly for transparency purposes. Not only the manufacturers and promoters of financial products but all large public interest companies under the scope of the Non-Financial Reporting Directive (NFRD/new CSRD) will have to publish the extent to which their activities are sustainable according to the EU Taxonomy. This means that the EU Taxonomy is directly applicable to banks that would also have to report on the alignment of their lending portfolios under the so called Green Asset Ratio.

Banks will have to disclose existing exposures as well as new originations including both specialised and general-purpose lending. Banks will also have to disclose forward-looking information and sustainability targets.

The extent of the reporting obligations for banks is still often either completely overlooked or not well understood as some perceptions remain that the Taxonomy and related disclosures are directed at investors and investment products only.

Impact of the EU Taxonomy on Banks' Clients

Overall, banks financing will continue to represent the majority of external funding for European corporates and SMEs. Banks will be supporting their clients in the ESG transition by providing considerable sustainable financial products such as green and social bonds and loans, sustainability-linked loans, and various types of ESG improvement loans as well as transition plan related capital structuring and advisory services that may or may not be based on the EU Taxonomy. Financial products that create incentives for companies to reduce their emissions, but do not explicitly prescribe the way to do so, are very useful in the transition and have a potential to materially impact the EU objectives of climate neutrality as they allow companies to innovate and choose their own paths in a most cost-efficient way.

When companies ask for loans with the specific intention that the loan is supporting an environmentally friendly investment, then there will be a requirement for the company to meet certain criteria or demonstrate planned improvements to meet them. Such loan may or may not be linked to EU taxonomy criteria and only those that qualify as taxonomy aligned could be reported by banks as such under the Green Asset Ratio.

Companies however often receive general credit facilities in the form of general purpose loans or revolving credit facilities provided by banks. These in fact represent the majority of banking transactions in terms of volume and banks' balance sheets. Such general-purpose loans are used by companies to cover diverse corporate expenditures and are not solely related to specific capital investments. These products provide companies with flexibility to finance their day-to-day operations.

Taking the example of a corporate loan used by a large corporate client for daily cash flow management, the loan proceeds may be directed at cash flow management for the Group entity which takes the loan facility, and whose activities encompass multiple types of infrastructure projects located in different parts of the world, or towards cash flow management for one of its subsidiaries that constructs commercial buildings in an EU country. Exposures whose purpose is not to fianance a specific identified activities will be included in the Green Asset Ratio to the exten thaeither the turnover or Capex of the borrower are taxonomy aligned (expressed as a pecentage).

In any case, when companies seek loans, banks will always assess the creditworthiness of the company regardless of whether they ask for loan for activities with positive environmental impact or not, a general purpose loan or loan financing a specific purpose. Assessment, management, transformation and absorption of financial risk is a key expertise and role of the banks that benefit the society at large. Such credit assessment includes credit history and the company's ability to repay the loan.

Following the revised EBA Guidelines on Loan Origination and Monitoring[6], the introduction of the Taxonomy and the related reporting obligations as well as the forthcoming regulatory expectations and guidelines in the area of risk management, the existing credit assessment processes will be complemented with ESG related assessment that is important for banks' risk management processes, reporting purposes and allocation of capital in line with banks' own strategies and targets (e.g. commitments to align their activities with Paris Agreement objectives or SDGs). This may include taxonomy related data, forward looking information such as on companies' investment plans as well as transition plans.

Financing the Greening

A paper by the Climate Bonds Initiative noted, "green finance frameworks and capital flows have been principally directed at activities which can be considered 'already green'. There has been significantly less investment into transitioning ac-

6 https://www.eba.europa.eu/regulation-and-policy/credit-risk/guidelines-on-loan-origination-and-monitoring.

tivities and assets that are associated with the highest carbon emitting industries and businesses."[7]

The majority of financing in support of the transition towards a more sustainable economy and society will have to be directed towards activities and assets that are associated with the highest carbon emitting industries and businesses. As repeatedly affirmed by financial regulators, notably in the context of NGFS, the Network of Central Banks and Supervisors for Greening the Financial System, banks' contribution to climate-related policies is to finance the greening of the economy, and not only the green economy. Debt and lending products are indeed well suited to raise funds for activities and assets that are not yet EU Taxonomy aligned.

Action is urgently needed on decarbonizing those sectors that contribute to a large share of global emissions, such as heavy industry, manufacturing and agriculture. There is significant business model innovation taking place in such sectors, which are in urgent need of sustainable finance. It is therefore important that the EU regulatory framework is not only supportive of financing green assets, but also of financing the transition towards a net zero emission economy.

In its report in response to the Commission's request to reflect on transition finance in the EU framework[8], the EU Platform on Sustainable Finance acknowledged some limitations to how the Taxonomy can currently be used for transition financing.

Indeed, the way that the current EU Taxonomy helps support finance to companies undertaking activities that do not yet meet the taxonomy criteria (R&D, CAPEX, enabling activities) is insufficient as it does not properly incorporate the notion of full transition pathways. Consideration should therefore be given to how to complement the current EU Taxonomy framework by an approach which will allow the assessment of a company alignment with net zero 2050 objectives- without relaxing the taxonomy thresholds. It is important that the EU Taxonomy indeed preserves its capacity to define a science-based target consistent with the 2050 objectives to maintain its credibility and the trust of institutional and retail investors who want to ensure that (a proportion of) their assets are invested in already green activities. This is a key benefit of the EU Taxonomy and it should not be compromised. Instead, a complementary approach to the current taxonomy framework, which defines not only "what is green", but provides an additional,

---

7 Financing Credible Transitions – A Climate Bonds / Credit Suisse Project | Climate Bonds Initiative.

8 https://ec.europa.eu/info/files/210319-eu-platform-transition-finance-report_en.

forward-looking dimension, defining "what is greening" (transition aligned or transition compliant) should be considered.

The EU Platform for Sustainable Finance report reflects on how to recognise a company's efforts to move its economic activities towards (but not reaching) substantial contribution criteria. The Platform also proposes to support companies transition by establishing transition pathways for certain environmental performance levels, that could be applied to specific economic activities. Also, to allow companies to demonstrate their transition plans, the Platform further recommends establishing and using other metrics than just Taxonomy-alignment percentage, like TCFD metrics, science-based targets and sector pathways or transition scenarios. In particular, the Platform recommends using the requirements in the Climate Transition Benchmark Regulation to define climate transition at company level.

The EU Taxonomy should indeed be enhanced by the creation of mechanisms that will incentivize investors and companies in the transition to a sustainable and low-carbon economy. Such mechanisms need to acknowledge both the transition needs and the capacity and willingness of companies that are at different stages of their transitional journey across sectors/geographies, and within sectors/geographies as well as recognize and support gradual improvements in companies' climate metrics that are consistent with the ambition of the EU's net zero emissions objective in 2050. Similarly, within activities currently addressed by the EU Taxonomy, the achievements of firms which are not meeting yet the ambitious thresholds set by the EU Taxonomy but have credible and binding corporate plans to adapt their business models over time, should be recognized. Those achievements may be the most effective in terms of impact -i.e., in terms of potential of carbon emission reduction.

A full transition pathway of corporates at the 2050 horizon should be considered to determine whether the company is "transition compliant"– a term used by the EU Platform on SF in its report. The respect of the transition pathway by the corporate should be monitored closely by the third-party evaluator, and, in case the commitments are not met, the company would lose its "greening or transition compliant" status. This would avoid any "greening-washing", a very important aspect to foster trust and closeup accountability.

These third parties should submit their assessment methodologies to an EU standard setter (as is the case for external credit assessment institutions, who are subject to ESMA authorization), and their methodologies should respect agreed standards: science-based, aligned with the Paris Accord/Net Zero emission strategy/ EU and Member States plans. The benefit of such an approach is that the KPIs used by those third parties in their transition pathway assessment may be more specific to each sector / company. This would create an alignment between the definition of "greening" in the taxonomy, and the key performance indicators typically used in sustainability-linked loans and other ESG related solutions. It would also create an alignment between the definition of "greening" and the specific pathways defined by Member States, which could vary depending on their starting point. All in all, it would provide a definition of "greening" that would reflect adequately the scope of investments needed to achieve the EU's ambition, and therefore would help channel funding to the right projects and companies.

To provide a full picture on the transitioning efforts, a complementary approach to the EU Taxonomy could be an explicit recognition of efforts in a credible transition path at company level (that would be consistent also with the DNSH principle and minimum social safeguards).

In terms of finance, this could for example be a general purpose loan to a company where interest rates are linked to the CO2 performance at the levels required by a net-zero 2050 scenario. An added benefit of this recognition is that it could very easily be applied to sectors that are not yet developed in the draft delegated acts for climate change mitigation or adaptation, like textiles, etc. In banking activities this type of financing could be usually covered by a KPI-linked loan (also referred to as "sustainability-linked loan" under the Loan Market Associations standard) where targets should be in line with EU climate targets (net zero by 2050).

The EU sustainability framework should therefore formally recognize corporates' decarbonization engagement in line with the Paris agreement providing that some conditions are met:

- KPIs measuring the engagement would be in line with indicators used in the Taxonomy (e.g., carbon intensity per unit of production for power, transport sectors).
- The decarbonation trajectory should include intermediate targets (until 2050) consistent with EU climate law (2030/2050 reduction objectives) and could be based on recognized scenarios and sectorial standards. This could take the form of (i) an intermediate threshold or (ii) "reduction target" (EU objective of 55 % reduction in 2030) in line with the low carbon plan developed by the EU Member States and the review of EU sectoral regulation.
- The credibility and robustness of the corporate engagement should be subject to the adoption of recognized approaches. Such approaches should not only define the targets at corporate level, but also define / evaluate realistic and ambitious decarbonation strategies and actions of the corporates as well as their alignment to the sectoral strategies consistently with the national decarbonation pathways and the Paris mitigation goals.
- In order to avoid greenwashing and "greening-washing", there must be a requirement to provide evidence on how this KPI-linked funding contributes

to the realization of the investment plan, and a requirement that a company cannot raise more sustainable funding than the amount of sustainable investments that they do (in a certain timeframe).

Companies should be encouraged to make their own emissions reduction engagement based either on scientific targets, for instance through the adoption of objectives aligned with science-based targets and robust governance. A formal EU recognition of such a complementary approach (including through the use of such an approach as a formal indicator for reporting purposes), would help investors and credit institutions to reorient capital flows toward the companies that are effectively engaged into a transition pathway.

It is not suggested that such financing would be considered "EU Taxonomy-aligned" as the EU Taxonomy is clearly defined for those activities that substantially contribute to environmental and social objectives. What is being proposed is to consider the financing of companies that are aligning their activities with the EU climate targets under the concept of "transition financing". In summary, if all banking clients were performing in line with net zero pathways by 2050, banks would succeed in helping them to achieve EU climate targets.

Sirpa Pietikäinen

Green is becoming the new Black – Sustainable Finance is a Global Opportunity and the Key to tackling Climate Change

At the moment we are living through a remarkable period of history. For the first time in history, global cash flows have been channeled in an environmentally friendly direction. Being a niche field some decade ago, sustainable finance is finally becoming a major trend in the global financial markets. In 2020, sustainable funds attracted a total of $51.1 billion in net inflows, that was more than twice the previous record set in 2019.[1] The direction is right, but there is still a long way to go.

What exactly is covered by the concept of sustainable finance, and why is it now arousing interest among the investors? In general, sustainable finance means taking into full consideration environmental, social and governance (ESG) factors within the investment strategy, and thus maximizing the positive impact of everyday business. Even though over decades, researchers and scientists have been predicting and warning of the threat of global warming, ensuring sustainable development was not a foregone conclusion for a regular investor. Instead, profit-making was measured as the primary objective of any investing activity, and international financial and environmental legislation were evolving as separate fields.

This was also the case of the EU until 2018. The EU Commission launched its very first Sustainable Finance Action Plan in March 2018, a package that introduced 10 concrete actions aligned with the goals of the European Green Deal, in order to drive carbon neutrality within the European Union by 2050. Outside the European Union, 2021 has started promisingly. In the beginning of the year, China committed to carbon neutrality by 2060, the US re-joined the Paris Agreement and is also now drifting towards standardization of the ESG disclosure under the Biden administration[2]. On a global level, there finally exists a common understand-

1 Jon Hale, 'A Broken Record: Flows for U.S. Sustainable Funds Again Reach New Heights', *Morningstar*, 28 January 2021, retrieved on 2 April 2021, https://www.morningstar.com/articles/1019195/a-broken-record-flows-for-us-sustainable-funds-again-reach-new-heights.

2 Bhakti Mirchandani, 'Five Ways The Biden Administration Advanced Sustainable Investing In Its First 50 Days, Including Two Last Week', *Forbes*, 15 March 2021, retrieved on 3 April 2021, https://www.forbes.com/sites/bhaktimirchandani/2021/03/15/five-ways-the-biden-administrati

https://doi.org/10.1515/9783110752892-013

ing that no economy can work if we exceed the planetary boundaries. Fundamental re-channeling of money flows and adequate legislative reforms to adjust the financial markets to tackle risks of climate change are more relevant than ever – and we're closer to success than ever before.

From different Paths to a similar Road – Sustainable Finance combining two Major Fields

Although today, environmental and financial legislation are more closely intertwined than ever before, it must be remembered that political decision-making, and thus reconciling different perspectives always remains the starting point for legislation. In other words, no decision is being made without taking into account both those who are taking climate change seriously, as well those who are not willing to lift a finger for a sustainable future. In order to combine these extremes and different ideologies, the effective targets of climate, biodiversity and resource efficiency should be defined by science and impartial researchers. In this way we can ensure that legislation is genuinely impactful, and meets the requirements to tackle all intertwined environmental challenges.

It has been estimated that the climate crisis will cost us $1 quadrillion over the next 80 years if we fail to meet the terms of the Paris Climate Agreement. This makes the yearly sum even more than twice per year what COVID-19 crisis is hitting us with now.[3] An unprecedented amount of resources is being needed to cope with both crises. If we want to prepare and help our political institutions, companies, financial actors, retail investors and industries to cope with global warming, the bar needs to be set high enough to provide ambitious and effective legislation. If we manage to seize the moment to mobilize our financial markets and societies in a sustainable and resilient way, we will be able to successfully tackle the climate crisis and prevent the destruction of biodiversity.

Environmental responsibility and measuring environmental impacts are as important as economic due diligence and disclosure, and might be even more important. This logic is based on the fact that if a company operates illegally, for instance, willfully evades paying taxes, the disadvantages of such actions are lim-

---

on-advanced-sustainable-investing-in-its-first-50-days-including-two-last-week/?sh=69bec663f0a0.

3 Steve Zwick, 'Think The COVID Catastrophe Is Expensive? The Climate One Could Cost $1 Quadrillion', 17 April 2020, *Ecosystem Marketplace*, retrieved 4 April 2021, https://www.ecosystemmarketplace.com/articles/20544/

ited and even compensable. However, if the company and its economic activities are killing the environment, and finally making it unviable, the damage is irreparable. Therefore, setting requirements for statutory measuring and reporting of environmental impacts is crucial.

Heretofore, the EU Taxonomy Regulation is the very first EU financial regulation that sets science-based green finance rules. It aims to halt climate change, conserve biodiversity, foster a circular economy, prevent pollution, and protect biodiversity by re-channeling cash flows from unsustainable to sustainable targets. The EU Taxonomy is the cornerstone of EU sustainable finance and introduces essential tools and methods to be reproduced in the other upcoming financial reporting regulation revisions as well. These tools and methods include the life-cycle analysis, environmental and sustainability indicators and the 'do no significant harm' (DNSH) principle. In the regulation, these tools and methods are included, but we have to ensure this is reflected in all the next steps, including the necessary delegated acts.

The life-cycle analysis is a method that should be incorporated into every regulation concerning financial reporting. It is an analytical tool to evaluate environmental impacts of any product thoroughly and systematically during its life cycle, from the processing of the raw materials to the final disposal of the product. Additionally, the EU Taxonomy Regulation obliges the Commission to take into account the existing, commensurate sustainability and environmental indicators when establishing the technical screening criteria of the regulation. These include also the international standards developed by, amongst others, the OECD and International Financial Reporting Standards (IFRS). Lastly, for the first time, an EU regulation introduces the DNSH principle, that explicitly states that financial activities should not have a negative impact on the environment or biodiversity. The EU Taxonomy is, therefore, a revolutionary step towards correcting the way financial sector and the real economy price in, or rather do not price in, negative environmental externalities

Financial Market Risks to be examined by using the Concept of 'Triple Materiality'

Now when we develop the concept of sustainable finance and the next steps of the upcoming EU Commission's Sustainable Finance Strategy, there are a few points we would need to take into account. Primarily, sustainability accounting needs to be incorporated in all relevant public and private reporting, and to become globally aligned with the same harmonized methodology. It should be included into consideration of national budgets and the European Semester, as well as of banks, credit rating agencies, prudential risk management in solvency concepts, et cetera. Therefore, we should make a review of all EU financial regulations, including MiFID, PRIIPs, Basel, and so forth to introduce sustainability standards. Finally, a top-down approach is required in order to successfully integrate sustainability into a company's activities. Environmental and social due diligence should be included in the list of responses of corporate management and board, for the purpose of securing adequate levels of meticulousness and responsibility of the business.

In addition, the heart of the EU Taxonomy is to support climate risk mitigation. Thus, the examination of risk concepts and reviewing the effects of different risks has become timely. Last year, the risk of a global pandemic became reality in a modern world and caused an unprecedented shock to our economies and societies. When the Covid-19 pandemic struck us, no government nor any business had prepared for such a massive long-term risk, and meanwhile the even more catastrophic global risk of climate change is looming in the shadows. It has been estimated that a runaway climate crisis would cost a hundredfold more to our economy than the Covid-19 crisis. This is why the risk of climate change and environmental destruction must be taken into account in the whole financial sector and thus become visible in the price of any financial product. Additionally, the concept of risk needs to be understood profoundly.

There seems to be a good understanding and willingness to incorporate sustainability risks, but the definitions used in the EU and the US tend to be different, and we would need to solve how to combine and understand these approaches. We could either develop the general concept of risk and materiality so that they include both the direct financial and technical risks, and the risks and negative consequential cost for society, "the double materiality", and as well the long-term existential risk like climate change, that will inevitably turn into a financial risk because of a negative turn in economy, the third level. Or we could develop a straightforward understanding of the three levels of materiality. I often refer to the concept of "triple materiality" that gives the most accurate definitions of different types of risks in financial markets.

The first level of triple materiality is the *financial and technical risks* that might have potential impacts on the credit or liquidity of the company. Secondly, there exists the level of *environmental risks* including the operational risks, such as potential accidents, and new hazards emerging from climate and environmental changes that have a direct impact on the business. Lastly, the third and most invisible, though the most important level is the fact that if you are part of the problem, by increasing and intensifying climate change, biodiversity loss and resource overconsumption, you are destroying our economic fundamentals and thus your own business activity. Or the other way around, if you are part of the solution by transforming the economy to be climate neutral, biodiversity-saving and compensating, and resource-efficient, you will create the sound economic bases and thus a successful business environment for yourself.

In my opinion, the triple materiality should become a guiding principle in assessing the risks of which financial actors need to be aware of and disclose the risks that might have a general negative sustainability impact in the economy. In the long run, triple materiality, amongst the other tools and methods mentioned above, needs to be incorporated in all present financial regulation in the EU, instead of creating new, detached sustainability legislation. This relates also to financial and company law, as well as auditing rules. However, the aim is not to complicate the work of professionals with new requirements for separate environmental and taxonomic reports, but to incorporate the ESG elements within the other mandatory financial reporting and statements. Hence, we are able to establish fair and impactful legislation, ensure consistency between the different regulations, avoid unnecessary administrative burden, and support financial actors to foster the transformation to sustainable finance.

Increasing Transparency and Effectivity needs Comparable and Real-Time Data

In March, the European Parliament adopted a legislative initiative calling for the Commission to prepare a directive proposal on mandatory supply chain due diligence. According to the European Parliament's position, not only the companies would become obliged to respect ESG criteria in their own activities, but also in their value chains and activities of their business relationships. Ideally, in the long run, the companies operating in the European internal markets would need to prove that they comply with the due diligence requirements, and address and remedy their actions that might neglect environment, human rights or good governance practices. These measures are not at odds with economic growth, but on the contrary. Investors are already attracted by companies in which ESG risks are being minimized. Moreover, from the company perspective, anticipating and avoiding the risks through its operations is yet feasible, before the accelerating climate crisis leaves no leeway nor options – better act sooner rather than later.

Not only do we need an increased amount of data, but also transparency, and thus comparability. Besides reforming the reporting requirements, it must be ensured that both the financial and ESG information are accessible and comparable, and in real-time and free of charge. Presently, the EU is pushing this idea forward as this year the European Commission launched a consultation on establishment of a European Single Access Point (ESAP)[4] for financial and non-financial information publicly disclosed by companies. When implemented well, the ESAP would provide consistent information on the financial and ESG information of the companies based on their standardized reporting. Ideally, with the new ESAP platform, an investor could crosscheck this information provided by the companies as easily as comparing the nutritional value of food. This would further increase transparency of company activities and accelerate the cash flow in a sustainable direction in the EU.

Slowly, but steadily we are getting there; we have taken only the first baby steps in the long road of transforming our economic and financial systems to measure and act within the planetary boundaries. The EU Taxonomy, together with the Sustainable Finance Disclosure Regulation (SFDR) that entered into force in March, will soon bring comparable and transparent information on environmental and social impacts and risks to financial markets. The Taxonomy and SFDR are the first and remarkable steps, and their objectives and methods need to be reflected in other regulation and accounting standards as well. This regards the upcoming Corporate Sustainability Reporting Directive, Corporate Due Diligence and Corporate Accountability Regulation, Basel IV Regulation, Solvency III, and so forth.

We do not lack the money, we lack the incentives. Still today, in the markets there are nearly $30 trillion tied up in unsustainable investments. From the climate point of view, we cannot afford the wrong investments any longer. Sustainable finance is the key to tackle climate change and preserve biodiversity, and we have no time to waste.

References

Jon Hale, 'A Broken Record: Flows for U.S. Sustainable Funds Again Reach New Heights', Morningstar, 28 January 2021, retrieved on 2 April 2021, https://www.morningstar.com/articles/1019195/a-broken-record-flows-for-us-sustainable-funds-again-reach-new-heights

Bhakti Mirchandani, 'Five Ways The Biden Administration Advanced Sustainable Investing In Its First 50 Days, Including Two Last Week', Forbes, 15 March 2021, retrieved on 3 April 2021, https://www.forbes.com/sites/bhaktimirchandani/2021/03/15/five-ways-the-biden-administration-advanced-sustainable-investing-in-its-first-50-days-including-two-last-week/?sh=69bec663f0a0

4 European Commission, 'Targeted consultation on the establishment of a European single access point (ESAP) for financial and non-financial information publicly disclosed by companies', retrieved on 4 May 2021, https://ec.europa.eu/info/consultations/finance-2021-european-single-access-point_en.

European Commission, 'Targeted consultation on the establishment of a European single access point (ESAP) for financial and non-financial information publicly disclosed by companies', retrieved on 4 May 2021, https://ec.europa.eu/info/consultations/finance-2021-european-single-access-point_en

Steve Zwick, 'Think The COVID Catastrophe Is Expensive? The Climate One Could Cost $1 Quadrillion', 17 April 2020, Ecosystem Marketplace, retrieved 4 April 2021, https://www.ecosystemmarketplace.com/articles/20544/

Matthias Kopp and Valentin von Massow

Setting the Scene and Speed for Greening the Finance Sector – what Governments must do

1. Introduction

1.1 The Case for Action

The science is clear – we are living beyond our planet's boundaries. We use resources equivalent to 1.6 times of what the Earth can provide and replenish year-on-year[1]. To secure a future for humanity as well as the habitats that support us, we must stop and reverse the climate crisis, the dramatic loss in biodiversity, and the over-usage of critical life systems like oceans and fresh water[2]. To return to a one-planet economy, we need to change the ways we produce, transport and consume, and the ways we assess values of goods and services. We need to design policies that achieve the structural changes needed across our economies to deliver tangible reductions of the stress to our planet.

The need for change has already been clear for several decades. But policy responses have been slow and typically uncoordinated. The adjustments to our economies have mostly been half-hearted and not living up to what was required even to date, let alone in future. The biggest shortcoming has been the lack of structural and transformational approaches to change: Many countries have instigated investments in renewables, but without re-designing their grids; incentivised low-carbon technologies, but without providing adequate financial instruments; established carbon trading, but without ensuring that prices really make a difference to investments. The list goes on.

Unless we want to enter the vagaries of a much more centrally planned economy, we have only one lever that can effectively ensure that all sectors and actors within our economies can be addressed and mobilised towards the one-planet economy. That lever is the financial system, which lubricates all physical transactions and the use of all planetary resources. But the financial system has hitherto not been fully mobilized, not been prepared for, or systematically equipped to de-

1 WWF Living Planet Report, https://livingplanet.panda.org/.
2 Rockström et al, 2009, https://www.stockholmresilience.org/research/planetary-boundaries.html.

https://doi.org/10.1515/9783110752892-014

liver its contribution to the degree required to truly transform towards one-planet economies.

The past approaches to green finance based on exclusions will not suffice. One segment of the market offering "sustainable investment" or "green financing solutions" is of no use, if the wider financial system operates under near complete ignorance of planetary boundaries. Structural transformation at scale requires mainstreaming one-planet financing to all industries and production processes; fully pricing externalities; and re-designing policies and regulations to address the true costs and values of natural as well as financial capital. The good news is that it can be done, and that the call for action is louder than ever.

1.2 Why now

In 2015 the UN General Assembly agreed 17 interlinked global Sustainable Development Goals (SDG) to be achieved by 2030, the UN's Agenda 2030. These structural transformations 'to achieve a better and more sustainable future for all' are characterised across six interdependent dimensions[3]:

Six transformations to achieve the SDGs:

1. Education, Gender, and Inequality
2. Health, Wellbeing, and Demography
3. Energy Decarbonisation and Sustainable Industry
4. Sustainable Food, Land, Water, and Oceans
5. Sustainable Cities and Communities; and
6. Digital Revolution for Sustainable Development.

Scientific backing, translating goals into actions, setting targets, and designing tracking systems all resulted in the realisation, that the approaches will have to be interconnected, mutually reinforcing, and linked by a coordinated and co-operative approach. Hence the need for holistic ESG standards – monitoring Environmental, Social and Governance performance – both at legislative and corporate levels. It has also become increasingly clear that we are falling behind. Stronger, more integrated efforts are needed, and fast.

The CoVID-19 pandemic substantially changed the playing field yet again. First, it has brought home for all to see that there can be no healthy humans on an unhealthy planet. The increasing evidence of zoonoses (virus transfer from wild

3 Six transformations to achieve the SDGs, 2018 https://iiasa.ac.at/web/home/research/twi/Report2018.html.

animals to humans), caused by dramatic loss of natural habitats and biodiversity, forces us to embrace the concept of 'one health'. Secondly, the large amounts of public funding to buffer the economic and social cost of serial Covid-lockdowns present a unique opportunity not to repeat the mistakes of 2008–11, when 'quantitative easing' mostly cemented existing capital misallocation – 'too big to fail' when it should have been 'not sustainable enough to survive'. We will not get away with that a second time.

Lastly, the regulatory framework in Europe is undergoing fundamental change. EU Commission and Parliament have agreed the cornerstones of the European Green Deal[4], which will have far-reaching consequences. The EU's 2018 action plan to finance sustainable growth, recent developments around the Sustainable Finance Disclosure Regulation, and the EU Taxonomy Regulation all push in the same direction[5]. Add to that the likely results of the UN CBD CoP15 (Convention on Biodiversity, Conference of Parties) and CoP 26 on climate in October/November 2021, supported by various national and multi-lateral activities, and the case for action now becomes irrefutable. And of course, with the EU's largest economy, Germany, going to the polls in September 2021, the greening of the economy is set to become an important election topic.

In the following sections, we argue that European governments must and can act in five priority areas of legislation and regulation, whereby they will ensure a fundamental shift towards 'greened finance' and sustainable economies:

- Set binding CO2 and ESG targets and enshrine them into law,
- Complete the taxonomy and make it a binding framework,
- Provide some critical tools to turbo-charge change,
- Encourage the markets to do what they do best, and
- Demand transparency and monitor progress on a regular basis.

In concluding, we will briefly reflect on how these changes will affect the role of Central Banks, and on the rewards we can expect at the end of the rainbow.

4 https://ec.europa.eu/info/strategy/priorities-2019-2024/european-green-deal_en.
5 https://ec.europa.eu/info/business-economy-euro/banking-and-finance/sustainable-finance_en.

2. Enshrine binding Targets into Law

Excursion: Banks' vs their Clients' Responsibilities

For the current redesign of rules and regulations to be successful, a fundamental understanding needs to be established about roles and responsibilities between the financial sector and the clients of the financial system. Most of the institutions in the banking sector felt that they have at best a very limited, if any, role with respect to climate change or planetary boundaries. They "only" financed what the 'real' economy, hopefully with a full license to operate and in full compliance with regulations, offered to the financial system to invest in, or requested funding for. Regulation was meant to address the needs for change at the source. However, given the interlinkages, the systemic nature of the transformations needed, the long-term nature of the structural changes, the need for continuous financing of the transitions, and the need for risk-sharing and mutual, cooperative and collaborative engagement, the role of the financial system has to change fundamentally – from 'hands-off' banker to 'integrated value-chain' partner. With that, the systems to assess risks and values, to provide continuous relevant information and data require a major overhaul. In future, the 'one-planet economy' responsibility cannot be passed on to a bank's clients. Banks and other financial institutions themselves need to resume a clearly defined role – and accept accountability – for enabling, accelerating, guiding, or preventing developments and change. Future regulation in the financial system will have to incorporate this fundamental paradigm shift.

As we have laid out in the introduction, assigning the right balance between governments' and markets' roles is critically important. Markets and market actors, in the 'real' economy and the financial system alike, need reliable, credible guidance, leaving little to no doubt about the direction of travel. They need to see that the entire system is addressed and will be requested to develop adequate responses, and that there are no regulatory loopholes. By the same token, the role of governments and regulatory authorities cannot be to define and predetermine every detail, but to provide clear and reliable guidance about the direction and speed of travel, based on stable and clearly articulated fundamental principles, and linked to a fully transparent set of objectives, targets and scenarios of how to achieve them.

Scenarios and their underlying mechanics are essential because the very nature of deriving policies and regulations must fundamentally differ from historic policy formulation. In the past, policy efficiency and effectiveness had mostly been open to trial and error. Adjustments were made following more or less regular ex-post reviews, and the definition of the desired state was a loose one. But it is a different challenge altogether to initiate transformations that recalibrate the economic system to return to a state within the specific definition of the planetary boundaries. This is a process of "legislate and review based on necessary outcomes". It requires a fundamental overhaul and adjustment of the regulatory framework to be based on projections and best available science. The earth's systems' ways of functioning through interdependencies, tipping points and delicate states of equilibrium (regional as well as global) do not allow for a 'design and react to failure' approach anymore. We must prohibit entry into dangerous territory (based on science) at absolute levels, for instance tipping points that might be triggered at warming levels beyond two degrees of atmospheric heating compared to pre-industrial levels. We cannot afford to 'try and test' those tipping points, simply because of their irreversible character. There will be no path back to stabilising the climate system at stable-state levels once triggered, for instance through the melting of permafrost or the loss of summer ice sheets in the arctic, and others (Tipping points in the climate system, Schellnhuber et al, 2008, UBA).

For the markets to take such levels as credible, absolute and binding, they need to be embedded into law and relevant guidance with non-negotiable targets. The key regulations to apply for the financial systems as well as any other parts of the economy are:

1. Setting targets, e.g. for CO2-emissions linked to the global carbon budget aligned with the 1,5 degrees path and based on best available science.
2. Mandating transparent sustainability performance assessments and compliance rating.
3. Setting rules and mechanisms for assuring accurate and correct data provision.

2.1 Setting Targets for CO2 Emissions

The 2015 Paris climate accord brought governments together to a legally binding agreement to limit global warming to well below 2 degrees, and to aim at stabilising climate change by no more than 1.5 degrees warming compared to pre-industrial levels. It also included the ambition to make financial flows consistent with that degree of warming (Art. 2.1.c). Various regulatory instruments on limiting greenhouse gas emissions for the 'real' economy have long been in existence, the EU Emissions Trading Scheme (ETS) is only one example. However, almost all have lacked credibility in the eyes of private market actors when assessing their embedded "signalling effect": are policy makers seriously and consistently willing to set regulation which achieves the climate change targets? Will there be consequences if the regulated entities show inadequate responses? The EU ETS for instance, through the way it was structured in the past, signalled to the market, that there seemed to be ample time for marginal improvements to production processes, as opposed to the required large investments in new technologies, delivering significantly higher and long-term emission reductions. The EU ETS regulation failed to demonstrate to the 'real' economy as well as the capital and financial markets, what a clear and consistent decarbonisation pathway aligned to a warming limit of 1.5 would consist of. This should have happened by ensuring a target-oriented pricing mechanism, which would have included full emissions auctioning, no or very restrictively capped free allocations of emission rights, strict and consistent retiring of surplus emissions based on reduction targets, and establishing floor prices, to name but a few key requirements for establishing that market effectively.

At the same time, to align the financial system, banks should have been required to consistently apply a shadow carbon price, or use scenarios for carbon price developments, when conducting the credit risk and investment appraisal of projects or business partners. They should also have been mandated to adjust the time horizons beyond the typically required 1-to-3-year assessment period. The decarbonisation transition risks will materialise over longer time horizons and will be structurally more significant, given that the changes affect entire sectors in a similar way. For private banks to adjust their processes, however, the supervisory authorities and central banks, who are in charge of financial institutions and markets oversight, stability and risk, need to adjust their supervisory mechanisms accordingly. Adjusting the supervisory instruments and practices should not be done lightly, and does require very serious design and testing. That assessment process involves careful definition of the scenarios to be applied, and a clear understanding of interpreting results and deriving conclusions. We are under no illusion how difficult any, let-alone far-reaching, adjustment in banks' supervisory regimes actually is to agree upon[6]. On the other hand, such adjustments will signal the seriousness of the change very clearly to the markets. And a further element comes into play here, too. It concerns the independence of central banks from policy makers and general regulation. Central banks demonstrate their independence on a day-to-day basis, carefully managing markets' expectations and interpretations as to how they act and what decisions they take, within their frameworks of targets around monetary stability, exchange rates etc. Continuing their roles independently will require central banks to internalise the targets for industrial-scale decarbonisation and real estate asset decarbonisation, for in-

6 It should be noted, explicitly, that ongoing discussions on "green support factors", if not aligned with the risk assessment function of capital, seem to be ill-advised.

stance. The realisation of their independent role in this has only recently set in with central banks adjusting their stress testing as well as risk management expectations with the ECB guidance (or the BaFin recommendations) on dealing with sustainability risks. But in the field of monetary policy, for instance in the rules and underlying decisions of the ECB's asset purchasing programs, the full consequence of this role change has not yet been internalised: there the "market neutrality approach" is still applied. As if such a thing ever existed. By pursuing 'market neutrality', central banks inadvertently replicate existing market structures, technologies, and their unaccounted for 'external costs' to society and the health of the planet. They are not at all 'neutral', let alone addressing the financing needs of the transformation to a one-planet economy.

2.2 Setting Targets for mandatory ESG Rating

An efficient and effective integration of sustainability and climate change objectives with the financial system will not happen without providing solid and forward-looking data, as well as clear requirements for those institutions processing such data, to provide relevant and reliable intelligence to the wider market. The key regulatory fields here are mandatory company reporting requirements and the rules and regulations addressing rating agencies. Current reporting requirements still very much differentiate between financial reporting requirements, in existence for over 100 years with established audit procedures; vis-à-vis the "non-financial" reporting, like ESG and sustainability reporting. As if a company's (future) financial performance could be separated from its sustainability. The latter is regulated through the Non-Financial Reporting Directive in the EU (NFRD), which suffers from several insufficiencies in how it is set up. Those range from the limitations to the companies it applies to – which are not set according to their exposure to risks from the transitional changes, but number of staff – to the fact that NFRD does not (yet) mandatorily require emissions targets over time, or the disclosure of the transition pathway through which decarbonisation is being pursued. The devil is in the detail and not every information here should be made available to the wider market. These are increasingly commercially sensitive, yet this kind of information is key for well-informed business, financing, and investment decisions. Addressing the shortcomings of the NFRD must also aim to significantly empower the system to process and apply such data and information. Whether triple or integrated single bottom-line: The reporting has to be relevant to decision making, including short- as well as long-term financial, social and environmental sustainability, e.g. risks of increasing carbon pricing, and open to independent external scrutiny (within bounds of strategic sensitivity). The existence of specialised ESG rating agencies trying to compile data through questionnaires and rifling through Annual Reports and other company brochures to profile sustainability performance, is further proof how unfit the current system is. Both companies and their financial partners will benefit from a binding, effective and efficient, integrated and auditable finance and sustainability information system, which allows guidance and oversight in strategic as well as daily decision making.

It goes without saying, that regulation on credit risk assessments by ratings agencies must also address the application of CO2 price-scenarios and the assessment of how technology choices are aligned with sectoral and company pathways resulting from 1,5-degree policies in sectors.

These few spotlights already demonstrate the interdependencies of regulatory instruments needed to live and operate within planetary boundaries. They also highlight the transformational rather than incremental nature of change, requiring continuous oversight and a bold yet considered assessment of when and how to intervene and adjust.

2.3 Setting Targets for Compliance and Assurance Mechanism

The final element to address in careful calibration of regulatory regimes is the need to ensure that requirements for market actors are not only forced upon them but are also enabled from within, by the respective systems and processes. Take the assurance mechanisms for annual financial reporting: a mandatory requirement for financial accounting, but widely absent in the field of ESG or so-called non-financial reporting. For data to be reliable for internal as well as external decision making (e.g., by banks), the underlying systems and processes require a solid degree of openness to comparability and thus third-party assurance. Classifying critical data wrongly as "non-financial" and not subject to a mandatory assurance mechanism gives a false sense of security. ESG data will be financially extremely relevant if banks want to understand the technological and process adjustments required in the oil, gas, coal and other mining, automotive, chemicals, steel and various logistics industries, to name only a few that will undergo fundamental changes or simply cease to exist once we design policies to stay within the planetary temperature limits. The same will result from policies to address resource use and the circular economy, as well as producer responsibilities for lifetime product uses.

Accountants and auditors, as well as the standard setters for accounting principles, have been picking up on these issues, with the EU currently on its way to develop new ESG reporting standards. These standards are essential, and they will need to address what to report, as well as the assurance mechanism for the quality of data collection and reporting.[7]

3. Complete the Taxonomy as a binding Framework

The European Commission's plan to finance sustainable economic growth for the first time presented a comprehensive regulatory approach to including sustainability in financial market regulation. The approach chosen in 2018 addressed ten key areas (see figure) and was a steep change in promoting the concept of sustainability structurally as well as embedding it at the very heart of regulation.

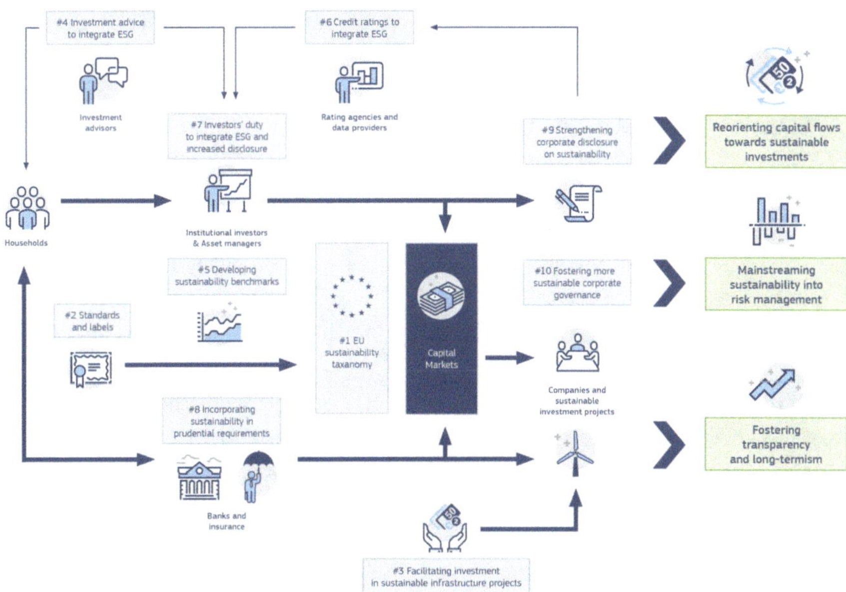

The core of the action plan has been to establish a taxonomy for a sustainability performance assessment framework[8]. The taxonomy is to address one shortcoming identified by the EU – to ensure one set of standards and assessment logic for

7 Since writing this text the EU Commission presented the revision of the NFRD with the proposed new Corporate Sustainability Reporting Directive (CSRD) addressing some of the aspects raised here.

8 https://ec.europa.eu/info/business-economy-euro/banking-and-finance/sustainable-finance/eu-taxonomy-sustainable-activities_en.

defining "sustainable" such that financial and investment products labelled as "sustainable" can only invest in underlying companies, projects or assets that comply with the assessment guidelines. This standardised approach to definitions is vital and addresses one key weakness of previous regimes. Even more importantly, developing a taxonomy that can be applied to assess each and every financial product, and the underlying asset or company for their respective contribution to the necessary transitions, will be the biggest game changer for the entire financial system.

The initial "first phase" of the taxonomy development has been to establish technical screening criteria that are characteristic for economic activities as classified by the EU's industry sector and activities classification system NACE. By applying those screening criteria, benchmark values have been set which define the level of "substantial contribution" for all environmental objectives. The taxonomy addresses six such objectives:

1. Climate change mitigation
2. Climate change adaptation
3. The sustainable use and protection of water and marine resources
4. The transition to a circular economy
5. Pollution prevention and control
6. The protection and restoration of biodiversity and ecosystems

The first two objectives have been developed to the level of delegated acts, to be adopted by the EU in Q2 2021.

Activities contributing substantially to one or several of the six objectives must pass two further tests before being taxonomy-compliant: they must not have harmful effects to any other objective ("do no significant harm", also defined for a first set of applications); and they have to comply with a set of social norms as per the taxonomy regulation.

As of March 2021, the taxonomy's status is under intense pressure from industry lobby groups, who have come to realise how powerful and impactful the taxonomy will be once fully applied across investment and financing decisions, public and private. While it is obvious that these backward lobbying efforts will ultimately be the industry shooting itself in the foot, it is, to date, still open whether the regulation will manage to be finalised in a meaningful way. However, the opportunities and benefits to establishing a strong foundation for financial market regulation, to get to a new integrated sustainability footing are immense.

Whatever the current discussions, the EU will have to complete the taxonomy development with its application across the entire financial system in mind. Equally important is its applicability as one assessment framework, fully consistent with other regulatory developments such as the EU ETS benchmark regulation, buildings performance, circular economy regulation, vehicle emissions regulations and many more. Such a taxonomy would allow to assess the transformation contribution – i.e., the alignment with the required transformation path per sector, in a regionally differentiated way – and would thus allow the financial system to guide financial flows to where they are most needed, have the highest transformation contribution and exactly when they are required. It would also allow the financial system to smartly leverage scarce public resources, thus guiding capital flows towards sustainable transformation rather than financing projects and infrastructure most likely not aligned with science-based projections and needs of the transformation, as is most often still the case today. The taxonomy would make it hugely unattractive, if not illegal, to invest in oil exploration in biodiversity hotspots like the Central African rainforest and the Okavambo basin, or in a new coal port right by the Great Barrier Reef, or in a dam in Selous National Park. It is in the financial sector's deepest interest to be able to rely on a taxonomy that protects their balance sheets from unsustainable debts and investments. Because they will be called out, sooner or later.

4. Provide some critical practical Tools

Concrete mechanisms and tools to support the necessary regulatory developments described are manifold, while some are indeed crucial to be made available to the wider market. We want to highlight just two which are very critical to enabling a system-wide approach and uptake of adjusted processes: a) widely available and commonly understood targets and scenarios delivering insights at sector and regional level, b) a data infrastructure that allows access to critical company, activity and asset data at the detail required by, and according to parameters coordinated with the needs and computations conducted in the scenario analyses and planetary boundary compliance assessments.

a) Scenarios are applied abundantly in financial markets today, but most reflect neither the time structure nor interdependencies that are necessary for assessing transformational developments towards a one-planet economy. Mark Carney already coined the term "tragedy of the horizons" back in 2015[9]. Yet the scenario instruments have barely improved their quality, be it of financial market risk assessments, combining micro- as well as macro-economic perspectives, from a system stability perspective all the way to incorporating sec-

9 https://www.bankofengland.co.uk/speech/2015/breaking-the-tragedy-of-the-horizon-climate-change-and-financial-stability.

tor interdependencies and second- and third-order effects. The 'tragedy of the horizons' applies today as it did then. There is still only a very limited number of providers of globally consistent scenarios when it comes to decarbonisation transformation, let alone other sustainability dimensions. Notably, the network for greening the financial system (NGFS), the group of financial market regulators set up in late 2017, issued guidance in 2020 how to apply scenarios, which is a first step to making much more widespread use of them. This will become even more important once we expand beyond the decarbonisation transformation towards an ever more regionalised perspective on ecosystem services, like freshwater basin integrity or land use effects of industrial and agricultural activities.

b) To enable the financial system to interact with the data available in the wider economy at a very different scale and frequency of data exchange, some access at an industrialised and real time basis will eventually be required. Information technology as well as machine learning hold the potential to enable a more integrated system. Yet, today's regulation and established practices rely on ring-fenced annual financial reporting, with non-existing sustainability reporting standards. The EU has initiated two processes in this regard, the afore-mentioned NFRD with the development of an NFR-standard, and the EU Single Access Point as a database for such data access. Both processes should be recalibrated to deliver at the scale and detail necessary, or at least be aligned over time and through a clear outline and roadmap. All transformation actors (those exposed to the transformations as well as those driving them on) should be mandated to make clearly defined data accessible to eligible data users, i.e. the financial system, in a standardised, cost effective confidential, if need-be, and non-discriminatory way. For these data may originate within private entities, yet their application in the regulatory process makes them a public good and will need to be regulated as such.

5. Encourage the Markets

Market players, specifically in the financial system, should be incentivised and supported to actively address the need for and the potential of the transformations towards sustainability. Such incentives should still be done in a coherent way, i.e., not interfering with, or weakening existing regulations, for instance those addressing systemic and market-wide economic risks. Nor should they lead to public money crowding out private financing or capital flows.

Some examples for active market encouragement are given here: leveraging risk coverage at scale by the public sector where private capital will not be able to engage; promotional programs to roll out technologies at early stages in the development cycles; export credit guarantees; fund structures with risk tranches reserved to public funding; and there are many more. These incentives should typically be catering to requirements that are specific to asset classes, as well as taking regional specifics into account.

Equally relevant as financial incentives are the market structures and reliable transaction processes that allow for a physical asset base to develop, that is transformation-compliant and available for investment and financing in the first place. As the EUs High Level Expert Group on sustainable finance recommended back in 2018[10], critical capacity must be made available in the planning stages across the EU, in some countries more than in others, for actual projects and assets to go through a professional strategic environmental impact assessment. And to be granted timely approval to being developed further for funding. The same applies to stable and reliable regulatory conditions, as for instance a predictable regime for expansion of renewable energies as well as their funding.

6. Monitor Progress

As mentioned earlier, the transformations we must initiate and drive forward, differ in one central element from past transformations, structural changes and economic revolutions. This time, we need to accomplish structural change aligned with concrete targets and projections, like the 1.5 degrees path which is based on best available science and expertise. We do not really have the luxury to allow the market to try and fail yet again, like the ETS. Or to let the more short-term competitive yet unsustainable player to prevail until the sustainable one has had time to invest, like automotive over public transport. Meeting the 2050 objectives and staying within the carbon budget consistent with a 1,5 degrees warming pathway, to recap some of what we have argued here, is characterised by some central conditions: 1) the challenge is a fundamental systemic transformation; 2) it is cross cutting and interdisciplinary/ intersectoral; 3) it depends on progress at the required pace over the whole period in question; 4) it needs to be based on technologies that are available or within reach, given that the scalability to industrial dimensions has to be achieved within one or two investment cycles; 5) some strategic decisions will have to be made to guarantee privileged access to scarce resources based on the availability of technological alternatives (such as green hydrogen for use in industry rather than for individual mobility, which can move to electric).

10 https://ec.europa.eu/info/publications/sustainable-finance-high-level-expert-group_en.

Bearing these criteria in mind makes it very clear that such transformation processes require continuous progress tracking to allow for adjustments to regulation, capacities, incentives, or sanctions. Structured monitoring based on inputs, effects and outcomes has yet to be established in regulation development.

Similarly, monitoring the consistency and alignment of capital flows with the objectives of the Paris climate agreement has not been established within the financial system either. Monitoring financial and capital flows is, however, critically important for two reasons: First, regular and meaningful monitoring will have to be based on a solid understanding of which numbers to track. Defining these metrics and establishing the processes of data gathering will in itself be critically important to establish the sensitivity for the relevance of capital allocation in relation to the transitions. Statistical reporting or data gathering formats for instance on lending processes and portfolios in banks, as conducted today by central banks (such as the supervisory or statistical register of Germany's Bundesbank), could be a good entry point to add such transformation analytics. It would allow supervisors and authorities to be aware of developments and possibly intervene in a timely fashion. Second, from a market risk perspective it would indeed be very valuable to establish a continuous assessment of risk exposure to transitions within lending portfolios, given this segment of the financial markets is not particularly transparent. Supervisory authorities do have a role to play here, as individual data or information may not be made publicly available, yet the central bank should be enabled to intervene should the need arise.

7. What's the Reward at the End of the Rainbow?

The case for, as well as economic assessments of some key policy actions to correct the market and policy failures with respect to the climate crisis have been known and established for almost two decades now. From the Stern Review in 2006, up to individual assessments of assets at risk in sectors ranging from coal, oil and gas via automotive all the way to agriculture over recent years, the economics are clear – it is much less costly, and much less uncertain, to mobilise the resources for transitions timely and decisively, than sitting it out and adapting later. The numbers clearly show that it is literally worth "fighting for" every digit of avoided warming. The assessments of the cost and social damages resulting from unabated climate chaos, covering aspects such as political instability, forced migration, shortages of food supply etc. are not even as comprehensive as the assessments of the mitigation cost and the transformation investment needs. But even the rough estimates, combined with the remaining uncertainties about the habitability of a world of significantly more than 2 degrees of warming – which is the current 'business as usual' trajectory – clearly point to the fact that we must try all we can to avoid that development.

In addition to the assessments of investment needs to finance the decarbonisation, the effects and costs of degrading ecosystem services and the loss of biodiversity are also becoming increasingly clear. The results of the TEEB study (The Economics of Ecosystems and Biodiversity, led by Pavan Sukhdev between 2007 and 2011[11]), recently confirmed by the Dasgupta review, demonstrate the urgent need to act on averting the biodiversity crisis as well. It should not have needed the current Covid-19 pandemic to demonstrate the social and economic cost of zoonoses, which are caused by habitat and biodiversity loss. Inversely, in 2020 the Dutch Central Bank (DNB – Indebted to nature – Exploring biodiversity risks for the Dutch financial sector – 2020 – DNB-PBL) conducted a first analysis of the risks of biodiversity loss to the Dutch financial markets. The assessment concluded that € 510 bn of investments by Dutch financial institutions alone are highly or very highly dependent on one or more ecosystem services (DNB, 2020). Taken differently, if we do manage the restoration of our ecosystems, and establish economic ways of production aligned with the planetary boundaries, huge amounts of assets will be prevented from having the value impaired or ending up stranded altogether.

Last but not least, there is an opportunity for Central Banks, who have multiple roles to play as they oversee the financial sector and regulate that market for risks and stability. They determine, or at least intervene with monetary policy developments in most countries. To date, only a small, even if increasing, number of Central Banks have addressed linking their role in monetary policy to the transitions described here. Three obvious links should be explored, however: First, the structural changes resulting from the transitions towards sustainability will affect economic growth potentials and outlooks for sectors and regions in very different ways, even whole economies depending on how well the transitions are managed by their governments. Central Banks need to pay close attention, in order to be able to fulfil their broader monetary role which cannot be separated from the specifics of economic development. Second, given the fact that as a consequence of the 2007/8 financial crisis active monetary policy has been a regular field of engagement of Central Banks, they are required to assess and evaluate the effects of their interventions: Do they inadvertently cement existing structures with much more costly adaptation later, or do they fuel the necessary transformations. Third, by conducting asset purchasing programs and quantitative easing, hence actively engaging in (re-)financing sectors and industries, Central Banks directly interfere with the need and speed of transitions, which they must take much more into ac-

11 http://teebweb.org/publications/teeb-for/synthesis/.

count. Claiming to only reactively financing the market, and hence staying neutral to the nature and structure of the economy is, in fact, a myth. In today's reality, any general provision of funds means an active decision to finance an economy which is too carbon intensive and overuses our natural resources.

8. Summary and Outlook

This article argues for a more active and robust approach to involving the financial system more strategically into managing the necessary economic transitions to stay within the planetary boundaries. Developing the rationale, we hope to have demonstrated that there are no alternatives to rising to that challenge. The financial system, especially banking, is so inherently linked to the 'real' economy and thus to the necessary transitions towards sustainability we are confronted with, that it appears highly necessary and indeed beneficial to involve it as a key enabler. Failing to take this pro-active approach carries significant risks of re- and devaluation of major portfolios of assets, and whole sectors and economies in their wake. Capturing that enabling potential requires a very different approach from what we observe today, i.e. not a fostering of the 'Green Banking' segment, but to consistently pursue a systemic approach to 'Greening All Banking', or rather financial institutions and their client interactions. Governments must shape and regulate this evolving role of the financial system. The timing of 2021 is perfect: The CoP26 on the climate crisis and CoP15 on biodiversity towards the end of this year will set new targets and procedures; the recent developments in the financial system provide momentum as well as policy challenges, be it the private sector side through Net Zero Commitments of Asset Owners, Asset Managers and banks, the race-to-zero campaigns and others, or the public sector through new financial regulation such as in the EU, in Australia, New Zealand, UK, and others. That momentum needs to be translated into changes to regulation, to market processes, into scenarios and infrastructures and redirecting capital flows. The European Commission is finally preparing the delegated act to the Taxonomy Regulation, which is critically important. The renewed sustainable finance strategy of the EU is expected for release in June 2021, following Germany's expected sustainable finance strategy towards end of April 2021.[12] The momentum exists, critical sectors and companies have begun to embrace transitional strategies, science-

12 The renewed EU Sustainable Finance Strategy was published in June '21 and maintains the momentum, even though it is not clear and concrete enough. The German SF-Strategy, released in late April '21 falls significantly short of the required ambition in the eyes of the authors.

based targets and programmes. This year has all the markings to becoming a critical turning point, from concepts to delivery at scale. There is every good argument to pursue the holistic 'Greening of the Financial Sector' now and at speed. The science is there, and the concepts, and the majority of market players are yearning for clarity, and for confidence in our planet's and thus their own future.

IV. The Role of Central Banks, Regulators and Supervisors

Christine Lagarde

Climate Change and Central Banking

Keynote speech by Christine Lagarde, President of the ECB, at the ILF Conference on Green Banking and Green Central Banking, Frankfurt am Main, 25 January 2021

In the famous fable "Belling the Cat",[1] a group of mice gather to discuss how to deal with a cat that is eating them one by one. They hatch a plan to put a bell on the cat so they can hear it coming and escape before being caught. When it comes to who will actually do it, however, each mouse finds a reason why they are not the right mouse for the job, and why another mouse should do it instead. The cat never does receive a bell – and the story ends poorly for the mice.

In many ways, that fable describes mankind's reaction to the threats posed by climate change. Already in 1986, the front cover of Der Spiegel showed Cologne cathedral half-submerged by water and the headline declared a "Climate Catastrophe".[2] This is just one example, among many, that demonstrates that people were aware of the risks posed by climate change a generation ago. Yet, while many people agreed on the seriousness of the issue, and that something had to be done, concrete action has been much less prevalent.

It is with this history in mind that I want to talk about the role of central banks in addressing climate change. Clearly, central banks are not the main actors when it comes to preventing global heating. Central banks are not responsible for climate policy and the most important tools that are needed lie outside of our mandate. But the fact that we are not in the driving seat does not mean that we can simply ignore climate change, or that we do not play a role in combating it.

Just as with the mice in the fable, inaction has negative consequences, and the implications of not tackling climate change are already visible. Globally, the past six years are the warmest six on record, and 2020 was the warmest in Europe.[3] The number of disasters caused by natural hazards is also rising, resulting in $210 billion of damages in 2020.[4] An analysis of over 300 peer-reviewed studies

1 Also known as the Council of Mice.

2 Der Spiegel (1986), 11 August.

3 Source: Copernicus Climate Change Service.

4 Source: MunichRe.

https://doi.org/10.1515/9783110752892-015

of disasters found that almost 70 % of the events analysed were made more likely, or more severe, by human-caused climate change.[5]

That said, there are now signs that policy action to fight climate change is accelerating, especially in Europe. We are seeing a new political willingness among regulators and fiscal authorities to speed up the transition to a carbon neutral economy, on the back of substantial technological advances in the private sector.

This increased action is often considered as a source of transition risk, which we need to take into account and reflect in our policy framework. This is not "mission creep", it is simply acknowledging reality. Yet the transition to carbon neutral is not so much a risk as an opportunity for the world to avoid the far more disruptive outcome that would eventually result from governmental and societal inaction. Scenarios show that the economic and financial risks of an orderly transition can be contained. Even a disorderly scenario, where the economic and financial impacts are potentially substantial, represents a much better overall outcome in the long run than the disastrous impact of the transition not occurring at all.[6]

It now seems likely that faster progress will be made along three interlocking dimensions. Each of them lies outside the remit of central banks, but will have important implications for central bank balance sheets and policy objectives.

Including, informing and innovating

The first dimension along which we expect rapid progress is including the true social and environmental cost of carbon into the prices paid by all sectors of the economy.

Appropriate pricing can come via direct carbon taxes or through comprehensive cap and trade schemes. Both are used to some extent in the EU. It is likely, though, that the next steps in Europe will come mainly via the EU's Emissions Trading System (ETS), a cap and trade scheme. The ETS is an essential infrastructure, although it has not always been successful in the past at delivering a predict-

5 See https://www.carbonbrief.org/mapped-how-climate-change-affects-extreme-weather-around-the-world.

6 See recent climate scenario analysis, including: Vermeulen, R., Schets, E., Lohuis, M., Kölbl, B., Jansen, D.-J. and Heeringa, W. (2018), "An energy transition risk stress test for the financial system of the Netherlands", *Occasional Studies*, Vol. 16, No 7, De Nederlandsche Bank; Allen, T. et al. (2020), "Climate-Related Scenarios for Financial Stability Assessment: An Application to France", *Working Paper Series*, No 774, Banque de France; European Systemic Risk Board (2020), "Positively green: Measuring climate change risks to financial stability", June.

able price of carbon. Moreover, it currently covers only around half of EU greenhouse gas emissions and a significant amount of allowances continue to be given for free.

The effective price of carbon is expected to rise if the EU's targets for reducing emissions are to be reached. Modelling by the OECD and the European Commission[7] suggests that an effective carbon price between €40–60[8] is currently needed, depending on how stringent other regulations are. The introduction of the ETS Market Stability Reserve and the review of the ETS scheduled for this year should provide the opportunity to deliver a clear path towards adequate carbon pricing.

The second dimension where we expect to see progress is greater information on the exposure of individual companies. At present, information on the sustainability of financial products – when available – is inconsistent, largely incomparable and at times unreliable. That means that climate risks are not adequately priced,[9] and there is a substantial risk of sharp future corrections. Yet for an open market economy to allocate resources efficiently, the pricing mechanism needs to work correctly.

This requires a step change in the disclosure of climate-related data using standardised and commonly agreed definitions. While TCFD-based[10] disclosures have underpinned public/private efforts to better inform, disclosure needs to be at a far more granular level of detail than is currently available. In Europe. climate disclosures are governed by the Non-Financial Reporting Directive (NFRD), which is currently under review.[11] The Eurosystem has advocated for mandatory disclosures of climate-related risks from a far greater number of companies, including non-listed entities. Moreover, disclosures should be complemented by forward-looking measures that assess the extent to which both financial and non-financial firms are aligned with climate goals and net zero commitments.

The European Taxonomy Regulation[12] that entered into force last year is also an important milestone along this path. But it still needs to be fleshed out with

---

7 OECD (2019), "Taxing Energy Use 2019"; European Commission (2020), "Stepping up Europe's 2030 climate ambition", *Staff Working Document*, 17 September.

8 Per tonne of CO2.

9 See the Eurosystem's reply to the European Commission's public consultations on the Renewed Sustainable Finance Strategy and the revision of the Non-Financial Reporting Directive.

10 Task Force on Climate-related Financial Disclosures.

11 European Commission (2020), "Consultation Document – Review of the Non-Financial Reporting Directive".

12 Regulation (EU) 2020/852of the European Parliament and of the Council of 18 June 2020 on the establishment of a framework to facilitate sustainable investment, and amending Regulation (EU) 2019/2088 (OJ L 198, 22.6.2020, p. 13).

concrete technical criteria and complemented by an equivalent taxonomy for carbon-intensive activities. A further essential step is the consistent and transparent inclusion of climate risks in credit ratings. Here, again, we have high hopes that progress will now speed up.

While adequate carbon prices and greater information on exposures will help provide incentives to decarbonise, that economic transformation cannot take place without the third dimension: substantial green innovation and investment. Both, however, require a complex ecosystem of which finance is a key element,[13] so we expect to see increasing availability of green finance. Green bond issuance by euro area residents has grown sevenfold since 2015, reaching €75 billion in 2020 – this represents roughly 4 % of the total corporate bond issuance.[14]

We need to see funding for green innovation increasing from other market segments as well, especially as recent analyses point to the beneficial role of equity investors in supporting the green transition.[15] Assets under management by investment funds with environmental, social and governance mandates have roughly tripled since 2015, and a little more than half of these funds are domiciled in the euro area. Completing the capital markets union should provide a further push to support equity-based green finance by fostering deep and liquid capital markets across Europe.

Simultaneous progress along each of these three dimensions increases the likelihood of substantial economic change in the near term. That is so because movement along each dimension reinforces progress along the others and magnifies the effectiveness of climate policy.

For example, the economic impact of higher carbon prices depends on the availability of alternative green technologies. In the past, a sudden and substantial increase in carbon taxes could have resulted in an economic downturn, substantial stranded assets and threats to financial stability. Today, however, solar power is not only consistently cheaper than new coal or gas-fired plants in most countries, but it also offers some of the lowest cost electricity ever seen.[16] Green finance and innovation are also developing rapidly. Introducing well-signalled carbon pricing therefore becomes more feasible and could further sharpen incentives

13 See Lagarde, C. (2020), "Fostering sustainable growth in Europe", Keynote speech at the European Banking Congress, Frankfurt, 20 November.

14 The majority of this issuance – €67 billion – is denominated in euro, representing 6 % of euro-denominated issuance by euro-area residents.

15 See De Haas, R. and Popov, A. (2019), "Finance and carbon emissions," *Working Paper Series*, No 2318, ECB, September; and Popov, A. (2020), "Does financial structure affect the carbon footprint of the economy?", *Financial Integration and Structure in the Euro Area*, ECB, March.

16 International Energy Agency (2020), "World Energy Outlook 2020".

both to develop new technologies and to carry out the substantial investment required for the widespread adoption of the green technologies that already exist.

Climate Change and Central Banks

Today, then, central banks face two trends – more visible impacts of climate change and an acceleration of policy transition. Both trends have macroeconomic and financial implications and have consequences for our primary objective of price stability,[17] for our other areas of competence including financial stability and banking supervision, as well as for the Eurosystem's own balance sheet. Central banks are both aware of those consequences, and determined to mitigate them. Much has already been accomplished and more is under way:

The founding of the Network for Greening the Financial System (NGFS), with membership including all major central banks, is testament to that collective engagement with climate change.

At the ECB, we are now launching a new climate change centre to bring together more efficiently the different expertise and strands of work on climate across the Bank. Climate change affects all of our policy areas. The climate change centre provides the structure we need to tackle the issue with the urgency and determination that it deserves.

In the area of financial stability and banking supervision, the ECB has taken concrete steps towards expanding the financial system's understanding of climate risks and its ability to manage them. We have issued a guide on our supervisory expectations relating to the management and disclosure of climate-related and environmental risks.[18] A recent survey of the climate-related disclosures of 125 banks suggests there is still a way to go. It evaluated climate disclosures across several basic information categories. Only 3 % of banks made disclosures in every category, and 16 % made no disclosure in any category.[19] ECB Banking Supervision has requested that banks conduct a climate risk self-assessment and draw up action plans, which we will begin assessing this year. We will conduct a bank-level climate stress test in 2022.

The ECB is also currently carrying out a climate risk stress test exercise to assess the impact on the European banking sector over a 30-year horizon. Prelimin-

---

17 Lagarde, C. (2020), Opening remarks at the ECB Conference on Monetary Policy: bridging science and practice, Frankfurt, 19 October.

18 ECB Banking Supervision (2020), Guide on climate-related and environmental risks, November.

19 ECB (2020), ECB report on institutions' climate-related and environmental risk disclosures.

ary results from mapping climate patterns to the address-level location of firms' physical assets show that in the absence of a transition, physical risks in Europe are concentrated unevenly across countries and sectors of the economy.

But there is more: climate change also impacts our primary mandate of price stability through several channels. This is why climate change considerations form an integral part of our ongoing review of our monetary policy strategy. Climate change can create short-term volatility in output and inflation through extreme weather events,[20] and if left unaddressed can have long-lasting effects on growth and inflation. Transition policies and innovation can also have a significant impact on growth and inflation. These factors could potentially cause a durable divergence between headline and core measures of inflation and influence the inflation expectations of households and businesses.

The transmission of monetary policy through to the interest rates faced by households and businesses could also be impaired, to the extent that increased physical risks or the transition generate stranded assets and losses by financial institutions. According to a recent estimate by the European Systemic Risk Board, a disorderly transition could reduce lending to the private sector by 5% in real terms.[21]

And climate change can also have implications for our monetary policy instruments. First, the Eurosystem's balance sheet itself is exposed to climate risks, through the securities purchased in the asset purchase programmes and the collateral provided by counterparties as part of our policy operations.

Furthermore, several factors associated with climate change may weigh on productivity and the equilibrium interest rate, potentially reducing the space available for conventional policy. For example, labour supply and productivity may diminish as a result of heat stress, temporary incapability to work and higher rates of mortality and morbidity.[22] Resources may be reallocated away from productive use to support adaptation, while capital accumulation may be impaired by rising destruction from natural hazards and weaker investment dynamics related to rising uncertainty.[23] And the increase in short-term volatility and accelerated structural change could hamper central banks' ability to correctly identify

---

20 Parker, M. (2018), "The Impact of Disasters on Inflation", *Economics of Disasters and Climate Change*, Vol. 2, No. 1, pp. 21–48.

21 ESRB, (2020), "Positively green: measuring climate change risks to financial stability", European Systemic Risk Board, June.

22 See, e.g. Hsiang et al. (2017), "Estimating economic damage from climate change in the United States", *Science*, Vol. 356, Issue 6345, pp. 1362–1369.

23 Dietz, S. and Stern, N. (2015), "Endogenous Growth, Convexity of Damage and Climate Risk: How Nordhaus' Framework Supports Deep Cuts in Carbon Emissions", *The Economic Journal*,

the shocks that are relevant for the medium-term inflation outlook, making it more difficult to assess the appropriate monetary policy stance.

Our strategy review enables us to consider more deeply how we can continue to protect our mandate in the face of these risks and, at the same time, strengthen the resilience of monetary policy and our balance sheet to climate risks. That naturally involves evaluating the feasibility, efficiency and effectiveness of available options, and ensuring they are consistent with our mandate.

The ECB is also assessing carefully, without prejudice to the primary objective of price stability, how it can contribute to supporting the EU's economic policies, as required by the treaty. Europe has prioritised combating climate change and put in place targets, policies and regulations to underpin the transition to a carbon-neutral economy. While the Eurosystem is not a policy maker in these areas, it should assess its potential role in the transition.

We recognise that our active role in some markets can influence the development of certain market segments. The ECB currently holds around a fifth of the outstanding volume of eligible green bonds. Standardisation helps nascent markets gain liquidity and encourages growth. And our eligibility criteria can provide, in this context, a useful coordination device. For example, since the start of this year, bonds with coupon structures linked to certain sustainability performance targets have been eligible as collateral for Eurosystem credit operations and for outright purchases for monetary policy purposes.

We have also taken action with regards to our non-monetary policy portfolio, namely our own funds and pension fund. The ECB raised the share of green bonds in its own funds portfolio to 3.5% last year and is planning on raising it further as this market is expected to grow in the coming years. Investing parts of the own funds portfolio in the green bond fund of the Bank for International Settlements marks another step in this direction. A shift of all conventional equity benchmark indices tracked by the staff pension fund to low-carbon equivalents last year significantly reduced the carbon footprint of the equity funds. Other central banks are also aligning decisively their investment decisions with sustainability criteria.[24]

Vol. 125, No 583, pp. 574–620; Benmir, G., Jaccard, I. and Vermandel, G. (2020), "Green asset pricing", *Working Paper Series*, No 2477, ECB, October.

24 See, for example, Jordan, T. (2020), Introductory remarks, Swiss National Bank, 17 December; Sveriges Riksbank (2020), Sustainability strategy for the Riksbank; Banque de France, Responsible investment policy: reinforcing exclusions with regard to fossil fuels, Press Release, 19 January 2021. NGFS (2019), A Sustainable and Responsible Investment Guide for Central Banks' Portfolio Management, Network for Greening the Financial System; NGFS (2020), Progress report on the im-

Conclusion

Let me conclude.

Climate change is one of the greatest challenges faced by mankind this century, and there is now broad agreement that we should act. But that agreement needs to be translated more urgently into concrete measures. The ECB will contribute to this effort within its mandate, acting in tandem with those responsible for climate policy.

Unlike the mice in the fable, not only do we have to recognise that we cannot keep waiting for someone else to act, we also must recognise that the burden cannot fall on one party alone. There is no single panacea for climate change, and combating it requires rapid progress along several dimensions. Relying on just one solution, or on one party, will not be enough to avoid a climate catastrophe. And here we can actually learn something from mice. As the Roman playwright Plautus wrote, "How wise a beast is the little mouse, who never entrusts its safety to only one hole."[25]

plementation of sustainable and responsible investment practices in central banks' portfolio management, Network for Greening the Financial System.

25 "Cogito, mus pusillus quam sit sapiens bestia, aetatem qui uni cubili nunquam committit suam." Plautus, *Truculentus*, Act IV, scene iv.

Jens Weidmann

What Role should Central Banks play in Combating Climate Change?

Remarks at the ILF Online-Conference "Green Banking and Green Central Banking: What are the right Concepts?", Goethe University Frankfurt, 25 January 2021

1. Introduction

Ladies and gentlemen,

I would have been only too happy to meet you all in person. Even more so, as from my office it would only have been a short walk to the campus of the Goethe University.

And allow me the following side remark: There can hardly be a better person to name a university after than Johann Wolfgang von Goethe. Goethe combined many disciplines and subjects, and not just as a poet, dramatist, novelist and critic. He also conducted research in various natural sciences, studying minerals, plants, human anatomy and meteorology, to name a few. And let's not forget that he reflected on the nature of money, even serving as finance minister in the Duchy of Saxe-Weimar-Eisenach, a small, former state in what is now Thuringia. Goethe seems to be a true all-rounder, able to turn his hand to any number of things.

Some would like to see central banks in a similar role. In their view, not only are we supposed to ensure price stability, help with supervising banks and safeguarding financial stability, foster growth or promote employment. Some also expect central banks to act as a rapid response unit for every economic crisis, keep sovereign financing costs low or provide savers with adequate interest rates. Recently, another item has been added to the wish list: we are being called upon to assume an active role in climate policy.

One thing is clear: climate change presents a challenge for all of humanity. The Swiss playwright Friedrich Dürrenmatt wrote in an appendix to his play *The Physicists*: "What concerns everybody can only be solved by everybody." Therefore, every institution is right to ask itself what contribution it can make to mitigating climate change within the remit of its mandate.

https://doi.org/10.1515/9783110752892-016

2. Dealing with climate-related Risks

The mandates of central banks and financial supervisors vary, but they typically include price stability, financial stability and the soundness of financial institutions. Climate change and climate policies can affect all of these mandates, as they may have an impact on macroeconomic and financial variables such as output, inflation, interest rates and asset prices, while altering the underlying structure of our economies. It is therefore essential for central banks to gain a full understanding of these repercussions for the functioning of the economy and the financial system.[1] We need to embed climate-related developments and risks in our analyses and update our analytical and forecasting toolkits accordingly.

Regarding the impact on the financial system and the economy, climate change entails both physical and transition risks.[2] First, physical risks result from persistent changes in climate and more frequent extreme weather events. Goethe himself experienced first-hand the enormous impact extreme weather can have. In his day, this was caused by a volcanic eruption far away on an Indonesian island. The year 1816 went down in history as the "Year Without a Summer". People suffered from the cold and from persistent rain; crops failed and famine broke out.[3] Second, transition risks relate to the process of adjustment towards a lower-carbon economy.

Both the physical impact of climate change and the transition to a less carbon-intensive economy can be a source of financial risk.[4] For example, the ECB found in a sample of euro area banks that the exposures to the twenty largest emitters of carbon account for 20 % of total large exposures.[5]

Clearly, it is in every market participant's interest to properly protect themselves against climate-related financial risks by adjusting their risk management accordingly. Thus, first and foremost, it's up to the financial sector to recognise and take into account such risks. Whether and how this is done has a bearing on several of our tasks as a central bank.

---

1 Deutsche Bundesbank (2020), The significance of climate change for the Bundesbank's tasks, Annual Report 2019, pp. 22–24.

2 Network for Greening the Financial System (2019), A Call for Action: Climate Change as a Source of Financial Risk – First Comprehensive Report; Deutsche Bundesbank (2019), Impact of climate-related risks on financial stability, Financial Stability Review 2019, pp. 107–120.

3 Badenhop, P. (2016), Als der Tambora den Himmel verdunkelte, Frankfurter Allgemeine Zeitung, 11. September 2016, https://www.faz.net/aktuell/rhein-main/das-jahr-ohne-sommer-als-der-tambora-den-himmel-verdunkelte-14422262.html.

4 Network for Greening the Financial System (2020), Overview of Environmental Risk Analysis by Financial Institutions, September 2020.

5 European Central Bank (2019), Financial Stability Review, May 2019, pp. 120–133.

In banking supervision, we do not regard climate-related financial risks as a new risk category, but as a driver of classic categories such as credit risk and market risk.[6] We already expect banks to incorporate such risks into their risk management framework appropriately and to back them with adequate capital.

However, climate-related risks have certain characteristics that hamper their inclusion in ratings and internal risk models. First, historical data do not capture them adequately. Second, physical risks are potentially non-linear and expected to primarily materialise in the medium to long term. And third, the future pathway of climate change and climate action is highly uncertain, not least because it heavily depends on political decisions.

In this context, scenario analysis is a particularly useful tool.[7] Furthermore, it is important that banks take a forward-looking approach and consider a longer than usual time horizon. The ECB Guide on climate-related and environmental risks outlines the supervisory expectations and sets an ambitious goal: to fully integrate all relevant climate-related risks into banks' risk management, business strategy and internal organisation.[8]

Every new beginning is difficult. But, to echo the king in Lewis Carroll's "Alice in Wonderland", we have to "Begin at the beginning." According to a survey conducted by the ECB and the EBA, only a small number of institutions have fully incorporated climate-related risks into their risk management framework already.[9] In 2019, the stress test conducted by the Bundesbank and BaFin for small and medium-sized banks (less significant institutions, LSIs) yielded a similar result: only one third of the German credit institutions had incorporated climate-related risks into their risk management at least to some degree. Two-thirds did not take them into account at all.[10]

Clearly, an ambitious goal cannot be reached overnight. However, supervisors do expect continuous progress to be made. Therefore, addressing climate-related risks will continue gaining in importance in banking supervision. This year, we will use the supervisory dialogue to discuss the banks' self-assessments and

6 Network for Greening the Financial System (2020), Guide for Supervisors: Integrating climate-related and environmental risks into prudential supervision, May 2020.

7 Network for Greening the Financial System (2020), Guide to climate scenario analysis for central banks and supervisors, June 2020.

8 European Central Bank (2020), Guide on climate-related and environmental risks – Supervisory expectations relating to risk management and disclosure.

9 European Central Bank (2020), op. cit.

10 Deutsche Bundesbank (2019), Ergebnisse des LSI-Stresstests 2019, press conference on 23 September 2019, https://www.bundesbank.de/resource/blob/807590/8cd2b931f02825341c51c1de19b62354/mL/2019-09-23-stresstest-anlage-data.pdf.

plans to meet the supervisory expectations. And next year, the ECB will conduct its supervisory stress test on climate-related risks.

Obviously, central banks are not commercial banks. But our financial assets can be just as exposed to financial risk as those of commercial banks. In this regard, central banks should practise what they preach. Hence, I believe that central banks should factor climate-related financial risks into their risk management. That should also apply to financial risks arising from monetary policy operations.

For this purpose, the Eurosystem has a legitimate interest in making climate-related financial risks more transparent: In my view, we should consider only purchasing bonds or accepting them as collateral for monetary policy purposes if their issuers meet certain climate-related reporting requirements. In addition, we could examine whether we should use only those ratings that appropriately include climate-related financial risks.

By taking such measures, the Eurosystem would help foster market transparency and standards at rating agencies and banks. In this way, we could act as a catalyst for change in the financial system and support climate policies in the EU without overstretching our mandate.

3. Central Banks cannot substitute for stringent carbon Pricing

But problems arise when monetary policy, financial supervision or banking regulation are pressed into service for other purposes. Each of these domains already has a clearly defined objective. This focus is also consistent with the Tinbergen rule, named after the first Nobel Laureate in economics, Jan Tinbergen. His rule stipulates that for each separate economic policy target, there must also be at least one separate instrument.[11]

If the instruments are overloaded with multiple targets, conflicts of objectives will emerge sooner or later. At worst, the existing core tasks could end up taking a back seat without the new targets being met. To quote Jean Tirole, who was also awarded the Nobel Memorial Prize: "We must resist this trend of governmental agencies becoming jacks of all trades and masters of none."[12] Metaphorically speaking, the man who chases two rabbits catches neither. Using banking regula-

---

11 Tinbergen, J. (1952), On the Theory of Economic Policy, North-Holland Publishing Company, Amsterdam.

12 Tirole, J. (2019), Institutional and economic challenges for central banking, European Central Bank, Monetary policy: the challenges ahead (Colloquium in honour of Benoît Cœuré, held on 17–18 December 2019), pp. 34–40.

tion to pursue climate policy objectives could represent a "chase for the second rabbit".

For example, one might aim to make green investments more attractive for banks by offering a discount on the bank capital required for such exposures. However, a green supporting factor could distort the risk-based capital requirements and thus might undermine efforts to reinforce the stability of the banking sector.

Moreover, lowering capital charges may not be immediately effective, as the EU's experience with a similar supporting factor for SME lending has shown. In its initial assessment of the available data, the EBA found no sufficient evidence that this move provided additional stimulus for lending to smaller firms relative to larger firms.[13] Banking regulation should retain its risk-oriented focus. It should not be used as an instrument to promote other policy objectives.

It would be just as wrong to use monetary policy as a means of pursuing climate policy, for example, by favouring "green" securities and excluding bonds issued by carbon-intensive enterprises. For one thing, the impact of such measures on emissions should not be overestimated, as I have already explained on previous occasions.[14] For another, the measures could come at a high price: here again, conflicts of interest may arise, this time with our primary objective of price stability. Asset purchase programmes are part of our expansionary monetary policy, and this is not meant for perpetual use. Indeed, it would be short-sighted to assume that inflation rates will hover at very low levels forever.[15]

When necessary in order to maintain price stability, the Eurosystem needs to apply the brakes and scale back its asset purchases or portfolio. But if the programmes were favouring green assets, that would also mean less support for the transition of the economy. Should the scale of climate action really depend on inflation developments? Certainly not! A clear and credible path of transition is essential for businesses, as they need reliable perspectives to make the necessary long-term investments.

In this context, we should remember that Robert Mundell, yet another Nobel Laureate, extended Tinbergen's rule significantly, as "instruments (...) should be

---

13 European Banking Authority (2016), EBA Report on SMEs and SME Supporting Factor, EBA/OP/2016/04, https://eba.europa.eu/eba-publishes-the-report-on-smes-and-the-sme-supporting-factor.

14 Weidmann, J. (2020), Combating climate change – What central banks can and cannot do, speech delivered at the European Banking Congress on 20 November 2020.

15 Weidmann, J. (2020), Too close for comfort? The relationship between monetary and fiscal policy, speech delivered at the OMFIF Virtual Panel on 5 November 2020.

directed at those targets (...) on which they have the most direct influence."[16] Climate action crucially depends on carbon emissions becoming more expensive. In order to raise carbon prices, both emissions trading systems and carbon taxes are effective and efficient tools. The decisions to use these tools are a matter for governments and parliaments. As elected representatives, they have the democratic legitimacy needed to make such wide-ranging decisions.

Many believe that not enough climate action is being taken at the political level. Some go further, claiming that central banks therefore need to "step in". As tempting as this idea might sound, it is not up to independent central banks to correct or replace political decisions. We were not granted independence to make the decisions that politicians are unwilling to make. We were granted independence because independent central banks are best equipped to safeguard price stability. An active role in climate policy could undermine our independence and, eventually, jeopardise our ability to maintain price stability.

4. Central Banks as a Blueprint for independent carbon Agencies?

Ladies and gentlemen,

I am very disappointed when I see half-hearted climate policies and a lack of commitment to a clear transition path. Why is it so difficult for politicians to take ambitious and credible climate action? One reason is what Mark Carney described as the "tragedy of the horizon": "the catastrophic impacts of climate change will be felt beyond the traditional horizons of most actors – imposing a cost on future generations that the current generation has no direct incentive to fix."[17]

In addition, the literature points to a time inconsistency problem, which may resemble the one facing monetary policy: after policymakers have set climate targets, they may have an incentive to put them on the back burner in order to boost employment in the short run or avoid unwelcome distributional effects.[18] Being aware of this incentive and the multitude or fuzziness of the government's objectives, businesses could lack confidence in a long-term climate policy. In this case,

16 Mundell, R. A. (1960), The Monetary Dynamics of International Adjustment under Fixed and Flexible Exchange Rates, Quarterly Journal of Economics, Vol. 74, pp. 227–257.

17 Carney, M. (2015), Breaking the tragedy of the horizon – climate change and financial stability, speech delivered at Lloyd's of London on 29 September 2015.

18 See for example Helm, D., C. Hepburn and R. Mash (2003), Credible carbon policy, Oxford Review of Economic Policy, Vol. 19, pp. 438–450; Brunner, S., C. Flachsland and R. Marschinski (2012), Credible commitment in carbon policy, Climate Policy, Vol. 12, pp. 255–271.

they will not make the investments needed for the transition to a carbon-neutral economy.

Against this backdrop, there is an academic debate on how to enhance the credibility of climate policy and whether monetary policy provides a suitable blueprint. Indeed, central banks were granted independence in order to solve monetary policy's time inconsistency problem.[19] From then on, they were able to safeguard price stability insulated from political influences. And it paid off.[20]

Some economists have suggested that this success story could be emulated by delegating climate policy to a new independent institution at the European level. Parliaments would have to equip it with both a clear mandate and the necessary instruments for carbon pricing. This agency could then pursue a stringent climate policy, with no regard for short-term electoral considerations. It would be committed to the long-term targets for reducing carbon emissions. For businesses and financial markets, this could create greater planning certainty for long-term investment.

Such an independent carbon agency would need to be transparent, publicly accountable and led by renowned experts in this field. The institution – just as in the case of central banks – would also need to rest on a broad political and societal consensus, as well as a solid legal foundation. However, in contrast to monetary policy in general, ambitious carbon pricing will significantly alter the distribution of resources and income – even across multiple generations. To what extent can we and should we forego democratic decision-making processes here?

Indeed, recommendations have come from other quarters for politicians not to hand over responsibility for setting the path of emissions. These observers stress the importance of retaining the flexibility to amend policy and having direct political accountability.[21] Essentially, governments can resolve commitment problems by curbing their discretionary powers via delegation. But having their hands tied like this also comes at a cost. Moreover, an independent European institution would not be a panacea for all the ailments climate policy suffers. Just think of the free-rider problem at the international level.

---

19 Weidmann, J. (2020), Zu möglichen langfristigen Folgen der Coronakrise für Wirtschaft und Geldpolitik, speech at the Humboldt University of Berlin on 16 December 2020.

20 Alesina, A. and L. H. Summers (1993), Central Bank Independence and Macroeconomic Performance: Some Comparative Evidence, Journal of Money, Credit and Banking, Vol. 25, pp. 151–162; Cukierman, A. (2008), Central bank independence and monetary policymaking institutions – Past, present and future, European Journal of Political Economy, Vol. 24, pp. 722–736.

21 Ergas, H. (2010), New policies create new politics: issues of institutional design in climate change policy, The Australian Journal of Agriculture and Resource Economics, Vol. 54, pp. 143–164.

Overall, there are important pros and cons to weigh up when thinking about an independent carbon agency. At least, the case for delegation and independence does not appear as clear-cut as it is in the context of monetary policy. Indeed, a recent paper lists several conditions that would make an independent carbon agency a preferable option to strengthen commitment. And according to the researchers, it is debatable whether an institution can be designed to meet those requirements.[22]

However, without precluding further discussion, these considerations make one point quite clearly: Central banks should not slip into the role of a carbon agency. Ultimately, broadening the tasks of central banks could raise the impression that we are striving for multiple or fuzzy objectives, jeopardising the focus that is needed to establish credibility in the first place. It might also weaken accountability as discretionary decisions could then be justified by referring to one or the other of various objectives. To quote Jean Tirole once more: "[...] well-managed agencies may resist being granted new tasks."

Let me be clear: Like Christine Lagarde, I am convinced that we all can do more to mitigate climate change, without risking conflict with our very own tasks. And we should do more!

At the same time, we need to safeguard the division of labour and the boundaries of clearly assigned responsibilities between policy areas. As economist Clemens Fuest put it recently: "Environmental policy [should] provide guidance by setting the carbon price. Other policy areas should incorporate the climate issue to the extent that it affects their core tasks, but they should not compete with environmental policy."[23]

5. Conclusion

Ladies and gentlemen,

Did you know that Goethe was very proud of his scientific research? He valued his *Theory of Colours* even more than his poetry.[24] The irony is that his scientific explanation of light, colours and their origin is widely regarded as incorrect.

---

22 Edenhofer, O., M. Franks and M. Kalkuhl (2021), Pigou in the 21st Century: a tribute on the occasion of the 100th anniversary of the publication of The Economics of Welfare, International Tax and Public Finance, published online, https://doi.org/10.1007/s10797-020-09653-y.

23 Fuest, C. (2020), Klimapolitik: Vorzüge der richtigen Arbeitsteilung, Frankfurter Allgemeine Zeitung, 11. December 2020.

24 Donat, S. and H. Birus (1999), Goethe – ein letztes Universalgenie?, Wallstein-Verlag, Göttingen.

Looking back, it is plain to see that Goethe overestimated his abilities as a natural scientist. You could say that Goethe was a "jack of all trades and master of some". But even he was not a universal genius.

Applied to our current topic, it could be interpreted as warning central banks against overburdening themselves. We should not convey the impression that central banks are the better carbon agencies and can solve the problem of climate change on the side. This would raise expectations that we cannot meet.

Thank you for your attention.

Jose Manuel Campa

Enhancing ESG Governance, Disclosure and Risk Measurement in Credit Institutions

The current circumstances remind us that the risks posed by sustainability issues are real threats. If anything, the covid-19 crisis is showing how challenging the management of environmental and social crises is going to be in the future. The pandemic has highlighted that existing vulnerabilities in terms of environmental, and social sustainability are not only potential risks that we need to avoid so that they don't arise at some point far away in the future but salient challenges that pose serious difficulties and need to be addressed today with an increasing sense of urgency.

Climate risk, and more broadly sustainability challenges, tend to be global in nature. Large and different type of externalities are prevalent when analysing these problems. The policy difficulties that this complexity bring should not be underestimated. However, these difficulties cannot serve as an argument for inaction. On the contrary, action and coordination need to play a prominent role precisely to overcome those difficulties in addressing the problem. This applies to all agents in our society, governments and international regulators, corporates, investors and consumers.

In that context, we need to ensure that the banking sector is well-prepared. Banks need to be able to adjust their governance, risk measurement and business models so as to ensure that they confront these challenges in terms of the direct risks that they face. As financial intermediaries, with an essential role of channeling savings to investment opportunities. They also need to be able to assess those investment opportunities from a risk perspective, evaluate their overall riskiness and impact on their business models and clearly communicate them. A swift execution of those steps will assure that the credit/financing channel performs its role. Being up to this task is essential for banks to support the transformation of the real economy and the future living standards of European citizens.

Awareness needs to be raised within the banking sector and among financial market participants of the need for immediate action to promote, more generally, a sustainable finance agenda. In my view this should imply that banks need to: assess their strategy and risk management on ESG related issues; implement key metrics for monitoring and disclosure to stakeholders; enhance their risk measurement and modelling techniques for regular risk assessment of their portfolios and stress testing and scenario analysis.

https://doi.org/10.1515/9783110752892-017

The rationale for this sequence is the need firstly to better embed sustainability factors and risks in institutions' practices and better understand institutions' exposures. Institutions need to have metrics that can be clearly comprehended – including by the public– measured and managed in relation to the banks' chosen strategy. Disclosures will be absolutely key in driving change given the heightened interest of stakeholders in sustainability considerations. Finally, proper risk measurement, with well-tested modelling techniques and proper assessment of the financial risks involved will help assure that banks are correctly managing those risks. Any adjustments to the prudential treatment could only come later, based on appropriate evidence.

In the rest of this article, I would like to briefly elaborate on each of these three areas briefly.

Governance and Management of ESG Risks

Environmental, social and governance (ESG) factors materialize at many levels, such as international, country, sectoral or entity level. Therefore, the financial materiality of ESG risks will need to be carefully assessed by institutions and supervisors. Since not all financing activities are likely to be equally affected by ESG risks, it is important that institutions and supervisors are able to distinguish and form a view on the relevance of ESG risks, following a proportionate, risk-based approach that takes into account the likelihood and the severity of the materialization of ESG risks. Credit institutions are directly exposed to ESG factors as companies and these risks need to be covered by the related management arrangements. Credit institutions are also exposed to ESG risks via the impact of ESG factors on their counterparties and they need to assess how these factors can also be sources of risk for themselves.

Institutions need to enhance the incorporation of ESG risks into their business strategies, business processes and proportionately incorporate ESG risks in their internal governance arrangements. Board oversight, proper committees and other internal governance procedures need to be set up to ensure that ESG risks are measured, assessed, and decided upon. ESG policies need to be developed and enforced. Management knowledge and skills on ESG issues must be upgraded. Remuneration policies need to be reviewed.

Adjusting the business strategy of an institution to incorporate ESG risks as drivers of prudential risks can be considered as a progressive risk management tool to mitigate the potential impact of ESG risks. Risk appetite on ESG issues, and related risk policies and risk limits need to be established. Credit institutions also need to gradually develop methodologies and approaches to a climate risk stress test, while considering the methodological and data constraints. The objective of a climate risk stress test should be to inform on the resilience of institutions' own business model and investment strategies. Finally, credit institutions need to engage actively with their customers and other relevant stakeholders. An engagement policy should consider the internal perspective, what are the capacities the institution needs to build up to understand and execute on their ESG strategy, and the external perspective of how it should interact with investors, customers, employees and possibly other stakeholders to mitigate ESG risks.

Prudential supervisors need to proportionately incorporate the ESG factors and considerations into their supervisory toolkit. In particular, with regards to the supervisory assessment of the business environment in which an institution operates; its current business model and its related sustainability; and the analysis of the existing strategy from an ESG perspective. However, the existing assessment under the Supervisory Review and Evaluation Process (SREP) of credit institutions might not sufficiently enable supervisors to understand the longer term impact of ESG risks, their breadth and magnitude, on future financial positions and related long-term vulnerabilities. In my view, the evaluation of the long term resilience of the business model of credit institutions against the time horizon of the relevant public policies or broader transition trends, needs to be further developed and incorporated in the supervisory approach.

Measurement and Disclosure of ESG Exposures

A second area in which further progress needs to be made is in the measurement and disclosure of exposure to ESG related activities and potential risks. A lot of work has been done on the development of a Taxonomy, particularly in the EU, to translate the Paris agreement into a mechanism for disclosing information on the relative size and exposure of activities exposed to climate-related risks. Banks like other nonfinancial corporations are expected to provide information based on this taxonomy and other disclosure requirements. In addition, banks need to also provide information on the composition and evolution of their loan portfolios and activities in regards to ESG risks. At this stage, most of the progress has been on climate and environmental related exposures.

In my view, institutions need to make progress in communicating where they believe they are in terms of their ESG agenda, where they would like to be in the medium and long term and what are the specific actions they will put in place to execute the transition needed to accomplish those objectives. This should imply at a minimum the disclosure by institutions of: qualitative disclosures on environmental, social and governance risks; quantitative disclosures on climate change transitional and physical risk; as well as a set of Key Performance Indicators (KPIs) that institutions will use to assess their climate change mitigating measures and the performance on those KPIs over time.

The European Banking Authority (EBA) has also proposed along these lines the reporting by credit institutions of a green asset ratio (GAR) on EU taxonomy-aligned activities. The provision of this information may be difficult in the short term. Uncertainty on the timing and effect of the materialization of these risks is high. The scarcity of relevant, comparable, reliable data is high. Metrics are not well defined. Furthermore, the materialization and quantification of the risks related to these exposures, particularly for transitional risks, are likely to be very different depending on the policies effectively implemented to facilitate such transition. Counterparties may not be in a situation to provide the information needed by credit institutions to properly classify and report the risks. Methodological difficulties also exist. Some of the existing taxonomies are activity based which for large corporates engaging in a large number of activities may account for very different percentages of their overall turnover. Therefore, the classification of counterparties into an activity-based taxonomy may be challenging. Furthermore, clear benchmarks do not currently exist for classifying activities exposed to climate change physical risk.

These difficulties should not divert us from the key priority. The recognition that the provision of ESG related exposures and the vision of credit institutions on where they want to be in the future is very relevant information for stakeholders and the disclosure by institutions of meaningful and informative data, at least using estimates, is urgent for managing those exposures and their related risks.

ESG Exposures: From Disclosure to Risk Assessment

A sound and resilient financial sector is key in facilitating a smooth transition to a low-carbon economy and mitigate the potentially disruptive impacts of environmental risks. This requires the credit institutions to ensure themselves on their resilience to the environmental risks and to engage in the necessary assessment of the measures they need to engage in to ensure their resilience through the transition. Even though these risks are generally perceived to be a long-term threat for financial stability, some of them have already started to crystallize and others could significantly increase in the short and medium term.

As discussed in the previous section, institutions need to quantify the potential impact of climate risks on their existing loan portfolios and their business models going forward. They need to accurately manage the financial risks associated with those portfolios and manage them actively. Modelling ESG related risks poses novel and additional challenges to the traditional risk modelling used by credit institutions. Historical data on the materialization of risk events is scarce. Furthermore, ESG related risks tend to be better analyzed in a context of general equilibrium rather than as individual idiosyncratic risks affecting specific exposures. Therefore, general equilibrium, scenario type, methodologies are more suited than the traditional historical, time series based analysis. Credit institutions need to develop those methodologies, test them, understand them and assess how best to use them to accurately measure the financial risks arising from these exposures.

For supervisory authorities, assessing the banking sector and testing bank readiness to classify, evaluate and manage these risks is a priority for policy makers. The process of integrating climate risks into standard financial stability monitoring and supervision has been already kicked-off, building on recent EU initiatives on sustainable finance. Authorities also need to develop appropriate qualitative and quantitative criteria, like stress testing processes and scenario analyses, to assess the impact of ESG risks under scenarios with different severities. A number of national authorities have taken and/or announced initiatives to assess the exposure to climate related risks and assess the impact that these risks may have on financial stability[1].

At the EBA, our founding regulation has been aligned with these new tasks and it mandates the EBA to develop common methodologies for assessing the effect of risks stemming from adverse environmental developments on an institution's financial position. Last year, the EBA launched a pilot exercise on climate risk designed as a learning exercise to investigate how existing and newly developed climate risk assessment and classification tools perform, and to test banks readiness to deal with related data and methodological challenges. The exercise involved 29 EU banks from 10 countries and focuses on corporate non-SME exposures towards EU obligors. The sample provides a good picture of the EU banking landscape as it includes different business models (commercial banks, public banks, saving banks, cooperative banks).

According to the outcome of the mapping exercise, more than a half of banks' exposures (55 % of total) are allocated towards NACE level 4 classes that might be sensitive to transition risk, while a parallel analysis, based on greenhouse gas (GHG) emissions, reveals that 32 % of the exposures is towards obligors with GHG

---

1 For instance, in the European Union, the European Central Bank, European Insurance and Occupational Pensions Authority, and the European Systemic Risk Board have all announced initiatives on this front as have the Central Banks of the Netherlands and France.

emissions above the median of the distribution.[2] Finally, the sensitivity analysis results show that the impact of climate related risks across banks has different magnitude and is concentrated in some particular sectors. Tools for scenario analysis are quickly developing and further progress should be made on modeling the transmission channels of climate risk shocks to banks balance sheets.

Given the nature of the exercise and the related data and methodological limitations, these results must be interpreted with caution and should be considered as starting point estimates for future work on climate risk.

Conclusion

In the previous sections I have highlighted the need for credit institutions to make specific progress in their ESG agenda along three areas: assess their strategy and risk management on ESG related issues; implement internal governance mechanisms and key metrics for monitoring and disclosure to stakeholders; and enhance their risk measurement and modelling techniques for regular risk assessment of their portfolios and stress testing and scenario analysis. Timely progress by all institutions along these lines is a necessary condition to address the challenges they confront. However, while these are necessary conditions for success credit institutions by themselves cannot achieve the ultimate goal. Progress needs to happen in two additional dimensions.

First, coordination at the global and cross-sectoral level among authorities to design and implement proper policies to address the underlying risks are paramount. Most of the challenges related to ESG are inherently global or at least require large cross-border and cross-sectoral coordination. The range and importance of economic externalities in dealing with many of these problems show that neither purely private nor partial solutions to address the problem will ultimately achieve the intended goals. Much progress in international coordination has been achieved but a much larger momentum is needed.

Second, credit institutions allocate savings to investment and provide financing to corporates across all sectors of economic activity. For them to properly assess ESG related risks and allocate financing, credit institutions need to assess the investment opportunities and receive adequate, comparable, information with regards to ESG exposures. Progress needs to be made on the best way for corporates

2 For a summary of the results, see: https://www.eba.europa.eu/sites/default/documents/files/document_library/Risk%20Analysis%20and%20Data/Risk%20Assessment%20Reports/2020/December%202020/961060/Risk%20Assessment_Report_December_2020.pdf.

to provide the relevant information. We need to progress beyond the non financial reporting requirements for large corporates to determine how best to assess relevant risks for SMEs and retail exposures.

Sylvie Goulard

Climate Change and Central Banks: From Financial Stability Considerations to a global Response?

Introduction

Central banks are independent institutions with a generally strictly defined mandate: under Article 127 of the Treaty on the Functioning of the European Union, the primary objective of the European Central Bank and the Eurosystem is to maintain price stability. For the US Federal Reserve or the Bank of England, there is also an objective of supporting employment. Combating climate change, biodiversity loss or pandemics are all tasks that, in a democracy, are primarily the responsibility of the elected authorities and not of central banks. To this end, governments have various tools at their disposal to put in place the incentives and prohibitions needed to influence the behaviour of companies and households.

However, there are several reasons why central banks should take this challenge up and considerable progress has already been made, starting with the preservation of financial stability. Although less clearly defined in the mandates, this mission belongs to central banks' core responsibilities and has actively justified reforms since the 2008 financial crisis.

In a seminal speech on "The Tragedy of the Horizon", Mark Carney, then Governor of the Bank of England, was the first to warn that climate change creates new, serious risks for financial systems and economies. Thus, central banks cannot limit their actions to the short or medium term without taking into account the profound and irreversible changes created in the long term by an unsustainable economy. The systemic nature of the effects of climate change therefore jeopardizes the stability of the financial system and the ability of central banks to pursue their primary objective. This is what we recalled with Sabine Mauderer, member of the Board of the Deutsche Bundesbank, in an article published in July 2019.

Under the Treaties, European central banks must, without prejudice to their primary objectives, support the general policies of the European Union. The recent adoption of the Green New Deal by the von der Leyen Commission, as well as numerous statements by the European Council (Michel, 2020), clearly demonstrate the political will at the European level to promote sustainable development, and in particular to achieve zero net greenhouse gas emissions by 2050. Achieving this goal requires a general mobilisation of all actors, each in its own sphere of competence, including the central banks.

https://doi.org/10.1515/9783110752892-018

Global awareness is quickly gaining ground in our community. Created late 2017 by eight founding members -including the Banque de France, the Deutsche Bundesbank and also the People's Bank of China, the Banco de Mexico and Bank Al Maghrib- the Central Banks and Supervisors Network for Greening the Financial System (NGFS) now consists of 89 members including the US Federal Reserve, which recently joined. A dozen international organisations are also observers of the Network -including the Bank for International Settlements, the International Monetary Fund and the World Bank. The NGFS has developed shared analytical tools and has enabled the dissemination and cross-border exchange of best practices among peers.

In the field of monetary policy, too, reflections on the climate have emerged and could materialize in the European Central Bank's Strategic Review, which was launched in early 2020. Christine Lagarde has strong convictions in this area: "I want to explore every avenue available in order to combat climate change".

In addition to the individual moral imperative to contribute, in one's own capacity, climate change will not be curbed without a combination of actions. Measures taken by elected governments, at national or European level, to integrate the price of negative externalities, for example through a carbon tax, are necessary but, even if properly implemented, may not be sufficient.

Finally, the Covid-19 pandemic illustrates the risks for humanity and for our economies of the potential consequences of the resurgence of virus transmissions from animals to humans, encouraged by the destruction of natural habitats and biodiversity. Hence, the development of new thinking encompassing all climate-related and ecological risks in what some authors have called "Green Swans". (Bolton et al, 2020a)

Financial Stability and Climate Change

The community of central banks and supervisors now recognizes the need to address a new type of financial risk: climate-related risk. There are two main types: physical and transition risks (see Figure 1).

Physical risks are the economic and financial losses associated with the increased frequency and intensity of extreme weather events (hurricanes, floods, etc.) as well as long-term changes in climate trends (e.g. rising sea levels, desertification or disruption of agricultural production conditions). The risk of catastrophic losses cannot be excluded, especially if the increase in average temperature exceeds 1.5 °C or 2 °C.

Transition risks refer to the risks that could materialize in the event of a rapid transition to a low-carbon economy (e.g. due to sudden public policies, technological disruptions or brakes, etc.). In particular, limiting the increase in average temperature to 1.5 °C or 2 °C implies that a large part of the existing reserves of fossil resources cannot be extracted. These would then become "stranded assets", reserves that could quickly become worthless and trigger massive fire sales.

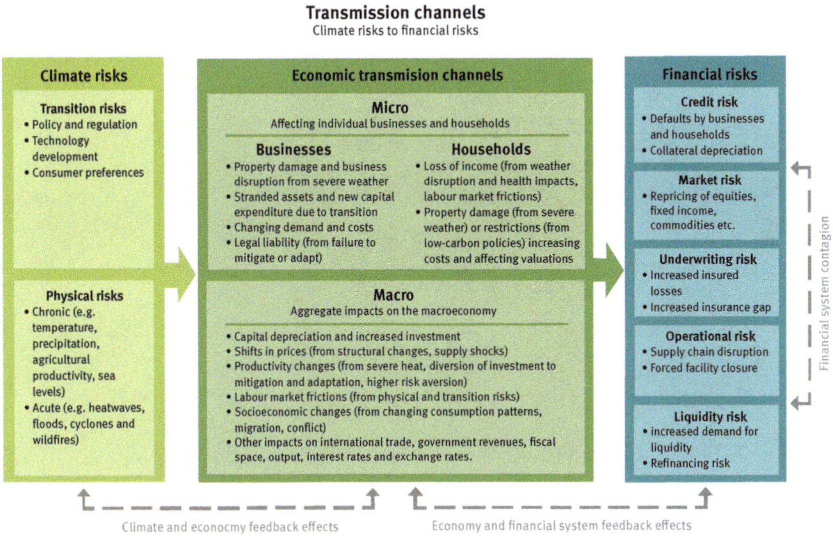

Figure 1: Transmission Channels climate risks to Financial risks, NGFS (2020).

This threat to global financial stability was the catalyst for the NGFS, as an international coalition of the willing. After having made a joint diagnosis on the relevance of climate-related risk for the mandate of central banks and supervisors in April 2019 (NGFS, 2019), the members of the network have worked on a series of guides, in order to display existing leading practices. In particular, the NGFS published a first set of climate scenarios in June 2020 to provide a common starting point for measuring and integrating climate-related risks into financial stability monitoring.

These scenarios were chosen to show a range of lower and higher risk outcomes. Although in reality there is a continuum of physical and transition risk outcomes, there are two main factors from these scenarios that determine the potential impact on the economy and financial system. One is the total level of mitigation attained (leading to a particular climate outcome), the other is whether the transition occurs in an orderly or disorderly way (Figure 2).

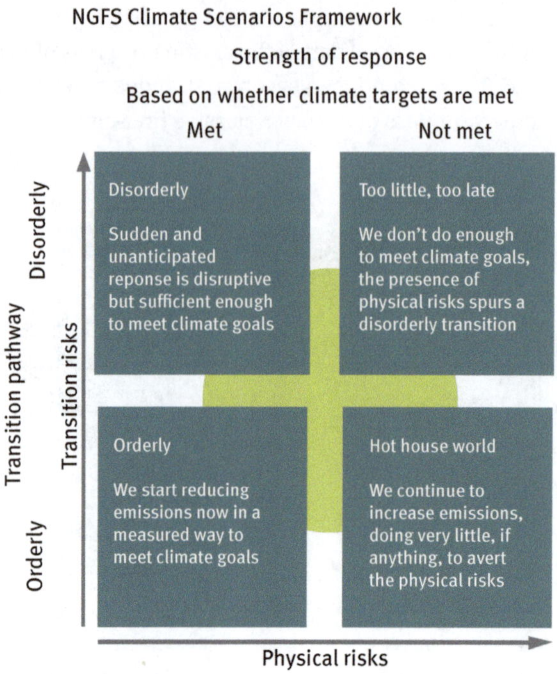

Figure 2: NGFS Climate Scenarios Framework (2019).

In its first comprehensive report published in April 2019, the NGFS has also stressed the importance of a robust and internationally consistent framework for financial disclosures related to climate and environmental risk. It then encouraged all companies issuing public debt or equity as well as financial sector institutions to disclose in line with the recommendations of the Task Force on Climate-related Financial Disclosures (TCFD). In practical terms, the TCFD articulates its disclosure recommendations around four pillars: (i) governance around climate issues within the company, (ii) strategic implications, (iii) climate-related risk management processes and (iv) metrics and targets followed by the company.

What about green Monetary Policy?

While the inclusion of climate-related risks in the financial stability mandate of central banks is advancing rapidly, their relevance to monetary policy is still being debated. In particular, the NGFS is catalyzing discussions among willing central banks that resulted in the publication in March 2021 of a new report assessing various options to factor climate-related risks into monetary policy operational framework. Building on previous NGFS work on possible effects of climate change on the determinants of monetary policy and on a survey on monetary policy operations and climate change, this report assesses nine options based on four criteria: (1) Consequences for monetary policy effectiveness; (2) Contributions to mitigating climate change; (3) Effectiveness as risk protection measures and (4) Operational feasibility.

The Eurosystem stands out with numerous speeches such as those of Benoit Coeuré (ECB, 2018), Philip R Lane (BoI, 2019) or more recently Isabel Schnabel (ECB, 2020) and François Villeroy de Galhau (BdF, 2021) underlining the repercussions, which are already visible, of climate change on price stability and inflation, and therefore its relevance in the conduct of monetary policy. In a speech delivered in January 2021, the President of the European Central Bank herself, Christine Lagarde, stated that "Climate change also impacts our primary mandate of price stability through several channels. This is why climate change considerations form an integral part of our ongoing review of our monetary policy strategy".

The strategic review of the European Central Bank should give concrete expression to these thoughts later this year. In addition to strengthening our economic analysis of the effects of climate change on macroeconomic variables, we also need to reflect on the alignment of monetary policy operations with the low carbon transition. If we consider that climate change is a source of financial risk, as the NGFS has pointed out, the path of adapting our rules on collateral would be in line with the sound management of the risks to which central banks are exposed. Thus, by systematically integrating climate-related risk into the evaluation of the collateral taken by the Eurosystem and by modulating haircuts accordingly, we would send a more powerful global signal than just buying green assets, while respecting our mandate.

All in all, adjusting central bank operational frameworks to more adequately reflect climate-related considerations appears relevant, legally possible and, eventually, practically feasible. However the climate-related adjustments of central bank operations will have to overcome a range of practical and analytical challenges, including data gaps and uncertainties with regard to risk quantification.

Climate-related Risks call for a global coordinated Response

Despite the unhedgeable and far-reaching nature of climate-related risks, climate change is in fact only the 'tip of the iceberg' of ecological issues. Many biogeochemical cycles other than the carbon cycle, but just as essential, are affected by human activity. The overstepping of several 'global limits' could thus lead to other systemic crises, triggered for example by the massive decline in biodiversity (IPBES, 2019) or accelerated soil erosion (UNCCD, 2019). Economic decision makers and, among them, central bankers are also beginning to recognize the multiplicity of ecological crises beyond the climate, with for instance the publication of report on biodiversity risks in June 2020 (DNB, 2020).

World Health Organization-Europe, which brings together 53 countries, announced the creation of a multidisciplinary working group in the summer, bringing together physicians, health experts, policy makers, economists and finance experts to examine, among other things, the interactions between public health and the economy, its codependency with other environmental issues (e.g. climate) and the means of financing more resilient health systems.

In this context, the joint Bank for International Settlements and Banque de France working paper entitled "The Green Swan", published early 2020, proposes a conceptual framework for understanding the nature and dynamics of the new global environmental risks we face.

The Green Swan concept developed by the authors of the report refers to the Black Swan concept (Taleb, 2007). It shares three main characteristics with the latter: (i) events that are unexpected in the light of past experience; (ii) with considerable or even extreme impacts and (iii) which could be rationalised ex-post. In addition to these three characteristics of Black Swans, Green Swans incorporate two additional elements of severity. Firstly, a high degree of certainty that the risk exists and a high degree of uncertainty as to how it will materialise. This is both an invitation to face them and a difficulty in doing so. Secondly, Green Swans can be even more extreme than Black Swans as they are often irreversible, resulting in loss of human and non-human life. As a result, no single actor can protect itself against such unhedgeable risks, which calls for global and coordinated responses.

The Covid-19 crisis appears to be a Green Swan for several reasons (Bolton et al, 2020b). First, many scientists point out that the pandemic was largely predictable and that it is due to widespread destruction of natural habitats (Grandcolas and Justine, 2020), which increases the possibility of zoonoses (FRB, 2020). Secondly, with regard to the materialisation of the risk: Covid-19 highlights the inability of traditional models to measure the extent of the risk involved. Who would have predicted that, following the outbreak of a virus in China, the vast majority of the world's governments would choose to shut down the economy, air traffic and a great deal of trade? The pandemic also illustrates the impossibility for a single agent to protect itself from these risks. Finally, this crisis raises profound and systemic questions about the world "after", and thus calls for a coordinated and global response.

In this context, the action of central banks and the financial system to deal with climate-related risks must be accompanied by multiple actions. If these actions are lacking or fall short of the required ambition in the implementation, the action of central banks and the mobilization of the financial system will be severely impeded or could even be irrelevant. The priority, according to many economists (Gollier and Tirole, 2015), should be to introduce a carbon price. In Europe, it is the European Union Emission Trading Scheme, which still needs to be improved. The European Commission has recently proposed extending the scheme to imported goods and the transport sector and will present further reform proposals as part of the Green New Deal in June 2021. However, the widespread belief that a carbon price is sufficient is probably illusory and increasingly contested (Hepburn, Stern and Stiglitz, 2020). Indeed, climate change is not an externality like any other (that can be solved by a price mechanism and 'other things being equal') but probably 'the greatest market failure the world has ever seen' to quote the 2006 Stern Review. Given the scale of the challenge and the shortcoming of the implementation, carbon prices may have to soar in a very short time, triggering a wide range of unintended consequences, including financial and income inequality.

Thus, the search for new policy mixes combining fiscal, regulatory, tax, monetary and prudential instruments becomes essential. For example, a greater role for multilateral development banks is vital to develop mitigation policies in a coordinated manner and to support the poorest countries in the event of ecological or health crises. Others point to the need to better account for the use and exhaustion of the "natural capital", whether at the national or corporate level, to make more visible the consequences of the actions of different actors in (over)consuming natural resources and enable them to take into account the degradation of this unpriced but immensely valuable capital.

These examples only underline the essential point: mitigating climate change requires thinking about profound transformations in our lifestyles, privileging long-term choices over short-term considerations, and thinking about new forms of local and international coordination to govern the commons. Such a task requires a transdisciplinary approach capable of better grasping the realities of transition.

Whatever the denial or wait-and-see positions of some, our societies are becoming ever more conscious of these challenges whose consequences are acutely felt by many and central banks and supervisors cannot consider themselves to be outside of such issues that are closely intricated in the economic and financial fabric that form a fundamental dimension of our human lives . Getting involved does not mean going to the opposite extreme and claiming to replace other actors, whether political or private. The challenge is rather, within the framework of the mandate received, and in all independence and rigor, to do their full share in the collective effort underway.

References

Bolton P., Després M., Pereira da Silva M., Samama F. et Svartzman R. (2020a) "The Green Swan, Central Banking and financial stability in the age of climate change", *Banque des règlement internationaux (BRI) et Banque de France*, ISBN 978-92-9259-326-1
Bolton P., Despres M., Pereira da Silva M., Samama F. et Svartzman R. (2020b) « Penser la stabilité financière à l'ère des risques écologiques globaux – Vers de nouveaux arbitrages entre efficience et résilience des systèmes complexes », *Revue d'Economie Financière* (à paraître)
Carney M. (2015) "Breaking the tragedy of the Horizon, Climate Change and Financial Stability", *Speech at Lloyd's of London*
Coeuré B. (2018) "Monetary policy and climate change", Berlin, 8 November 2018
DNB (2020) "Indebted to nature, Exploring biodiversity risks for the Dutch financial sector", DNB
FRB (Fondation pour la Recherche sur la Biodiversité) (2020). "Mobilisation de la FRB par les pouvoirs publics français sur les liens entre Covid-19 et biodiversité". FRB
Gollier, C., & Tirole, J. (2015). Negotiating effective institutions against climate change.
Goulard S. et Mauderer S. (2019) « Comment les banques centrales veulent « verdir » la finance », der Süddeutschen Zeitung, 8 Juillet 2019. https://www.bundesbank.de/de/presse/gastbeitraege/zentralbanken-werden-gruener-800808
Grandcolas P. et Justine J-L. (2020) "Covid-19 or the pandemic of mistreated biodiversity", *The Conversation*, 29 Avril 2020.
Hepburn C., Stiglitz J. et Stern N. (2020) "Carbon Pricing" Special Issue in the European Economic Review, European Economic Review, 103440.
IPBES (2019) "Summary for Policymakers of the Global Assessment Report on Biodiversity and Ecosystem Services of the Intergovernmental Science-Policy Platform on Biodiversity and Ecosystem Services", *IPBES secretariat.*
Lagarde, C. (2021) Keynote speech at the ILF conference on Green Banking and Green Central Banking, Frankfurt am Main, 25 January 2021
Lagarde, C. (2020a) "Interview with Financial Times". 8 July 2020
Lagarde, C. (2020b) "Interview with Le Courrier Cauchois". 31 July 2020
Lane, P. (2019) "Climate Change and the Irish Financial System", *Speech at the National University of Ireland Galway, 5 February 2019*
Michel, C. (2020) "Climate transition, transformation and convergence: Europe's path towards robust resilience", Speech via video conference on the occasion of the 20th Rencontres Économiques d'Aix-en-Provence, 5 July 2020
NGFS (2019) "NGFS First Comprehensive Report. A call for Action, Climate Change as a Source of Financial Risk", *NGFS.*
NGFS (2020) "Climate change and monetary policy: initial takeaways", *NGFS.*
NGFS (2020) "NGFS climate scenarios for central banks and supervisors", *NGFS.*
NGFS (2020) "Survey on monetary policy operations and climate change: key lessons for further analyses", *NGFS*

NGFS (2021) "Adapting central bank operations to a hotter world: Reviewing some options", *NGFS*

OMS (2020) "Annonce de la création de la Commission paneuropéenne sur la santé et le développement durable : repenser les priorités stratégiques à la lumière des pandémies » [Press Release], 11 Aout 2020

Schnabel I. (2020) "Never waste a crisis: COVID-19, climate change and monetary policy", Frankfurt am Main, 17 July 2020

Stern N. (2006) "Stern Review: The Economics of Climate Change", *HM Treasury*.

Taleb N. (2007), The Black Swan, Penguin Random House, New York.

UNCCD (2019) "Land in Numbers 2019, Risks and Opportunities", *UNCCD*, ISBN: 978-92-95110-00-4.

Villeroy de Galhau, F. (2021) "The role of central banks in the greening of the economy", Paris, 11 February 2021

Otmar Issing

Green Monetary Policy?

Climate change is probably the biggest challenge of our time. But should central banks also be worrying about the issue? If so, what should they be doing about it?

Central-bank representatives who make public speeches about climate change cannot deny the scale and scope of the problem; to do so would be to risk their own credibility. Beyond communicating with the public, the question, of course, is whether central banks should try to account for environmental considerations when shaping monetary policy. Obviously, climate change and corresponding government policies in response to it can have powerful effects on economic development. These consequences are reflected in all kinds of variables – growth, inflation, employment – that will in turn affect central-bank forecasts and influence monetary-policy decisions.

Likewise, natural disasters and other environmental events – actual or potential – can pose implicit risks to entire classes of financial assets. Regulators and supervisors charged with assessing risk and associated capital needs must take this environmental dimension into account. At a minimum, the high uncertainty stemming from these risks implies a huge challenge for assessing the stability of the financial system and corresponding macroprudential measures. And these risk factors are also increasingly relevant for monetary-policy decisions, such as when central banks should buy bonds or (in some cases) equities.

But the growing public demand that central banks contribute more actively to the fight against climate change leads to a different dimension. In theory, central banks could introduce preferential interest rates for "green" activities – thus driving up the prices of "green bonds" – while adopting a more negative attitude toward noxious assets, such as those tied to fossil fuels. And yet, assessing whether and to what extent an asset is environmentally harmful or helpful would be extremely difficult.

Putting aside these more technical issues, the broader question remains: Should central banks assume responsibility for implementing policies to combat climate change? A number of prominent central bankers have already argued that they should. And current proposals for accordingly extending central banks' responsibilities have come on top of growing concerns about income distribution and other issues tangentially related to monetary policy.

After having played a decisive role in preventing the world from falling into another 1930s-style depression, central bankers after the 2008 financial crisis have been held up as saviors of the world. The title of "maestro," once accorded just to former US Federal Reserve Chair Alan Greenspan, has now been extended

https://doi.org/10.1515/9783110752892-019

to the entire field. With central bankers at the height of their reputation, it is not surprising that many would now want them to make a substantive contribution to the fight against climate change.

But central bankers should never forget what they are appointed for: namely, to preserve price stability and, in some cases, to support high levels of employment. Central bankers are not omnipotent, and they should not be made to feel as if they were. Confronting climate change is above all the responsibility of governments and legislatures that are exposed to the risk of losing elections. Climate policies that will affect social and economic arrangements across all of society belong in the hands of those who are directly answerable to voters.

Central bankers who would assume responsibility for tackling climate change are acting out of hubris, and could well undermine the very independence upon which their institutions rely. Central banks were not made independent so that they could extend their own mandates. And where environmental issues are among their secondary objectives, central banks should warn against exaggerated expectations regarding their contribution. Making themselves publicly accountable beyond their limited capability in this field must lead to disappointment and undermine their reputation.

There can be no such thing as a "green" monetary policy. A policy domain far outside of central banks' proper mandate cannot be brought within it, and attempts to do so will inevitably end more or less badly.

Luiz Awazu Pereira da Silva

How are Central Banks helping to make the Recovery from the Covid-19 Pandemic more sustainable and inclusive?

Without the timely, coordinated, countercyclical and massive policy response to the Covid-19 pandemic by fiscal and monetary authorities around the globe, the downturn could have been much worse. On top of their own unprecedented monetary policy response, central banks are facilitating a sustainable and inclusive recovery in many ways. First, by raising awareness that climate-change related risks are a significant threat to global financial stability. Second, by showing that collective coordinated action, changes in supply and demand behaviour, and other public policies including adequate carbon pricing are required. Third, by fostering policies that ensure low financing costs of mitigation and transition and providing guidance that this will be maintained for an appropriately long horizon. Fourth, by developing analytical tools as public goods to improve the measurement, assessment and mitigation of such risks (such as new risk models, climate stress testing, climate scenarios, disclosure of carbon exposures and analysis of the redistributive impact of climate policies). And fifth, by engaging with the financial private sector to develop new financial instruments to accelerate adaptation and transition towards a net zero goal, which is increasingly endorsed by many countries.

For a long time, we believed that there was an infinite supply of natural resources and that their use entailed little to no cost. The consumption of air, water, forests and natural capital in general had very few restrictions and, amid those restrictions, technology would make it possible to use natural resources ad infinitum. Scepticism about "limits to growth" started in the 1970s with concerns about energy consumption from fossil fuels, and by the late 1980s, repeated warnings by climate scientists led to the creation of the Intergovernmental Panel on Climate Change (IPCC), which was established with the support of the UN Environment Programme and the World Meteorological Organization. The link between global warming and human activity – in particular through the emission of greenhouse gases (GHG) – continued to be analysed and gained traction thanks to further research by prominent social scientists.[1] By the end of the 1990s and 2000s, the cu-

1 The Stern Review on the Economics of Climate Change, issued on 30 October 2006 by Nicholas Stern, was the first economic report on climate change characterised as the greatest and widest-

Note: The opinions expressed here are those of the author and may not be attributed to BIS.

https://doi.org/10.1515/9783110752892-020

mulative growing evidence about GHG effects had changed social awareness of the risks related to climate change, the sustainability of the way we produce and consume, and the need for transitional solutions to a less risky, carbon-based economy, for all. Finally, this evolution of mindsets received further support, especially after the Global Financial Crisis, amongst the central banking community[2].

The reasons for central banks to become involved with climate change had to overcome two extreme viewpoints. On the one hand, by limiting its involvement a central bank was simply respecting its strict explicit mandate and preserving its independence. On the other hand, central banks were summoned to involve themselves even with no explicit mandate since they would be acting on a greater-than-the-Global Financial Crisis "emergency". De facto, many central banks have since pragmatically been addressing many climate issues interpreted within their mandates, while also recognising that there is no silver bullet against global warming and that they alone cannot mitigate all climate change-related risks.

Indeed, the impact of climate change directly undermines the objectives of most central bank mandates. Financial stability is potentially threatened by severe weather events, with massive losses of capital related to physical and transitional climate change-related risks. Moreover, price and macroeconomic stability are affected by climate change-related shocks and uncertainty, including food prices, shortages, mass migration, savings, lower employment and financial crises. Finally, and more importantly, central banks need to take into account rapid changes taking place in the real economy and financial sector. Both are moving faster than the official sector: demand is increasing among investors and consumers for greater commitments to sustainability, transparency and consistency; and the supply of green portfolios is growing, coupled with an evolving taxonomy, a higher volume of green financial assets, and an increased appetite to hold and manage them.

ranging market failure ever. The report had a large public repercussion. In 2005, Jared Diamond published *Collapse: how societies choose to fail or succeed*, which describes the causes of historical societal collapse, especially as related to the impact of man-made or other environmental changes.

2 In a seminal 2015 speech, "Breaking the tragedy of the horizon – climate change and financial stability", Mark Carney stated that "[c]limate change is the Tragedy of the Horizon" and that "once climate change becomes a defining issue for financial stability, it may already be too late".

"The green Swan" Contribution to the Debate: It is about Risk!

The publication The green swan: central banking and financial stability in the age of climate change[3] tried to move the climate change debate in the financial sector from an ethical to a risk-based discussion. The metaphor was inspired by Nassim Nicholas Taleb's black swans during the Global Financial Crisis – they represented the exceptional and rare nature of a sequence of financial meltdowns that nevertheless created a global financial crisis. A green swan also represents an event, but one that is bound to happen because it is the result of climate change and is therefore, according to today's science, a quasi-certainty. When and in what form the event will take place are unknown. However, in recent years we have seen numerous, glaringly obvious manifestations of these growing risks, including those related to natural weather catastrophes. In addition, cases of zoonosis – which can spark pandemics such as the one our world is currently witnessing – are also the result of the destruction of animals' natural habitat and the loss of biodiversity. The Covid-19 pandemic, which has paralysed the global economy over the last year, serves as a useful illustration of how expected events related to climate change, albeit unfolding at a very slow pace, can materialise suddenly and accelerate dramatically.[4]

The messages in *The green swan* come directly from today's best science. First, climate change calls for an epistemological rupture in risk models, breaking away from: (i) Gaussian distributions of risk (with fat tails or not); (ii) the linearity of transmissions of climate change-related risks; and (iii) the convenient extrapolation of the consequences of these events using historical data. Second, the best science warns us of: (i) the quasi-certainty of the occurrence of climate change-related catastrophic material and human losses; and (ii) the crossing for our societies of irreversible tipping points if we emit GHGs beyond the 420 billion tonne threshold of CO_2 equivalents. Indeed, the latest IPCC reports calculate that this emission budget is the maximum limit (at the 66 % confidence level) for average temperatures on the planet to grow by less than 1.5 °C. In a nutshell, *The green swan* alerted us to the reality that, given these risks, the "wait-and-see" attitude behind our benign neglect is itself very risky.

---

3 P Bolton, M Després, L Pereira da Silva, F Samama and R Svartzman, *The green swan: central banking and financial stability in the age of climate change*, Bank for International Settlements and Banque de France, 2020.

4 See L Pereira da Silva, "Green Swan 2 – climate change and Covid-19: reflections on efficiency versus resilience", speech based on remarks at the OECD Chief Economist Talk Series, Paris, 23 April 2020 and a research webinar at the BIS, 13 May 2020.

The green swan highlights that the risk of waiting too long is not worth taking, and that we need to act even in spite of radical uncertainty because climate change-related risks are asymmetrical. That is, we are faced with the quasi-certainty of incurring huge future losses versus paying a small mitigation cost today. Therefore, it is better to prevent risks, to insure against future losses and to build buffers now even in the absence of supportive optimal carbon pricing, better models than our integrated assessment models (IAMs), other models in a general equilibrium framework or even an ideal understanding of all the ramifications of climate change. We also need to act by moving towards financing the transition to a less carbonised economy and thinking about its complex coordination issues. There is no entity within society that can perform this transition by itself, no matter its influence – be it central banks, governments, global banks or private firms. We must work together for the common good – *all hands on deck.*

How Central Banks are and *should continue* contributing: Providing public Goods on climate change-related Risks, and Fostering global and local Coordination

Beyond promoting awareness and building consensus, central banks are providing guiding frameworks for the public and private financial sector and civil society. The Network for Greening the Financial System (NGFS), which regroups the community of central banks and supervisors, has been instrumental in offering such public goods. In addition, public interventions by central bank Governors have been explicit about the importance of climate change for central banks in both advanced and emerging economies.[5]

5 See C Lagarde "Climate change and central banking" keynote speech at the ILF conference on Green Banking and Green Central Banking, Frankfurt, 25 January 2021; L Brainard "Financial Stability Implications of Climate Change", speech at "Transform Tomorrow Today" Ceres 2021 Conference, Boston, 23 March, 2021; Y Gang "Make full use of China's monetary policy space and promote green finance", remarks at the Roundtable of China Development Forum, 21 March 2021; H Kuroda "Addressing climate-related financial risks – from a central bank's perspective", remarks by at the International Research Workshop on Climate-related Financial Risks, Bank of Japan, 25 March 2021; A Bailey "The time to push ahead on tackling climate change", speech at the Corporation of London Green Horizon Summit, 9 November 2020; F Villeroy de Galhau "Paris 2020 Climate Finance Day" speech at the Paris 2020 Climate Finance Day, Paris, 29 October 2020; J Weidmann "Climate change and central banks", address at the Deutsche Bundesbank's second financial market conference, Frankfurt am Main, 29 October 2019; A Díaz de León "Climate change and its impact on the financial system", remarks at the Conference on Climate Change and its Impact on the Financial System, Mexico City, 5 December 2019; R Campos Neto "BC# Sustain-

The central banking community is addressing climate change in five key ways. First, they are continuing to improve analytical tools to assess climate change-related risks and test the resilience of our financial sectors, in particular developing new macro models – beyond IAMs or DSGEs – as well as new risk metrics, climate-related stress tests, and scenarios for 1.5 °C with sustainable growth for the real economy and financial sector.

Second, central banks are continuing to discuss the scope and role of macroprudential tools and monetary policies, including those for collateral and asset purchase programmes. The Basel Committee, for example, has a task force on climate-related financial risks. These are not trivial issues, and the discussion has to weigh the pros and cons of introducing some form of shadow asset pricing while we still have not been capable of introducing an adequate global real carbon price.

Third, central banks are working on policies for disclosure and accounting standards, together with the Financial Stability Board and its Task Force on Climate-related Financial Disclosures (TCFD), and the International Financial Reporting Standards (IFRS) consultation on sustainability reporting.

Fourth, the central banking community is working to make the taxonomy on green investment products for investors and civil society more consistent, with an emphasis on such things as comparable environmental, social and corporate governance (ESG) criteria and green bond standards.

And finally, the central banking community is seeking a greening of its own assets, such as reserves and pension funds, while offering investment options for investors that favour green finance.

But it doesn't end there. The central banking community is also working to strengthen coordination between local and global agents to avoid free riding and problems arising from collective action, while favouring greater cooperation and helping to find a reasonable balance of burden-sharing for mitigation and adaptation policies. Central banks realise that climate change actions require a significant amount of coordination[6], especially in the light of governments' commitment to a net zero emissions approach. It requires the involvement of governments, treasuries and fiscal policy to address Pigovian carbon taxes, trading and pricing emissions. It requires international institutions and development banks to

ability Agenda", presentation at the launching of the Sustainability agenda, Brasília, 8 September 2020.

6 The need to address inclusion, the pandemic and climate change challenges is the priority of the G20 Presidency in 2021 see I Visco "The G20 under Italy's leadership in 2021", keynote speech at The Global Foundation – Rome Roundtable 2020 "Which way the world after the pandemic? Our inclusive human future", 16–17 November 2020.

help leverage the financing costs of transition and mitigation.[7] Lastly, but equally important, it requires real sector firms, banks, insurance companies, regulators, standard-setters and ratings agencies to ensure consistency with the commitments established.

While recognising the dramatic cost Covid-19 has had on human societies and the global economy, one collateral effect is that the pandemic may have triggered a behavioural change. It showed, overwhelmingly, the evidence of the huge costs of green swans and, amid the pain and suffering, helped relay to societies, policymakers and the private sector the asymmetric risk-return that global warming entails, and the need for immediate action.

The "first-best" Solution of Combating Climate Change faces Redistributive Challenges

Acting now comes with a warning: there *are* distributional consequences of climate change policies and for the transition to be successful, the political economy must be considered. The risks and impact of global warming disproportionately affect poor countries and poor households in rich countries. The global and local short-term social effects of mitigation policies might be regressive on impact before the medium- to long-term welfare benefits materialise. Therefore, there is an urgent need to think about and design such policies keeping in mind compensation and transfers, as these are important elements to build support and fairness. This is not specifically a central bank role, but this concern can be present in the overall coordination process with fiscal authorities.

To change relative prices in our economies to favour less carbon-based production and consumption, the textbook solution is to *fix a price* and internalise the negative externality arising from the emission of GHGs. A carbon price via tax or an emission right is needed, but we now know that it not only presents technical difficulties – such as its transmission to the whole economy – but has a redistributive and therefore also a political impact, particularly because of the diversity of social groups potentially subject to this tax and their uneven capacity to absorb its costs. Any transition to a new carbon regime in a new society has a

7 The coordination with United Nations agencies, eg UNEP, and the Bretton Woods institutions, as well as others, is essential. In November 2020, the first Finance in Common Summit assembled 450 public development banks whose annual total investments total about $2.3 trillion, about 10% of total global investments. The summit aimed at ensuring the recovery from the Covid-19 pandemic is in line with the principles of sustainable finance, the Paris Agreement and a key milestone ahead of the Glasgow Climate Change Conference (COP 26).

redistributive impact. In theory, changes happen seamlessly, free of adjustment cost and pain, and entail an instant reallocation of resources to different entities and sectors that emit less carbon. But there is de facto a transition cost with highly significant redistributive consequences. These effects must not be overlooked by economic policymakers as they can exacerbate the inequalities within our societies. If we were to implement good climate policies that could increase inequality and social fragility without considering compensation mechanisms, we could inadvertently trigger a backlash. That applies at both the national and international level. For example, the capacity to finance the transition to a lower carbon economy in India, Brazil or Indonesia is not the same as in Norway, Switzerland or France. That means while working on fixing a suitable price for carbon, we must also look at alternatives and use other complementary instruments, which are also required for this transition. That naturally raises the question of financing the transition and, subsequently, the role of finance. It is vital to know how to finance a transition to make it more likely that it will entail, not as many people fear, an economic contraction, but rather an expansion. It's not a minor issue.

Last but not least, while these are mostly issues for fiscal authorities, central banks are increasingly aware of how inequality can influence the effectiveness of their policies. For example, the issues of transmission across different groups and, implicitly, inequality have featured more prominently in major central banks' current reviews of monetary policy.[8] In practical terms, some central banks are extending their description of the monetary transmission channel to heterogeneous agents and thus are considering the role played by inequality.

Central Banks can enhance the positive Role of the Financial System in the Transition

For a start, it is vital to make the financial system more resilient in the face of the increasingly massive potential costs of accidents caused by extreme natural catastrophes (storms, hurricanes, forest fires etc). We need to reflect on the capital and other buffers that need to be put in place to face these climate shocks, so as to avoid a new global financial crisis. The central bank community is aware of this, and the pandemic has actually proved that the consolidation work undertaken after the Global Financial Crisis added resilience to the financial sector.

---

8 See J Powell, "New economic challenges and the Fed's monetary policy review", in *Navigating the decade ahead: implications for monetary policy*, proceedings of the Federal Reserve Bank of Kansas City Jackson Hole symposium, August 2020.

Then, we need to look at how to finance the numerous good ideas that are emerging from many quarters. Obviously, supporting innovation in new technologies (clean energy and climate-related R&D) is paramount, as is acting and investing in green infrastructure that uses better standards and lower-carbon production processes.[9]

Therefore, we need to develop new financial instruments to help us channel savings and invest them into these new fields and help alter investor behaviour. Green finance is, in general, the route the financial sector is thinking of taking in this transition. This sector is looking at new green instruments because it makes business sense as the demand is there. But the financial system's creativity is also responding to a reputational risk. Some governments, companies and portfolio managers are aware of a behavioural change among consumers and investors, for example in Norway with the sovereign wealth fund, or BlackRock or Amundi.[10] There is a growing willingness on the part of the entire financial sector to improve the clarity and taxonomy of these new instruments and central banks and regulators are helping to incentivise this process. How exactly can we improve the definition of a green bond? How can we better illustrate and bring together the various concepts behind ESG criteria in a given financial instrument? What are the implications of the risks and returns of investing in such a product? These new demands can improve investor behaviour and the way in which certain financial institutions present these products to finance a transition. When we put all this together, we are assembling the various pieces of what could later be a consistent new macroeconomic policy for addressing climate change.

---

9 Chapter 11 of Bill Gates' *How to avoid a climate disaster* (2021) provides an extensive list of practical ideas and suggestions with related institutional changes.

10 Regarding governments, 113 countries have committed to be mostly carbon-neutral by 2050, representing about 50 % of world GDP, and nine have set legally binding targets. Among asset owners, $5.1 trillion is committed through the Net-Zero Asset Owner Alliance, and among asset managers, $9 trillion is committed through the Net Zero Asset Managers Initiative. In June 2019, Norway's sovereign wealth fund (managing $1 trillion in assets) signalled a gradual fossil fuel divestment policy. In his annual letter to CEOs on 14 January 2020, BlackRock's Larry Fink said: "Climate change has become a defining factor in companies' long-term prospects ... awareness is rapidly changing, and I believe we are on the edge of a fundamental reshaping of finance." BlackRock's assets under management are around $7 trillion. In Europe, at Amundi (about $1.7 trillion under management), Frédéric Samama has been instrumental in the Portfolio Decarbonisation Coalition, the creation of low-carbon indices, and one of the world's biggest green bond funds.

Conclusions: Never "waste a Crisis". Use the Covid-19 Crisis as an Opportunity to aim at sustainable and more inclusive Recovery

Central banks have been acting in significantly to mitigate the pandemic's devastating effects. They have also coordinated with other actors, as mentioned above. They have been contributing to promote new ideas for green finance. Why is this transition so critical, and why is it important to find the means to finance it?[11] My short answer is because it will increase the likelihood of an expansionist outcome that, in turn, will help overcome the political economy and redistributive challenges alluded to earlier. Figure 1 shows a hypothetical example of the opportunities the Covid-19 crisis can offer.

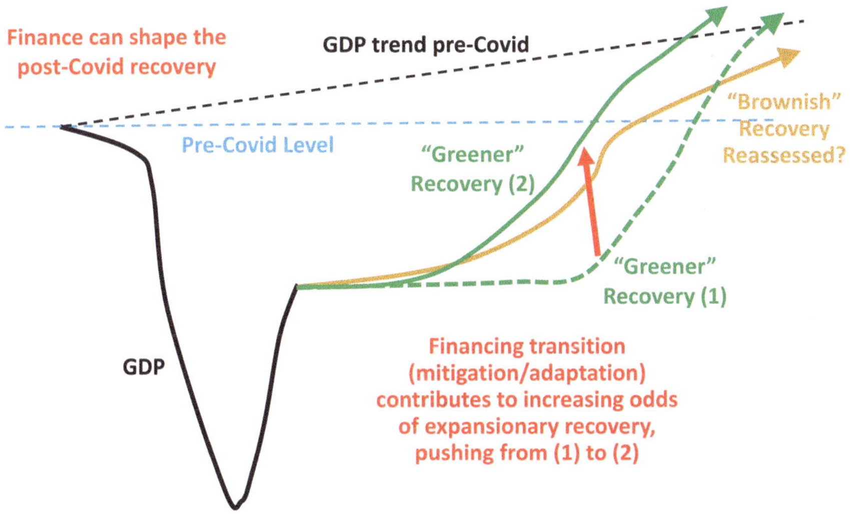

Figure 1: Post-Covid recovery: the role of green finance

As we already know, the Covid-19 pandemic made global GDP growth (solid black line in the stylized figure 1 above) fall dramatically. In an uneven way in many countries, we are beginning to witness a V-shaped recovery, or rather a "square

11 See K Georgieva (IMF Managing Director), "Securing a green recovery: the economic benefits from tackling climate change", remarks at the PBC-IMF High-Level Seminar on Green Finance and Climate Policy, 15 April 2021; and F Elderson (NGFS Chair), "A green light to lead us on the path of economic recovery", remarks at the 11th edition of the Petersberg Climate Dialogue: Financing Climate Ambition in the context of Covid-19, 29 April 2020.

root", as activity levels have yet to return to pre-Covid levels[12]. What type of recovery can we expect from now? Could it combine a rebound in activity, job creation and a greener economy? At first glance, this crisis is so severe that it would be better not to set extra goals and instead accept a more "brown" recovery, with an upturn based on the traditional instruments and technologies that stimulate employment and economic activity. A recovery powered in part by green investment is represented by the green dotted line: it would be slower as it would take longer to mobilise the technologies that are slightly more expensive. This figure, admittedly rudimentary and simplistic and which is not a forecast, illustrates how more green finance (with debt and equity) in the transition with more green technologies can hasten the availability and impact of new technological solutions.[13] Green financing instruments for investment in innovation and more risk-taking may offer the possibility to increase the pace of the recovery, substitute our existing capital stock faster, incentivise shifts in consumption and push it higher, to that solid green line, which would enable a recovery trajectory that would be quicker over the medium term than the traditional recovery fuelled by the type of consumption and production we had pre-Covid. The challenge is to use the current crisis as an opportunity to accelerate the transformation of our societies using new instruments to finance innovation, a kind of Schumpeterian creative destruction.[14] And indeed, in 2021 this is being implemented in the United States and Europe, with bold action being taken aiming at both sustainability and more inclusion.[15]

Is that path totally unrealistic? No, it isn't. If we move from a macroeconomic to a project perspective, a study by Nick Stern and Joseph Stiglitz[16] compares the different public policy measures that can be implemented to boost a recovery, for example research, infrastructure investments etc. Figure 2 shows the growth ac-

---

12 See IMF *World Economic Outlook: Managing Divergent Recoveries*, April 2021.

13 A more sober but still supportive view is J Pisani-Ferry, "A credible decarbonization agenda can help strengthen Europe's economy", PIIE, 9 December 2019.

14 This is the point made in P Aghion, C Antonin and S Bunel, "Innovation verte et croissance soutenable", in *Le pouvoir de la destruction créatrice*, 2020.

15 The European Green Deal is a multi-year package of at least €1 trillion in investment as a strategy committing to zero net emissions of greenhouse gases by 2050, betting on turning climate and environmental challenges into opportunities, and making the transition just and inclusive for all. The Biden infrastructure plan is a $2 trillion plan to overhaul and upgrade US infrastructure while taking into account climate risk and resilience. In addition US Treasury Secretary Janet Yellen reaffirmed President Biden's $1.9 trillion coronavirus relief package: "it's the right size to address the very significant problem that we have"; see J Yellen, ABC news interview by J Arnholz, 14 March 2021.

16 C Hepburn, B O'Callaghan, N Stern, J Stiglitz and D Zenghelis, "Will Covid-19 fiscal recovery packages accelerate or retard progress on climate change?", *Oxford Review of Economic Policy*, volume 36, number S1, May 2020.

tivity multipliers on the horizontal axis to the right, and the impact of the reduction in negative climatic effects on the vertical axis.

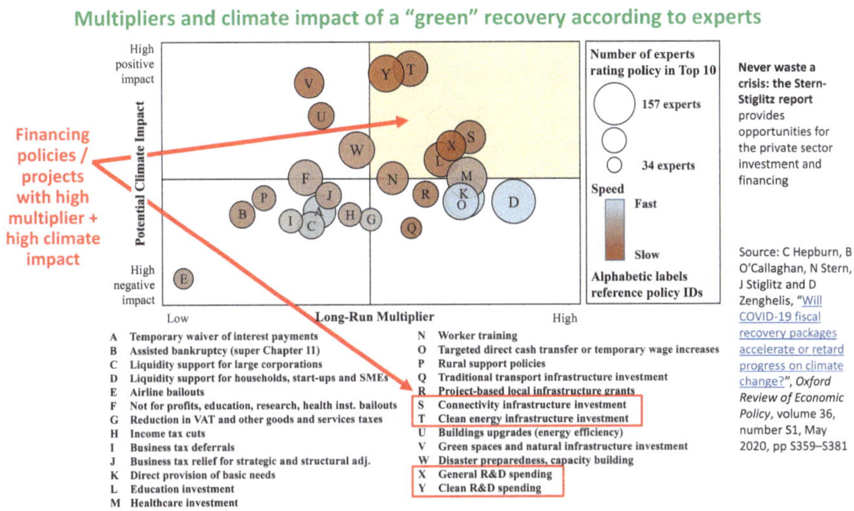

Figure 2: Possible projects for a green recovery

Different economic policy measures and eligible projects are points on this diagram, and we ideally would like these measures to be in the upper-right quadrant, where the projects have a strong impact on activity (high budgetary multiplier) and a strong mitigating impact on climate risk. The study provides at least four good examples of that: greener infrastructure, the search for alternative energies, research and development led by the private sector but also by the public sector, and connectivity and virtual infrastructure.

That means there are projects for relaunching the economy and, at the same time, carefully choosing the effects of this relaunch from the perspective of a transition and fighting climate change. Therefore, having the debt and equity financing for these projects is key since most of these new endeavours will represent a higher risk. The private financial sector has a role to play, but green R&D innovation will also require a longer-term return horizon that the public sector can provide and the coordination of all these actions. This coordination must include governments, regulators, international organisations and central banks. It is indispensable, not only on the supply side, ie technology, including financial technology, but also on the demand side, meaning the behaviour of each one of us. What will each of us consume and how will we receive price signals and information that will enable us to adjust our consumption to the low-carbon option?

The Covid-19 pandemic has produced the unprecedented contraction that we long feared with the consequences of physical and transition risks related to climate change. So what is the lesson? It's simple: *never* waste a crisis. The macroeconomic conditions are favourable. For example, interest rates are low at the moment, savings are higher in many rich countries, demand and awareness is increasing for green products, and there is growing ambition in the United States, European Union, China etc. There are also a number of projects, such as those involving green infrastructure, greener cities, carbon footprint tracing, new technologies and new ways to act using social networks. On the demand side, consumer information and incentives favour a lower-carbon economy and are increasingly aligned. For example, public awareness has risen to allow progress on carbon pricing, GHG emission taxation and emission certificates etc. On the supply side, green finance investors are asking for practical diversification for their portfolios and more projects to lower carbon content and finance the transition. There is more green research and R&D, and new technologies emerging, such as carbon capture.

Conditions seem to be emerging for an expansionary, green and more inclusive recovery, and central banks have played an important role in shaping them. Today, due to the Covid-19 crisis, the urgency is to finance an expansionary, sustainable and inclusive transition, find the good instruments and the best interlocutors, and coordinate and act in a way that actually reverses and stops the current trend of CO_2 emissions. However, as a final point, we also have to change the way we think and we measure our performances. If natural capital is not free, we must innovate and change, from our national accounts to our models, and analyse the effects of climate on our economies. How can we measure the utilisation and depreciation of natural resources? How could we also value our activity with other metrics beyond market prices?[17] How can we better understand the risk in our models connecting the macroeconomy with the climate in measuring happiness and our wealth?[18] We need to use our time well, because time is not on our side. The pandemic has served as a glaring warning that we don't have eternity before us, that we really are living on borrowed time, and that we need to act decisively to put in place measures that can mitigate the catastrophic risks of global warming.

---

17 This is the key question that, after pioneering work in alerting the central banking community about climate change, Mark Carney asks in *Value(s): building a better world for all* (2021).

18 This change will occur through dialogue between macroeconomists and scientists specialising in climate change. The best models we have for transitions are the Nobel Prize-winning contributions by William Nordhaus, for example the IAMs. We also have to place more emphasis on research on new frontiers where we take disequilibrium into account, non-linear trajectories, cascade and amplifying effects, slightly reminiscent of the Mandelbrot set.